M578

2-50

ROYAL HISTORICAL SOCIETY
GUIDES AND HANDBOOKS

No. 4

HANDBOOK OF DATES
FOR STUDENTS OF ENGLISH HISTORY

HANDBOOK OF DATES
FOR STUDENTS OF ENGLISH HISTORY

EDITED BY
C. R. CHENEY

LONDON
OFFICES OF THE ROYAL HISTORICAL SOCIETY
UNIVERSITY COLLEGE LONDON, GOWER STREET, W.C.1
1970

First Published . 1945
Reprinted . . 1948
Reprinted . . 1955
Reprinted . . 1961
Reprinted . . 1970
with corrections

Made and Printed in Great Britain by Butler & Tanner Ltd., Frome and London

TABLE OF CONTENTS

v

PREFACE

The plan of this book is the direct result of a suggestion made in January 1944 by Mr. D. L. Evans, of the Public Record Office. Mr. Evans observed that the older English handbooks of dates (notably E. A. Fry's *Almanacks for students of English history*, 1915) were out of print, and that a new volume containing some of the same tables was urgently required. He suggested, moreover, that a new compilation need not follow slavishly the form of the existing books and that it might well include the more strictly chronological parts of Professor F. M. Powicke's *Handbook of British chronology* (1939, cf. below, p. xvii). The Council of the Royal Historical Society approved the project and the present volume is the result. In its planning the editor has had the advantage of help and advice from many quarters. The chapters on reckonings of time and saints' days are essentially the work of Professor Hilda Johnstone and were published in their original form in the *Handbook of British chronology*; as they now appear, they embody revision and addition by the editor, made with the author's consent. Professor Johnstone's list of saints' days and festivals has been republished practically as it stands in the former handbook. Professor T. F. T. Plucknett has likewise contributed a revised version of the chapter on legal chronology which first appeared in the *Handbook of British chronology*. The same book has been laid under contribution for the list of rulers of England before A.D. 1154; here Professor R. R. Darlington has given his advice on the presentation of material which is extracted wholly from his section of the earlier handbook. The editor is deeply obliged to these contributors and also to all those other scholars who have given help; he wishes to thank especially Mr. D. Bonner-Smith, Professor V. H. Galbraith, Mr. A. V. Judges, Mr. I. G. Philip, Mr. H. G. Richardson, Professor M. A. Thomson, and Dr. M. Tyson.

The plan of the book has of necessity been rigorously exclusive, and those who wish to use it deserve to be warned about the things it does not contain. In the first place, one must emphasize the fact that it does not set up to be a systematic treatise on chronology. It is intended, rather, to provide a compact and convenient means of verifying dates, a work of ready reference which is required as much by the expert as the novice in the daily handling and checking of historical material. But the lists and tables which form the greater part of the book cannot safely be used unless the reader constantly remembers that at different times and in different places and in the minds of different people a single date may mean different things. Thus 28 December 1190 would be reckoned by the English chancery clerk of that day as falling in the second year of King Richard I, but for a clerk of the exchequer the accounts covering this date belonged to the Pipe Roll of 3 Richard I, and a Benedictine chronicler would include the events of that day in the year of grace 1191. Cervantes and Shakespeare did not die on the same day, although each died on 23 April 1616, according to the computation of his country. An English document dated 28 January 1620 would be written on the same day as a document dated in Scotland 28 January 1621 or a document dated in France 7 February 1621.

vii

These examples indicate some of the pitfalls. To afford some guidance in the difficult paths of chronology the book provides chapters on reckonings of time, festivals, regnal years, and so forth. But varieties of practice, both in the reckoning of time and in the presentation of chronological data, are innumerable. For further details of a subject far too complex to be completely covered in a volume of this size and character, the reader is referred to the works cited in the select bibliography which follows this preface.

The book is strictly limited to the dating of records which a student of English history will commonly encounter. Even so, it cannot claim to be complete, since the student will sometimes handle documents dated according to a French or German or Russian calendar, or may even be called upon to translate a date from the Jewish or Muhammadan to the Christian era. Moreover, the year of an episcopate, mayoralty, or shrievalty may be introduced into a document to perplex the historian. Any historical fact imaginable may be, not only a clue to the date of a record, but an element deliberately introduced by the writer to date it; so, for instance, we have a charter dated 'in the seventh year of the translation of the blessed Thomas the martyr', and a mortgage reckoned from 'the Easter after Henry the son of the king of England espoused the daughter of the king of France'.[1] Clearly, a handbook of this kind can only include the commonest chronological material, together with such general directions as will help the student to use other material for dating.

Nor is it within the scope of this work to discuss how undated or imperfectly dated documents may be dated accurately by the application of paleographical or diplomatic tests. Even when the student is not able, by handling the original, to draw inferences from handwriting, he learns to distinguish between the royal styles employed by the various Henries of England, to distinguish between one Pope Innocent and another by reference to their itineraries, and he can date an undated London private charter by finding among its witnesses the mayor and sheriffs of a particular year. These are but instances of a principle which applies to all documentary records: that a comparison with other records of the same class almost always produces at least an approximate date. And the student will often find that the work of assembling these records and of fitting them into the chronological scheme has been done for him already; he must simply learn his way about a library. All this, however, pertains not to chronology but to diplomatic. The reader must be referred once and for all to the classics of that subject, with the advice that where these fail to provide infallible tests, he must have recourse to the great collections of *Regesta*, to cartularies of private charters, and so on.[2] Nor is this method applicable only to the records of the Middle Ages. In modern times the undated or incompletely dated letter is as common as it ever was; but, to quote Professor L. B. Namier, 'there is hardly an undated document which, given reasonable care, cannot be dated, at least approximately, from internal evidence'. The reader may be directed to this scholar's *Additions and corrections to Sir John Fortescue's edition of the correspondence of George III (vol. I)* (Manchester, 1937) for examples of deficient dating and models of method in the establishing of dates.

[1] Brit. Mus., Add. charter 7593; *Essays in history presented to R. L. Poole* (Oxford, 1927), p. 205.
[2] For books on diplomatic, etc., see below, pp. xvi, xviii; for the *regesta* of kings and popes, see pp. xiii, xiv, xviii.

PREFACE

It will be observed that this handbook contains no detailed discussion of the *significance* of dates in official documents. Yet it behoves the historian to bear this matter well in mind. The fact that a charter of King Henry VI is dated at a certain place on a certain day does not mean that the king (or, indeed, any of the witnesses named) was at that place on that day. The date has a meaning, but not the obvious one, and to understand it we must understand the workings of the royal chancery and the privy seal and signet offices. So also with the written products of any highly organized government : when the student (with the help of this book) has translated the dates of the documents into modern terms, he has still to find out what the dates signify.[1]

Not only are we able by diplomatic tests to date the undated document and appreciate the significance of dates ; it sometimes happens that the dating clause of a document provides an important diplomatic test of authenticity. For the forger can be detected by the use of anachronistic forms of date. He may add a date to a soi-disant writ of William the Conqueror, whose writs were undated, or he may give the year of grace instead of the imperial year in fabricating an early papal bull. But this, after all, is only one among many tests of authenticity and is more fittingly discussed in a treatise on diplomatic than in a handbook of dates.

Finally, to come to an end of warnings, the reader must consider the causes of errors in dating. He will certainly encounter in the course of his work inconsistencies and downright impossibilities in the dates before him. As regards inconsistencies, a word may not be amiss. Where a date is expressed with a wealth of detail, as in the solemn diplomas of the later Anglo-Saxon kings, those elements in the date which are most remote from ordinary usage are the elements most likely to be wrong. Let no one suppose that these errors necessarily bespeak the forger's work. Even the chancery of Pope Innocent III was at sea in the reckoning of indictions in A.D. 1206 and A.D. 1207, whereas it never made a mistake in calculating the year of the pontificate. When we are presented with a date in which the day of the week and the day of the month do not harmonize, it is generally the day of the week which is right. Thus, Lord Halifax dated a letter to George III Friday 3 April 1765, but 3 April 1765 fell on Wednesday and the date of the letter was Friday 3 May.[2] The student must also be prepared to find whole statements of date which for one reason or another are inadmissible. He will make due allowance for human error, remembering how he has occasionally misdated his own correspondence, especially at the beginning of a month or year. But he will do more than this if he wants to make constructive criticism ; he will consider the conditions in which the date is transmitted, whether in an original document or in a later copy, whether expressed in words or in roman or arabic numerals, whether written in good faith or with the intention to deceive. Of all these points he must take account ; but they do not concern us in this handbook of dates.

Throughout this work the terms Old Style and New Style are used with the primary meanings attached to them by the *Oxford English Dictionary* ; that is to say, by Old Style we mean the Julian calendar and by New Style the Gregorian,

---

[1] The work of Maxwell-Lyte on the great seal (see p. xii) is particularly important for this question, so far as the English chancery is concerned.

[2] Namier, *op. cit.*, p. 23, cf. *ibid.*, p. 63 (nos. 384–5).

irrespective of the date adopted for the beginning of the year where these systems are in use. The practice of historians, both in England and on the Continent, has varied in the past, and the result is confusion. To use 'New Style', as is often done, to denote simply the historical year, which begins on 1 January is, strictly speaking, incorrect and to be avoided. If the reader will consider the variations in the practice of England, Scotland, and France between the years 1600 and 1752, he will realize at once the danger of laxity in this matter.

Photographic reprints of this book have provided the opportunity of correcting several errors, in particular dates, but have not permitted thorough revision. A few additions have been made to the select bibliography on page xvii, and the table of regnal years has been brought up to date.

SELECT BIBLIOGRAPHY

These lists may serve to direct students to further reading on chronological matters, and to indicate where material may be found for the interpretation of dates and the dating of undated documents. Works which are particularly useful are marked with *

I. GENERAL AND MISCELLANEOUS WORKS.

L'art de vérifier les dates et les faits historiques, par un religieux de la congrégation de St. Maur. 4th edition, by N. V. de St. Allais and others. 44 vols. (Paris, 1818–44).

> A great repository of detailed information, sometimes inaccurate but not altogether superseded. Mainly of use to the student of continental history.

Burnaby, S. B., *Elements of the Jewish and Muhammadan calendars with rules and tables and explanatory notes on the Julian and Gregorian calendars.* (London, 1901).

> A full and useful treatise. Tables of corresponding Jewish-Christian dates (A.D. 610–3003) and Muhammadan-Christian dates (A.D. 622–3008). For a simple concordance of Muslim and Christian years see Sir Wolseley Haig, *Comparative tables of Muhammadan and Christian dates.* (London, 1932).

Cappelli, A., *Cronologia e calendario perpetuo.* 'Manuali Hoepli' series. (Milan, 1906).

Fry, Edward Alexander, *Almanacks for students of English history.* (London, 1915).

Ginzel, F. K., *Handbuch der mathematischen und technischen Chronologie. Das Zeitrechnungswesen der Völker.* 3 vols. (Leipzig, 1906–14).

> Vol. iii contains a valuable chapter of nearly 200 pp. on medieval reckonings of time, and a series of detailed tables.

*Giry, A., *Manuel de diplomatique.* (Paris, 1894, reprinted 1925).

> Livre ii Chronologie technique (pp. 79–314) is an elaborate and valuable study, with lists and tables.

*Grotefend, H., *Taschenbuch der Zeitrechnung des deutschen Mittelalters und der Neuzeit.* (Hannover, 1898; 10th edition, 1960).

> An excellent manual, accurate and full, based on Grotefend's larger *Zeitrechnung des deutschen Mittelalters und der Neuzeit,* 2 vols. in 3 (Hannover, 1891–8).

Mas Latrie, J. M. J. L. de, *Trésor de chronologie, d'histoire et de géographie pour l'étude et l'emploi des documents du moyen âge.* (Paris, 1889).

> A vast work, chiefly of use for French history.

*de Morgan, Augustus, *The book of almanacs.* (London, 1851; 3rd edition, 1907).

> The work of a great mathematician, with admirable tables and the material for calculating phases of the moon.

Nicolas, Harris, *Chronology of history*. (London, 1833 ; 2nd edition (quoted in this work) 1838, and later reprints).

A deservedly popular handbook, now somewhat out of date and not always accurate in detail.

*Poole, Reginald Lane, *Medieval reckonings of time*. S.P.C.K. 'Helps for students of history ', no. 3. (London, 1921).

A lucid little guide by a great scholar.

——, *Studies in chronology and history*. (Oxford, 1934).

Stamp, A. E., *Methods of Chronology*. Historical Association pamphlet no. 92. (London, 1933).

Designed as a series of practical hints and warnings for historical students, by a former Deputy Keeper of the Public Records.

II. The beginning of the year.

In addition to the principal general works given above see

Anscombe, Alfred, ' The Anglo-Saxon computation of historic time in the ninth century ', *British Numismatic Journal*, 1st series, iv (1908), 241–310 ; v (1909), 381–407.

Beaven, Murray L. R., ' The regnal dates of Alfred, Edward the Elder, and Athelstan ', *English Historical Review*, xxxii (1917), 516–31.

——, ' The beginning of the year in the Alfredian chronicle (866–87) ', *ibid.*, xxxiii (1918), 328–42.

*Hodgkin, R. H., ' The beginning of the year in the English Chronicle ', in *Eng. Hist. Rev.*, xxxix (1924), 497–510.

Pollard, A. F., ' New Year's day and leap year in English history ', in *Eng. Hist. Rev.*, lv (1940), 177–93.

Poole, R. L., ' The chronology of Bede's *Historia ecclesiastica* and the councils of 679–680 ', *Journal of Theological Studies*, xx (1919), 24–40, reprinted in Poole's *Studies* (see above), pp. 38–55.

*——, ' The beginning of the year in the Middle Ages ', *Proceedings of the British Academy*, x (1921), reprinted in *Studies*, pp. 1–27.

III. Regnal years.

*Richardson, H. G., ' The exchequer year ', *Trans. R. Hist. Soc.*, 4th series, viii (1925), 171–90, ix (1926), 175–6.

Wallis, J. E. W., *English regnal years and titles, hand-lists, Easter dates, etc.* S.P.C.K. 'Helps for students of history ', no. 40. (London, 1921).

Not always accurate, especially in the matter of exchequer years.

The problems raised by the dating of documents of the chancery, privy seal office, etc., are discussed in

*Maxwell-Lyte, Sir Henry C., *Historical notes on the use of the Great Seal of England*. (London, 1926).

For detailed itineraries of English kings the student should consult the following :

*Delisle, Léopold and Berger, Elie (ed.), *Recueil des actes de Henri II roi d'Angleterre et duc de Normandie concernant les provinces françaises et les affaires de France.* 4 vols. (Paris, 1909–27).

> The introductory volume by Delisle (of fundamental importance for the whole study of twelfth-century royal diplomatic) demonstrates the means of dating undated documents.

Eyton, R. W., *Court, household, and itinerary of King Henry II.* (London, 1878).

Gough, Henry, *The itinerary of King Edward I.* 2 vols. (Paisley, 1900).

> Should only be used after reference to Maxwell-Lyte's work.

Hardy, T. Duffus, *A description of the Patent Rolls* [and] *an itinerary of King John.* Record Commission. (London, 1835). The itinerary is also printed in *Archaeologia*, xxii (1829), 124–60 and in *Rotuli litterarum patentium 1201–16.* Record Commission. (London, 1835).

Landon, Lionel, *The itinerary of King Richard I.* Pipe Roll Soc. Publications, new series, vol. 13. (London, 1935).

Regesta regum anglo-normannorum 1066–1154 : vol. i. *1066–1100*, ed. H. W. C. Davis (Oxford, 1913) ; vol. ii. *1100–1135*, ed. Charles Johnson and H. A. Cronne (Oxford, 1956) ; vol. iii. *1135–1154*, ed. H. A. Cronne and R. H. C. Davis (Oxford, 1968).

For lists of the rulers of Wales, Scotland, and the Isle of Man, see *Handbook of British chronology* (2nd ed., cf. below, p. xvii), pp. 46–64, with a note on the Scottish regnal year, p. 53. For lists of continental rulers, see Mas Latrie (cited in section I above).

IV. PAPAL CHRONOLOGY.

Annuario pontificio per l'anno 1969. (Vatican City, 1969).

> This official annual, replacing the earlier *La gerarchia cattolica*, contains a dated list of popes from St. Peter to the present. The list has been taken into account (but not followed at all points) on pp. 34–39, below.

*Duchesne, Louis (ed.), *Le Liber Pontificalis. Texte, introduction, et commentaire.* 2 vols. (Paris, 1886–92).

> Provides a list of popes to the thirteenth century which improves on Gams's list.

*Eubel, Conrad and Gauchat, Patricius, *Hierarchia catholica medii et recentioris aevi.* Vol. i. *1198–1431.* (2nd edition, Münster, 1913) ; vol. ii. *1431–1503* (2nd edition, 1914) ; vol. iii. *1503–1600.* (2nd ed., 1923) ; vol. iv. *1592–1667* (1935). Continued by R. Ritzler and R. Sefrin, vol. v. *1667–1730* (1952) ; vol. vi. *1730–1799* (1958) ; vol. vii. *1800–1846* (1968).

> More elaborate and accurate than Gams.

Gams, P. B., *Series episcoporum ecclesiae catholicae* (1873 and 1886, reprinted in one volume, Leipzig, 1931).

Menzer, A., 'Die Jahresmerkmale in den Datierung der Papsturkunden bis zum Ausgang des XI Jahrhunderts', *Römisches Quartalschrift*, xl (1932), 27–99.

*Poole, R. L., 'Papal chronology in the eleventh century', *Eng. Hist. Rev.*, xxxii (1917), 204–14, reprinted in Poole's *Studies*, pp. 144–55.

——, 'The names and numbers of medieval popes', *Eng. Hist. Rev.*, xxxii (1917), 465–78, reprinted in *Studies*, pp. 156–71.

——, 'Imperial influences on the forms of papal documents', *Proceedings of the British Academy*, viii (1917), reprinted in *Studies*, pp. 172–84.

For detailed itineraries of medieval popes the student should consult the published calendars and collections of their acts, particularly :

*Bliss, W. H., Johnson, C., and Twemlow J. A., (ed.), *Calendar of entries in the papal registers relating to Great Britain and Ireland*. Vols. i–xii. A.D. 1198–1471. (London, 1893–1933).

*Jaffe, P. (ed.), *Regesta pontificum romanorum ad annum 1198*. 2nd edition, by S. Loewenfeld, etc. 2 vols. (Berlin, 1885–6).

*Potthast, August (ed.), *Regesta pontificum romanorum* A.D. 1198–1304. (Berlin, 1874–5).

Pressutti, P. (ed.), *Regesta Honorii papae tertii*. 2 vols. (Rome, 1888–95).

Registers published by the *École française de Rome* during the past eighty years.

The *Bullarium romanum* provides material for the later period. The larger general histories of the papacy also provide a starting-point for chronological enquiries : the works of E. Caspar, H. K. Mann, and L. Pastor may be mentioned ; also, F. Gregorovius's history of the city of Rome (Eng. trans.), and C. J. Hefele's history of church councils in the French edition by H. Leclercq.

V. Saints' days and festivals.

Bishop, Edmund, *Liturgica historica* (Oxford, 1918).

Extremely important essays on the origins of the Feast of the Conception, on various Holy Week rites, etc.

The book of saints, compiled by the Benedictine monks of St. Augustine's Abbey, Ramsgate. (London, 1921).

An unpretentious little dictionary of saints, which includes many of post-medieval times.

Hampson, R. T., *Medii ævi kalendarium, or dates, charters, and customs of the Middle Ages*. 2 vols. (London, 1841).

A valuable collection of information, particularly useful for facts about festivals, and for the texts of calendars.

Wormald, Francis, *English kalendars before A.D. 1100*. Vol. i. (Henry Bradshaw Soc. Publications, lxxii, 1934).

——, *English Benedictine kalendars after A.D. 1100*. Vol. i. (Henry Bradshaw Soc. Publications, lxxvii, 1939).

SELECT BIBLIOGRAPHY

The following printed calendars from particular places have been used in the construction of the list of saints' days and festivals.

Canterbury :

Feltoe, C. L., *Three Canterbury kalendars*. (London, [1922]).

Gasquet, [F. A.], and Bishop, E., *The Bosworth psalter*. (London, 1908).

James, M. R., *The Canterbury psalter*. (London, 1935).

Hereford :

Frere, W. H., and Brown, L. E. G., *The Hereford breviary*. 3 vols. (Henry Bradshaw Soc. Publications, xxvi, xl, xlvi, 1904–15).

Oxford :

Wordsworth, C., *The ancient kalendar of the University of Oxford*. (Oxford Hist. Soc. Publications, xlv, Oxford, 1904).

Salisbury :

Frere, W. H., *Graduale sarisburiense*. (Plainsong and Medieval Music Soc. Publications, 1894).

York :

Lawley, Stephen, *The York breviary*. 2 vols. (Surtees Soc. Publications, lxxi, lxxv, 1880–3).

VI. LEGAL CHRONOLOGY.

There is no satisfactory treatise devoted specifically to this subject, and to discover the practice of the various courts at different periods the student must often have recourse to the actual records of legal proceedings. Some parts of the subject have, however, received attention from scholars, and the works which are here listed have been of particular use in the preparation of the chapter on legal chronology, below, pp. 65–74.

Alexander, J. J., ' The dates of county days ', in *Bulletin of the Institute of Historical Research*, iii (1925–6), 89–95.

Carr, Cecil T., ' The citation of statutes ', in *Cambridge legal essays in honour of H. Bond, W. W. Buckland, and C. S. Kenny*. (Cambridge, 1926).

Chronological table of the statutes (1235–1968.) (London, H.M.S.O., 1969).

A companion work is the *Index to the statutes in force*. 2 vols. (London, H.M.S.O., 1968.)

Finch, Henry, *Law, or a discourse thereof, in foure bookes*. (London, 1627).

Hopton, Arthur, *Concordancy of yeeres*. (London, 1612).

Also a new edition by John Penkethman, entitled *Hopton's concordancy enlarged* (London, 1635).

Jenkinson, Hilary and Formoy, Beryl E. R. (ed.), *Select cases in the exchequer of pleas*. (Selden Soc. Publications, vol. 48, 1932).

List of Plea Rolls of various courts. Public Record Office, Lists and Indexes, no. 4, revised edition. (London, H.M. Stationery Office, 1910).

Oughton, Thomas, *Ordo judiciorum.* 2 vols. (London, 1728–38).

Sayles, G. O. (ed.), *Select cases in the court of king's bench, Edw. I–Edw. III.* (Selden Soc. Pub., nos. 55, 57, 58, 74, 76, 82, 1936–65).

Spelman, Henry, 'The original of the four terms of the year', in *Reliquiæ spelmannianæ,* ed. Edmund Gibson. (London, 1723), ii. 69–104.

VII. DIPLOMATIC, ETC.

(*a*) The following list only gives a few of the most important general works and one or two essays of outstanding value.

de Boüard, A., *Manuel de diplomatique française et pontificale.* Tomes I and II, with plates. (Paris, 1929–52).

*Bresslau, Harry, *Handbuch der Urkundenlehre für Deutschland und Italien.* 2nd edition. 2 vols. (Leipzig, 1912–31).
  The most solid and trustworthy modern guide.

Galbraith, V. H., 'Monastic foundation charters of the eleventh and twelfth centuries', *Cambridge Historical Journal,* iv (1934), 205–22, 296–8.

*Giry, Arthur, *Manuel de diplomatique.* (Paris, 1894, reprinted 1925).
  Out of date in many details, but still the clearest and most elaborate general treatise.

Hall, Hubert, *A formula book of English official historical documents.* 2 parts. (Cambridge, 1908–9).
  A useful collection, rather confusedly presented.

*[Madox, Thomas], *Formulare anglicanum.* (London, 1702).
  An important collection of documents, preceded by an important introduction.

Maxwell-Lyte, Sir Henry C., *Historical notes on the use of the Great Seal of England.* (London, 1926).
  Discusses in great detail the significance of dates in documents of the English chancery, etc.

*Stenton, F. M., *Transcripts of charters relating to Gilbertine houses.* (Lincoln Record Society Publications, vol. xviii, 1922).
  The introduction contains a valuable note on the diplomatic of private charters.

——, 'Acta episcoporum', *Cambridge Historical Journal,* iii (1929), 1–14.

(*b*) For dating by study of handwriting the following amply illustrated works are recommended :

Jenkinson, Hilary, *The later court hands in England.* 2 vols. (Cambridge, 1927).

Johnson, Charles, and Jenkinson, Hilary, *English court hand a.d. 1066 to 1500.* 2 vols. (Oxford, 1915).

SELECT BIBLIOGRAPHY

Thompson, Edward Maunde, *Handbook of Greek and Latin palæography.* (Oxford, 1912).

——, ' The history of English handwriting A.D. 700–1400 ', *Trans. Bibliographical Soc.*, (London, 1901), 109–42, 213–53.

(*c*) For the possibilities of dating by tests applied to paper and ink, see

Mitchell, C. Ainsworth, *Documents and their scientific examination.* (London, 1922, new edition, 1935).

An admirable demonstration of detecting forgeries by applying dating tests to paper and printers' founts is to be found in :

Carter, John, and Pollard, Graham, *An enquiry into the nature of certain nineteenth century pamphlets.* (London, 1934).

ADDENDA

I. GENERAL AND MISCELLANEOUS WORKS (cf. p. xi above).

Handbook of British chronology, ed. F. M. Powicke and E. B. Fryde, 2nd edition (Royal Hist. Soc., Guides and Handbooks no. 2, London, 1961).

> This omits the sections on Reckonings of Time and Saints' Days and Legal Chronology and the Table of Regnal Years all contained in the first edition of 1939, which were revised for the present *Handbook of dates.* The second edition greatly enlarges the lists of office-holders and gives much more bibliographical matter.

Handbook of oriental history, ed. C. H. Philips (Royal Hist. Soc., Guides and Handbooks no. 6, London, 1951 and reprinted).

Wüstenfeld, F., *Vergleichungstabellen der muhammedanischen und christlichen Zeitrechnungen.* 2nd edition, revised by E. Mahler (Leipzig, 1926).

For the calendar used by the Society of Friends see Harris Nicolas, *Chronology of History* pp. 180–1.

For the reckoning by mayoral years in London judicial records of the seventeenth and eighteenth centuries see Hugh Bowler in *Publications of the Catholic Record Soc.*, xxxiv (1934), pp. xix–xx, and P. E. Jones in *Notes and Queries*, clxxxix (1945), 278.

For eclipses of the sun and moon :

Schroeter, J. Fr., *Spezieller Kanon der zentralen Sonnen- und Mondfinsternisse, welche innerhalb des Zeitraums von 600 bis 1800 n. Chr. in Europa sichtbar waren.* (Kristiania, 1923).

For storms, droughts and famines :

Britton, C. E. *A meteorological chronology to A.D. 1450.* Meteorological Office, Geophysical Memoirs no. 70. (London, Stationery Office, 1937.)

Titow, J. ' Evidence of weather in the account rolls of the Bishopric of Winchester, 1209–1350 ', *Economic History Review*, 2nd series, xii (1960), 360–407.

SELECT BIBLIOGRAPHY

II. The beginning of the year (cf. p. xii above).

Levison, Wilhelm, *England and the continent in the eighth century*. (Oxford, 1946.)

> Appendix vi : ' The beginning of the year of the incarnation in Bede's " Historia ecclesiastica " ', criticizes Poole's study (see above) and affects what is said below (p. 4) about Bede. See also Paul Grosjean, ' La date du colloque de Whitby ', *Analecta Bollandiana*, lxxviii (1960), 233–74.

Whitelock, Dorothy, ' On the commencement of the year in the Anglo-Saxon chronicles ', in *Two Anglo-Saxon chronicles parallel*, ed. C. Plummer, reprinted Oxford, 1952, vol. ii, pp. cxxxix–cxlii^c.

Vaughan, R., ' The chronology of the Parker Chronicle, 890–970 ', *Eng. Hist. Rev.*, lxix (1954), 59–66.

Wainwright, F. T., ' The chronology of the " Mercian Register " ', *Eng. Hist. Rev.*, lx (1945), 385–92.

IV. Papal chronology (cf. pp. xiii–xiv above).

Buzzi, G., ' Per la cronologia d'alcuni pontefici dei sec. x e xi ', *Archivio della Società romana di storia patria*, xxxv (1912), 611–622.

> Suggests some dates differing from the dating of Poole's studies (see above). Poole's dating is followed on pp. 36–37 below.

Cheney, C. R. and Mary G. (ed.), *The letters of Pope Innocent III (1198–1216) concerning England and Wales: a calendar with an appendix of texts* (Oxford, 1967).

VII. Diplomatic, etc. (cf. p. xvi above).

Bishop, T. A. M., *Scriptores regis: Facsimiles to identify and illustrate the hands of royal scribes in original charters of Henry I, Stephen, and Henry II* (Oxford, 1961).

Cheney, C. R., *English bishops' chanceries, 1100–1250* (Manchester, 1950).

RECKONINGS OF TIME

I. The Julian Calendar

Throughout the Middle Ages, and in some countries for much longer, the calendar in use was that known as the Julian, because it was originally introduced by Julius Cæsar in 45 B.C. This way of reckoning is now known as the Old Style, in contradistinction to the New Style, that is to say reckoning by the Gregorian calendar, introduced by Pope Gregory XIII in 1582.

The Julian calendar set up a common year consisting of 365 days, while every fourth year was to contain an extra day, the sixth calends of March (24 February) being doubled and the year therefore being described as *annus bissextilis*. This latter device was intended to rectify, at regular intervals, the accumulated discrepancy between the calendar year of 365 days and the solar year, calculated by the astronomers at $365\frac{1}{4}$ days. The mistake was made, however, of counting in the current year when deciding which was 'every fourth year', and in practice the bissextile years occurred in what we should call every third year. Thus an error rapidly accumulated, until the Emperor Augustus got rid of it by ordaining that twelve successive years should consist of 365 days only. The next bissextile or leap year was A.D. 4, and thereafter, as long as the Old Style lasted, every fourth year, in the modern sense, was a leap year.

II. The Year

The Christian era.

The use for dating purposes of the Christian year (*annus domini, annus ab incarnatione domini, annus gratiæ*) arose somewhat unexpectedly through the compilation of a table for calculating the date of Easter, made by the monk Dionysius Exiguus in A.D. 525. This was intended to continue to A.D. 626 the Easter Table then in use, of which the cycle would end in 531. Dionysius, a Scythian by birth, but living in Rome and *moribus omnino romanus*, constructed a list of years calculated not from the prevailing era of Diocletian, the pagan emperor, but from the Incarnation of Our Lord. A continuator carried on the table to A.D. 721. At the synod of Whitby, in A.D. 664, Wilfrid, as part of his advocacy of all things Roman, secured the acceptance in England of the Dionysian Easter Table, and with it, of course, came the accompanying list of years. Dionysius himself had had no thought of establishing a new era, but now his device was adopted for chronological purposes by Bede and even, it is possible, in a few instances before Bede. Starting from English usage in the eighth century, the new era gradually spread to the Continent until in every country of Western Europe except Spain (see below), Christians reckoned from A.D. 1.

In England this method was used for the dating of official documents long before it was adopted by continental chanceries. The year *ab incarnatione* is found in Anglo-Saxon diplomas very soon after the death of Bede to replace or supplement dating by indiction, and was commonly used for such royal documents as bore dates (even when they also used the regnal year) until late in the twelfth century.

Outside the royal chancery the reckoning is to be found in English legal instruments of all sorts in the exceptional cases in which a date of any kind is vouchsafed. Later in the Middle Ages documents of ecclesiastical provenance generally, and private charters occasionally, are dated by the year of grace. The era of the incarnation also regularly provided the chronological framework of English chronicles and annals.

The Spanish era.

In Spain, Portugal, and those southern parts of Gaul which were for a time under the rule of the Visigoths, an era was used which had been taken over by the latter from the Christians of Roman Spain. The era originated in an Easter Table of which the first cycle began, not at the year of incarnation, but at 38 B.C., and it was reckoned from 1 January 38 B.C. The era was in use in Catalonia to 1180, in Aragon to 1350, in Valencia to 1358, in Castile to 1382, in Portugal to 1420. The date is always given in the form ' era millesima octava ' not ' anno millesimo octavo ', and to find the equivalent year of the Christian era one must subtract 38 from the date in the Spanish era.

The indiction.

Unlike the Christian and Spanish eras, the indiction was originally a civil reckoning of time. It is a cycle of fifteen years, counted as *indictio prima, secunda*, and so on, to 15, reverting then to 1. The cycles were always computed from A.D. 312, but there were three chief methods of reckoning the opening date :

(a) The Greek, or Constantinopolitan, Indiction, beginning on 1 September. The popes seem to have used this fairly regularly till 1087, after which the practice of the papal chancery varied till Alexander III (1159–81).

(b) The Bedan, or Cæsarean, or Imperial Indiction, or the Indiction of Constantine, beginning on 24 September. This was probably introduced by Bede into England, where it became usual, and was adopted by the papacy under Alexander III.

(c) The Roman, or Pontifical, Indiction, beginning on 25 December (or sometimes on 1 January), was in fact only occasionally used in the papal chancery, but is found in other places at various periods.

The use of the indiction-year as an element in the dating of documents goes back to imperial Rome, when it was added to statements of the consular and imperial years. It continued to be used by the papacy and the royal chanceries of the West in the early Middle Ages for the more solemn privileges and legal records. It is also found in some private charters. But by the end of the thirteenth century it was generally ignored except in one class of document : the instruments drawn up by public notaries continue to exhibit the indiction together with other dating elements until the sixteenth century.

The dating formula, *indictio prima*, etc., simply shows the place which the year occupies in an unspecified cycle of fifteen years. The rule for calculating it is to subtract 312 from the number of the year of grace and divide by fifteen : the remainder will correspond with the number of the year in the indiction and the quotient will be one less than the number of the indiction (but the latter is seldom mentioned in documents). Since the beginning of the year of grace does not, in most systems of reckoning, coincide with the beginning of the indiction, the equation must take account of the day of the year. As an example, take a document dated 1 November 1094 : 1094 − 312 = 782 ; 782 ÷ 15 = 52 with a remainder of 2. Therefore, the number of the indiction *for the greater part of* 1094 is 2. But the date in question (1 November) falls in the lesser part of the year according to the Greek and Bedan indictions : it is therefore *indictio tertia* by these reckonings, *indictio secunda* by the Roman reckoning.

The regnal year.

From ancient up to modern times it has been a common practice to date official documents by the year of the rulers or magistrates from whom the documents emanated or within whose jurisdiction they were issued. Roman law demanded that certain classes of documents should bear the names of the consuls for the year ; and, in the absence of exact information, dating by reference to past consuls was sometimes preferred (e.g. *post consulatum Flavi Fausti iunioris*). In A.D. 537 Justinian provided that the years of the emperor's reign should be added and thereafter the *post-consulatum* element, though it lingered on in various forms, ceased to be of practical importance. But the system which had been used by the consuls of the Roman people and the emperors was copied by popes, bishops, kings, dukes, and lesser men. It found its way, moreover, from official documents to literary narratives. Sometimes the regnal year was used to the exclusion of the indiction or year of grace, sometimes it accompanied these elements. For the method of its use in the English chancery and the papal chancery the reader is referred to the notes which precede the lists of kings and popes.

III. The Beginning of the Year of Grace

Historians' errors in translating dates are most often due to carelessness about the various starting-points of the year of grace. Half a dozen different reckonings have been used at one time or another, and it is not uncommon to find two reckonings simultaneously used in adjacent countries or even in one country in different types of record. This has long been a matter for remark among historians. Gervase, the twelfth-century monk of Canterbury, bewailed the confusion arising from various computations : he himself had wavered between the systems of Christmas and the Annunciation before finally adopting the former for his chronicle and even then he made a concession to the more popular system for one famous event, the death of Thomas Becket on 29 December 1170. R. L. Poole furnishes an excellent illustration of the varieties in use in the Middle Ages : ' If we suppose (he says) a traveller to set out from Venice on March 1, 1245, the first day of the Venetian year, he would find himself in 1244 when he reached Florence ; and if after a short stay he went on to Pisa, the year 1246 would have already begun there. Continuing his journey westward, he would find himself again in 1245 when he entered Provence, and on arriving in France before Easter (April 16) he would be once more in 1244.' To take a case from the simpler conditions of the eighteenth century, a traveller who left England in January 1720 would arrive in France to discover that the French had begun the year 1721. The student must therefore do his best to discover what reckonings his authorities employ before he accepts their chronology as it stands.

3

1 January.

The historical year, the year now used by historians, begins on 1 January. It thus corresponds with modern chronological practice and also with the Roman civil year, which continued in general use till the seventh century A.D. and survived still longer where the Spanish Era obtained. Although the Church preferred one of its own major festivals to mark the beginning of the year and wished to make a break with pagan antecedents,[1] 1 January was occasionally treated as the beginning of the year of grace in the Middle Ages. In the sixteenth century it found favour again throughout most of the continent of Europe.[2] In Scotland it became the official beginning of the year 1600 following 31 December 1599. In England and Ireland the change was not effected until the day after 31 December 1751, which became 1 January 1752.

The universal return to the 1 January reckoning is explained by the persistence of the Roman calendar of months and the constant calculation of the ecclesiastical calendar on the basis of a solar year beginning on 1 January. Moreover, this day was everywhere in popular estimation associated with the New Year. Thus Samuel Pepys, who reckoned the years of his diary from 25 March, always made mention of New Year's Day when he reached 1 January.

Christmas Day.

Bede, in his chronological writings, took for granted that the year of grace must begin with the Nativity, Christmas Day, but in his *Ecclesiastical history*, since he was dealing with documents dated by the earlier reckoning from the Indiction of September, started his own year in September also. His chronological theory, however, proved to be more influential than his practice, and the reckoning from Christmas was soon in general vogue. It was used in the Empire till the second quarter of the thirteenth century, by the popes from 962 to 1098 (and even later in letters, as distinct from *privilegia*), in France and most of western Europe, except Spain, till the twelfth century. The Anglo-Saxon and Norman kings of England used it and Benedictine writers, with characteristic conservatism, still employed it after it had been abandoned in most quarters of Plantagenet England. This fact has too often been overlooked by later historians. Thus, for example, Edmund of Cornwall, cousin of Edward I, is very commonly said—on the authority of Matthew Paris—to have been born on 26 December 1250. But Matthew Paris used the Christmas reckoning, and the historical date is therefore 26 December 1249. The whole octave of the Nativity was, of course, a time of high festival, so that in practice the new beginning on 25 December and the older reckoning from 1 January sometimes shaded into each other.

The Annunciation.

Lady Day, the feast of the Annunciation on 25 March, was, in a sense, a more logical starting-point for years reckoned from the Incarnation than the feast of the Nativity, so long as the feast in question was that of the *preceding* 25 March. This way of reckoning started at Arles late in the ninth century, spread in Burgundy and northern Italy, was used, though with growing infrequency, in the papal

---

[1] 1 January was observed as the Feast of the Circumcision at least as early as the sixth century, and still earlier as the octave of the Nativity. Cf. *Decretum*, II. 26, 7, 14 and 16.
[2] Cf. below, p. 10.

chancery between 1088 and 1145, but remained a local use. It survived at Pisa till 1750, and has therefore been named the *calculus pisanus*. It is of little importance to students of English documents, though R. L. Poole found an isolated case of its use in a charter of Richard I. The grant, however, was to Pisan merchants in the Holy Land, so that the occasion was exceptional.

Less logical, but far more convenient, widespread, and important to the English historian was the use of 25 March *after* Christmas as the opening of the year. The origin of this practice is obscure, but may perhaps be traced to the influence of the abbey of Fleury, itself under Cluniac influence, and largely responsible for the increased emphasis laid upon devotions to the Virgin Mary in the early eleventh century.[1] In 1030 the style was in use at Fleury, and perhaps a few years earlier at Poitiers, which had connections with Fleury. Thus it long preceded the foundation of Cîteaux (1098), and cannot be due, as has often been suggested, to the Cistercians. The latter, however, gladly adopted the practice, as one more feature among many differentiating them from the earlier Benedictines. From a sense of a different kind of rivalry, Florence preferred the method as the opposite to that in vogue in Pisa, and so the new practice came to be called the *calculus florentinus*. It spread freely in France, though mainly in ecclesiastical circles, and from 1098 the papal chancery generally used it in its more solemn documents. In England it is found as early as the middle of the eleventh century, when certain annals of the *Anglo-Saxon chronicle* were apparently dated by this reckoning, but it only came into common English use late in the twelfth century and so continued to 1752. Medieval English writers using it sometimes defined their dating as *secundum consuetudinem* (or *secundum cursum et computationem) ecclesiae anglicanae*.[2]

From about the middle of the seventeenth century the practice of the continental countries, which had gone over to a year beginning with 1 January, must inevitably have had an effect on England. This influence was probably strengthened by English exiles abroad in the period of the Commonwealth. For official purposes, Englishmen continued till 1752 to use the old reckoning from 25 March, but they were wavering in their allegiance and found it convenient to give a double indication for the period between 1 January and 24 March; we commonly meet this in the form 29 February 167$\frac{5}{6}$ and we find it in all manner of official records and private papers of the period. Where no double indication is given, it is usually safe for the historian to assume that an Englishman writing in England reckons from 25 March, but it is worth remark that the printed almanacks started their year with 1 January and used the modern historical year, and so did some, at least, of the early periodicals and newspapers.[3]

Easter Day.

The *mos gallicanus*, which reckoned the year from the movable feast of Easter,[4] was introduced into the French chancery by Philip Augustus (1180–1223). It

---

[1] For full discussion, see Poole, *Studies*, pp. 13–17.

[2] The forms *ab incarnatione* and *incarnationis* normally (though not invariably) indicate the Annunciation style.

[3] Thus *The Spectator* begins in the historical year 1711 and bears the date '1 January 1711' on its first page; so also *The Gentleman's Magazine* begins the historical year 'January 1751' without any double indication of date.

[4] Those who used the Easter reckoning sometimes started their year on Good Friday (whence the term 'a Passione') or Holy Saturday.

spread to some regions, such as Holland and Cologne, where there were direct family or trading connections, but it never became uniform for the whole of France, or popular outside court circles. Its disadvantages are obvious, and if, as Poole has suggested, Philip chose it because he ' desired to mark his conquest of the English possessions in France by the use of a style different from those which had been current in them ',[1] he could hardly have made a gesture more disconcerting to his own subjects.

1, 24, or 29 September.

It is pointed out above (p. 4) that Bede, in his *Ecclesiastical history*, reckoned the year of grace as beginning at the same time as the year of the indiction. The indiction which he used for this calculation was either the Greek (beginning 1 September) or the Cæsarean (beginning 24 September), and more probably the latter. A similar reckoning is found in the Anglo-Saxon chronicles in the second half of the ninth century ; when the usage ceased is not exactly known ; the chronicles generally had reverted to the Christmas style by the beginning of the tenth century. According to the September style, the year of grace began in advance of the modern historical year. For example, A.D. 890 was understood to begin on 1 September or 24 September in the historical year 889. This practice has misled the older historians into post-dating by a year many notable events of Anglo-Saxon history.

Another September style appears as the aberration of an English chronicler of the fourteenth century, Adam de Murimuth. He did not equate the year of grace to any indiction-year, but began his year on Michaelmas Day (29 September) in advance of the historical year.

IV. DIVISIONS OF THE YEAR

The Roman calendar.

The division of the Julian year into months, as revised by the Emperor Augustus, has prevailed up to the present day. The Julian method of counting the days within the months also persisted for many centuries and was unaffected by the Gregorian reform. This calendar of the year is set out in full below (pp. 75–81).

Another method of counting the days is known as the *consuetudo bononiensis*, or custom of Bologna. So far as concerns England it may be termed the notarial method, for it is scarcely found outside documents drafted by public notaries. According to this reckoning, the day of the month was indicated by its position in the first sixteen days (or fifteen days in months of thirty days) reckoning forwards, or in the last fifteen days, reckoning backwards. Thus, *quarto die intrante Madio* indicates 4 May, and *quarto die exeunte* (or *stante*) *Madio* indicates 28 May.

The modern way of numbering the days of the month in one continuous series is found occasionally in very early times and gradually won acceptance during the Middle Ages as the most convenient and ' fool-proof ' method of numeration. But in the Middle Ages it never ousted other systems ; apart from the Roman system and the Bolognese systems, it had to compete with the ecclesiastical calendar.

The ecclesiastical calendar.

While the Christian Church could not drive out of use the Roman calendar, it introduced into common practice other methods of reckoning and stating dates.

---

[1] Poole, *Studies*, p. 23.

In the first place, the ecclesiastical calendar divided the year by weeks in the manner now universal.[1] Sunday was the first day of the week (*feria prima* or *dies dominicus*) and the chief day as regards liturgical observances. But the Church also consecrated certain days of the year (irrespective of their place in the week) to festivals of particular saints, and these became the material for dating events (see below, pp. 40–64). Finally, the Church attached special importance to commemorations connected with the life of Christ : Christmas, Good Friday, Ascension Day, and the like. Some of these, like the feasts of the saints, were fixed points in the Roman year : Christmas, for example, was always celebrated on viii kal. Jan., otherwise 25 December. But Easter Day was a 'movable' feast, and on Easter depended a whole series of other commemorations. Easter was 'movable' in the sense that it was fixed in relation to the moon's phases and the day of the week, and these do not recur at the same point in successive calendar years. After many disputes, which produced divergences in other parts of Christendom,[2] the Latin Church determined that Easter should be celebrated on the Sunday following the first full moon on or after the 21 March.[3] The result, in short, is this : that Easter never falls on the same day of the month in two successive years and it may fall on any of the thirty-five days between 22 March and 25 April (both included). The ecclesiastical calendar for the entire year is controlled by this fact of a movable Easter. To enable students to see clearly the ecclesiastical calendar for any given year from A.D. 500 to A.D. 2000, the series of tables at the end of this volume is provided. Confronted with a document dated on the Tuesday after Trinity, A.D. 1288, the student first discovers from the chronological table on p. 158 that Easter fell on 28 March in 1288 ; then, turning to table 7, he finds that the date in question is, in modern terms, 25 May 1288.

The medieval computists, faced with the problem of calculating the incidence of movable feasts, adopted various devices for relating the days of the week and the lunar month to the calendar. The scaffolding of the tables they compiled provided material for elaborating statements of date which for ordinary purposes were quite long enough already. Thus the Anglo-Saxon solemn diploma might set out not only the indiction year, the regnal year, and the day of the month in Roman form, but also the golden number, the epact, the dominical letter, and the con- currents. These elements also find their way into dating clauses of documents at other times and places during the Middle Ages. Used in this way, as parts of a dating clause, they indicate the position of the year in cycles of years, and thus might fittingly have found a place in the preceding section of this chapter ; but their original purpose was purely to establish the place of the Church's festivals in the calendar, and so they may logically be described at this point. We shall make

[1] We are of course only concerned here with the week as an element in the dating of records. For the observance of the week in the pagan Roman world and in Jewry, see F. H. Colson, *The week* (Cambridge, 1926).

[2] For the Easter of the Celtic British Church up to the year A.D. 717, see Giry, *Manuel*, pp. 212–13, or Wallis, *Eng. regnal years*, pp. 76–9.

[3] Because 21 March was taken to be invariably the date of the vernal equinox. In fact it is not ; and therefore some accurate astronomical calculations of the paschal moon differ from the approximate historical reckonings. But generally only the latter is in question when Easter is concerned. The Protestant states of Germany observed Easter according to an improved calculation in 1724 and 1744. The divergence of Swedish usage in the eighteenth and nineteenth centuries is more complicated (see Grotefend, *Taschenbuch*, pp. 27–8).

7

no attempt to do more than state how they are computed. For a more complete discussion the reader is referred to Giry's *Manuel*, on which this brief account is chiefly based.

Golden number (*numerus aureus, cyclus decemnovennalis*). For calculating the date of the paschal moon, which in turn governed the date of Easter, computists have made use of the close approximation of the lunar and solar cycles after a lapse of nineteen solar years. The slight inexactitude of their calculation has had no effect on the fixing of dates : the cycle of nineteen years has been generally accepted. The years of the cycle are numbered from I to XIX in direct series and the number for each year is known as the Golden Number. The cycle is computed from the year I B.C. and is usually held to begin 1 January in that year. To find the golden number of a year of grace, add 1 to the year of grace and divide by 19. The remainder is the golden number, unless the remainder is 0, when the golden number is XIX.

Epact (*Epacta lunaris*). The position of the year in the nineteen-year cycle is also represented in another way for the purpose of calculating the date of Easter. For this purpose it is necessary to establish the relationship between the solar year and the phase of the moon at 22 March, the earliest date for Easter. Since the solar year was estimated to have eleven days in excess of twelve complete lunar cycles, this relationship changed by eleven days annually ; the moon begins each year eleven days older than it was a year ago. When a new moon falls on 22 March the golden number is I (e.g., A.D. 1482 : 1483 divided by 19 leaves a remainder of 1), and the epact, which represents the age of the moon, is nil (*epacta nulla*).[1] In the next year the epact is eleven, and the next year twenty-two. The progression through the nineteen-year cycle is straightforward, except that thirty is deducted from numbers in excess of thirty.[2]

To find the epact of any year of grace, divide the year of grace by 19, multiply the remainder by 11, and divide by 30 : the remainder is the number of the epact.

While the annual mutation of the epact occurred, according to some medieval computists, on 1 January, it seems that other reckonings were also employed. When the calendar year began on 25 March or 1 September, the epact probably changed at that point.

Dominical letter (*littera dominicalis*). To determine the date of Easter one must know the sequence of the days of the week following the paschal full moon, and for this purpose special tables were devised in early Christian times. There are seven possible relationships of the days of the week to the calendar of the year, and the letters A to G were used to indicate the cycle of seven days beginning at 1 January. The dominical letter for the year is the letter allocated, according to this system, to the first Sunday in the year. Thus, Sunday fell on 4 January 1545 and the dominical letter for the year is the fourth letter, D ; in 1549 it fell on 6 January and the dominical letter is F, and so on. In the sequence of years the dominical letters run in retrograde series, for the year beginning on Monday (dominical letter G) is commonly succeeded by a year beginning on Tuesday (dominical letter F). A

---

[1] In some tables, e.g. those of Augustus de Morgan, the number 29 is given instead of zero.

[2] The cycle thus becomes 0, 11, 22, 3, 14, 25, 6, 17, 28, 9, 20, 1, 12, 23, 4, 15, 26, 7, 18. This cycle, and the above description, only hold good for the Old Style calendar. It seems unnecessary to enter into the complexities of the New Style reckoning of epacts, since the epact only appears as an element in the dating of documents during the Middle Ages.

complication is introduced in the leap year. The extra day, or *dies bissextus*, has the same letter assigned to it as has the day which it doubles. This produces a change in the cycle during February, so that the dominical letter for the period after *bis vi kal. Mar.* (24 February)—or after 28 February, if the modern system of dating is employed—differs from that for the preceding period. Thus the dominical letter for 1 January–28 February 1944 (a leap year) is B (1 January was Saturday), while for the remainder of the year it is A. The dominical letter for the next year 1945 (a common year) is G (1 January was Monday). It follows from the existence of leap years that the dominical letters move in cycles of twenty-eight, not seven, years.

Concurrents (*concurrentes septimanæ*). To each year was allotted by the computists a number (1 to 7) which represents the concurrents, or number of days between the last Sunday in the preceding year and 1 January. Since the concurrents are designed to serve the same purpose as the dominical letters, there is a regular correspondence between the two reckonings. This can be simply expressed as follows:

Dominical letter	.	.	.	F	E	D	C	B	A	G
Concurrents	.	.	.	1	2	3	4	5	6	7

It will be noticed that the concurrents are counted as 7 when the preceding year ends on a Sunday. It should also be observed that in leap years the concurrents correspond to the dominical letter for the *latter* part of the year.

V. FRACTIONS OF THE DAY

Early medieval custom divided the day into two periods, running from sunset to sunrise and from sunrise to sunset respectively.[1] Within each period were twelve hours, the length of which necessarily varied with the season. The hour which formed $\frac{1}{12}$ of the winter night, for example, would be longer than a similar fraction of the summer night. As a consequence of this, the seven 'canonical hours', or the times appointed for the services of the Church, similarly varied with the season, until the introduction of hours 'of the clock'.[2]

By the fourteenth century clocks with bells began to be displayed in churches and other buildings, and by this means a system of hours uniform in length came gradually into general use. The hours 'of the clock' have been usually counted in two series of twelve, from midnight and from noon respectively; but in recent times certain official records (a familiar example of this is the railway time-table) employ a single 24-hour series beginning at midnight. The development of telephony and wireless telegraphy has made it particularly necessary for the

---

[1] Cf. Anscombe, *Brit. Numism. Journ.*, 1st series, iv. 284–92. The *Digest*, 2, 12, 8 reckoned the period of 24 hours from midnight, but from early times the liturgical observance of a feast began (and begins) with first vespers (G. Schreiber, *Die Wochentage* (1959), p. 237). But Roger Wendover (*Flores historiarum* (Rolls series), i. 299) speaks of 'diem dominicum cum noctu sequente, qui dies dicitur naturalis'. See also L. C. Hector, 'The beginning of the " Natural Day " in the late fourteenth century', *Journal of the Soc. of Archivists*, II. iii. (1961), 87–9.

[2] The canonical hours are Matins, Prime, Terce, Sext, None, Vespers, and Compline. For a clear and detailed account of the early monastic time-table, David Knowles, *The Monastic order in England 943–1216* (1941), pp. 448–53, 714–15.

historian of modern times to pay attention to the exact hour of related events. In so doing he must of course make the adjustments demanded by discrepant methods of timing. Quite apart from the differences which arise from astronomical readings taken in different parts of the globe (Zone Standard Times), there is the difference between Greenwich Mean Time and the Summer Time which in recent times has been used during part or the whole of the year in the British Isles. The facts are conveniently set out in the annual volumes of *Whitaker's Almanack*.

Finally, the student of nautical records must take account of the system of reckoning found in ships' log-books from the seventeenth century until early in the nineteenth. Like the astronomer, the mariner determined his day by observation of the sun; and he recorded the events of twenty-four hours (on his log-board) from midday to midday. It was his practice to make the division of his log-book according to this scheme and to assign to each 24-hour period a date twelve hours in advance of the ordinary calendar-day. Thus, the battle of Trafalgar, fought in the afternoon of 21 October 1805, is recorded in the log-book of the *Victory* under 22 October. At about this very time, the Navy apparently began to date its log-book entries from midnight, following an Admiralty Order of October 1805; but in the merchant service it was still usual at a much later date for log-books to begin their day at noon.[1] This was, be it noted, a chronological arrangement peculiar to one class of record. Throughout the period in which it prevailed, sailors used the ordinary calendar-day in their letters and journals.

VI. The Gregorian Calendar: New Style

In the course of the Middle Ages various scholars interested in chronology pointed out that the calendar year was increasingly divergent from the solar year. The reckoning of the latter at $365\frac{1}{4}$ days was a slight over-estimate, and by the sixteenth century this annual error had caused, cumulatively, a discrepancy of ten days. It was not, however, until 24 February 1582 that a bull of Pope Gregory XIII ordered the use of a reformed calendar. This met the immediate trouble by cutting ten days out of the year 1582, so that 15 October followed immediately upon 4 October, while future difficulties were to be avoided by making only the fourth of the end-years of successive centuries a leap year. The bull allowed for A.D. 2000 to be a leap year, and this was adopted in later changes to the Gregorian calendar. The year was to begin on 1 January.

This desirable reform was proposed at an unfortunate date, when religious and political hostilities were so pronounced that even a measure so much to the general benefit was not regarded objectively as a mere matter of chronological accuracy, and was therefore at the time not accepted by any but states in the Roman obedience. The student of history from 1582 onwards, therefore, is in a worse plight than before, for he has to be sure, as he deals with the documents of Catholic, Orthodox, or Protestant states, whether at the date concerned that state was dating by the Gregorian calendar ('New Style') or by the Julian calendar ('Old Style'). Broadly speaking, Catholic states adopted the New Style in the sixteenth century, Protestant states early or late in the eighteenth century, Russia, the Balkan States, and Greece in the twentieth century.

[1] H. Raper, *The practice of navigation and nautical astronomy* (1840), p. 93.

It must be remembered that in every country an interval necessarily followed between the acceptance of the reform and its being put into practice, and that the methods of introduction were not uniform. In Great Britain and Ireland the change was effected by ' Chesterfield's Act ' (24 Geo. II, c. 23), passed in March 1751, which decreed that throughout the dominions of the British crown the following 1 January should be the first day of 1752 and 2 September 1752 should be followed by 14 September.[1] It must not be assumed that each European state, when it adopted the New Style calendar, acted like the Papacy and England in fixing 1 January as the beginning of the year. For in some countries this preceded the change from the Julian to the Gregorian calendar, while in a few it only followed long afterwards.[2]

Because the adoption of New Style had not synchronized in all countries, there came into being ' one of the most dangerous traps for students using original documents ',[3] to be avoided only by careful consideration of the origin of any document in use and the habits of its writer. A difference of dating may amount to 10, 11, 12, or 13 days according as the document is written after 1582, 1700, 1800, or 1900. Thus, when William of Orange had left Holland, where the New Style was in use, on 11 November 1688, he reached England, where it was not, on 5 November. In official communications with foreign powers and with its representatives abroad, the English government sought to obviate the confusion which might easily arise from this conflict of Styles. From Elizabeth's reign onwards English correspondence with the continent often gives both forms of date. Sir William Boswell writes from the Hague to Sir John Coke on ' $\frac{12}{22}$ Dec. 1635 '. Nearly three centuries later we find the same practice in a country which retained the Old Style : Isvolski, Russian minister of Foreign Affairs, dates a letter to the British ambassador ' 16/29 Août 1907 '. At times when the writer does not give a double date, he may indicate the Style employed by adding O.S. or N.S. ; but more often the date bears no such indication and the historian must decide what was intended according to the nationality and the circumstances of the writer.

[1] For the effect upon George II's twenty-sixth regnal year see below, p. 28, and for the complete calendar for the year 1752 see the special table on pp. 154–5.
[2] Cf. above, p. 4. Details of the changes on the continent will be found in the works of Cappelli and Grotefend. The Julian calendar to A.D. 2000 is given by Giry.
[3] Stamp, *Methods of chronology*, p. 6.

RULERS OF ENGLAND AND REGNAL YEARS

The regnal year is used in Anglo-Saxon royal charters early in the eighth century and the usage is based, one can hardly doubt, on contemporary Merovingian practice. The Anglo-Saxon kings continue to use this reckoning upon occasion until the tenth century, but thereafter it is only found exceptionally until the reign of Richard I.[1] From 1189 onwards it has been the approved method of expressing the year-date in documents of the civil government in England. Moreover, English private charters, which until Edward I's reign are usually undated, thereafter record the regnal year as a matter of course.

The scarcity of dated documents before the reign of Henry II prevents us from saying how the regnal year was reckoned in early days, i.e. at what point the reign was deemed to have begun. From Henry II to Henry III the regnal year was always reckoned from the day of coronation. With the death of Henry III a change of system occurred. Edward I's reign was deemed to begin four days after his father died and 'before the tomb had even been closed', although he did not return from abroad until two years later. Thereafter it was taken for granted that at the death of one king the next succeeded immediately and his first regnal year began.

The student of the thirteenth century should note a peculiarity of the reckoning for the reign of King John, which has often led historians into error. John was crowned on Ascension Day 1199 and this movable feast became the date at which his regnal years began. They are thus of unequal length, and we are faced with the confusing fact (to take one example) that 12 May 1206 and 12 May 1207 both fall within the eighth year of the king.[2] But it must be observed that when the regnal year runs, as it usually does, from a fixed point in the year, there is sometimes confusion of a contrary sort : the movable feasts of the Church, not the days of the month, are doubled in one regnal year. Thus, Easter Day occurs twice in 11 Henry VIII, and in 2 and 13 Charles I ; there was no Easter in 10 or 37 Henry VIII or in 3 or 14 Charles I.

One particular class of record introduces a complication into the reckoning of English regnal years. The exchequer period of account, which closed at Michaelmas, cut across the regnal year. Therefore, to date their annual account-roll, the Great Roll of the Pipe, the exchequer clerks reckoned according to the regnal year in which the accounts were either opened or closed. At different periods different practices prevailed. It follows that the student who refers to a Pipe Roll must take note of the system of dating which prevailed at the time. A table for this purpose is provided below (p. 32) But it cannot be emphasized too strongly that no evidence exists for the use of an 'Exchequer Year' dating for any other purpose than that

---

[1] It is found in Final Concords made in the King's Court in the reign of Henry II, but hardly ever appears in products of his chancery.

[2] The same phenomenon appears in the reckoning of regnal years of the Emperor Charles IV, who was crowned on Easter Day 1355. It may be that the same holds good for popes and bishops whose consecration occurred on the movable feasts of the Church, but this has not been verified.

of labelling records of the exchequer and the wardrobe.[1]   The year from Michaelmas to Michaelmas was not treated in the exchequer as the regnal year by which external events were dated.   Nor was it used for labelling all exchequer records ; the Issue and Receipt Rolls, while they necessarily take Michaelmas (as also Easter) for a terminal point, refer to the regnal year as it was reckoned in the chancery.   When, as often happened, a new regnal year opened in the midst of an exchequer term, the Issue and Receipt Rolls for that term either named both the regnal years involved or else named only the regnal year which was beginning.[2]

RULERS OF ENGLAND

FROM THE ENGLISH SETTLEMENT TO THE PRESENT DAY, WITH A TABLE OF REGNAL YEARS FROM A.D. 1154

KINGS OF KENT

Hengest	c. 455–488	Eadbert	? 725– ? 762 reigning jointly with Ethelbert II
Ceric surnamed Oisc	488–? 512	Alric	?
Octa	? 512– ?		possibly joint king with Ethelbert II and Eadbert
Eormenric	? –560		
Ethelbert	560–24 Feb. 616	Eardwulf	? reigning in 747 and 762 with Ethelbert II and Eadbert
Eadbald	616–640		
Earconbert	640–14 July 664	Sigered	? reigning in 762 with Eardwulf and Eadbert
Egbert I	664–July 673		
Hlothere	Summer 673–6 Feb. 685	Eanmund	? reigning 759 × 765 jointly with the preceding kings. Perhaps identical with Ealhmund, below
Eadric	685–(? Aug.) 686		
Suaebhard	reigning jointly, with Hlothere and with Wihtred respectively, on 1 March 676 and in July 692		
		Heaberht	reigning 764–765 jointly with Egbert II
Oswini	? 688–? 690	Egbert II	c. 765–780 or later
Wihtred	Autumn 690–23 April 725 first reigning jointly with Suaebhard	Ealhmund	reigning 784–786
		Eadbert (Praen)	796–798
		Eadwald	? 798 or 807
Ethelbert II	725–762 first reigning jointly with Eadbert	Cuthred	798–807
		Baldred	?–825

From 825 the kingdom of Kent, which had for long been dependent on Mercia, was a dependency of the West Saxon kingdom.

[1] E.g. the Memoranda Rolls of the remembrancers and certain of the Wardrobe Account Rolls are assigned to regnal years computed in this way.
[2] The whole matter of the so-called ' Exchequer Year ' is fully discussed by H. G. Richardson in the Society's *Transactions* of 1925 (see above, p. xii). Cf. *infra*, p. 69.

KINGS OF DEIRA

Aelli	559 or 560–588 or 590	Osric	late 632–Summer 633
Edwin	? 590–592 or 593	Oswald (St.)	633–5 Aug. 641 (with Bernicia)
Ethelfrith	592 or 593–616 (with Bernicia)	Oswine	644–20 Aug. 651
Edwin	616–12 Oct. 632 (with Bernicia)	Ethelwald	651–in or after Nov. 654

KINGS OF BERNICIA

Ida   547–559 or 560

(The order and regnal years of the kings between Ida and Ethelfrith are variously reported: for details, see *Handbook of Brit. Chronology*, pp. 9–11.)

Ethelfrith	592 or 593–616 (with Deira)	Oswald (St.)	633–5 Aug. 641 (with Deira)
Edwin	616–12 Oct. 632 (with Deira)	Oswiu	late 641–15 Feb. 670 (with Deira from 654)
Eanfrid	late 632–633		

KINGS OF NORTHUMBRIA

Ethelfrith	592 or 593–616	Elfwald I	778 or 779–788
Edwin	616–12 Oct. 632	Osred II	788 or 789–790
Oswald (St.)	633–5 Aug. 641	Ethelred I	790–April 796
Oswiu	654–15 Feb. 670	Osbald	796
Egfrith	Feb. 670–20 May 685	Eardwulf	? 26 May 796–806 (and see below)
Aldfrith	May 685–14 Dec. 704		
Osred I	Dec. 704 or early 705–716	Elfwald II	806–807 or 808
		Eardwulf	808 ?
Coenred	716–718	Eanred	807 or 808–840 or 841
Osric	718–9 May 729	Ethelred II	840 or 841–844 (and see below)
Ceolwulf	729–737		
Eadbert	737–758	Redwulf	844
Oswulf	757 or 758–24 or 25 July 757 or 758	Ethelred II	844–849 or 850
		Osbert	849 or 850–862 or 863
Ethelwald Moll	5 Aug. 758 or 759–30 Oct. 765	Aelle	862 or 863–21 March 867
		Egbert I	867–873
Alchred	765–774	Ricsig	873–876
Ethelred I	774–778 or 779 (and see below)	Egbert II	876–? 878

Egbert II is the last recorded king of Northumbria, much of which came under the rule of the Scandinavian kings of York (see below, p. 17).

RULERS OF ENGLAND

KINGS OF MERCIA

Cearl	*c.* 600	Egfrith	July 796–Dec. 796
Penda	? late 632–15 Nov. 654	Coenwulf	Dec. 796–? 821
(Oswiu of Northumbria ruled 654–657)		Ceolwulf I	821–823
Wulfhere	657–674	Beornwulf	823–825
Ethelred	674–704	Ludecan	825–827
Coenred	704–709	Wiglaf	827–840
Ceolred	709–716	Beorhtwulf	840–852
Ethelbald	716–? 757	Burgred	852–874
Beornred	757	Ceolwulf II	874–? before 883
Offa	757–July 796		

By 886 Alfred King of the West Saxons apparently was acknowledged king of all the English not under Danish rule.

KING OF LINDSEY

Aldfrith   reigning between 786 and 796.

This king's ancestors may have ruled Lindsey, but the kingdom was normally subject to Mercia or Northumbria.

KINGS OF THE EAST ANGLES

Redwald	late 6th century–616 or later		
Earpwald	? 616–627 or 628	Ethelred	?
Sigeberht	630 or 631– ?	Ethelbert	? –794
Ecgric	? reigning jointly with Sigeberht	Eadwald, Athelstan, Ethelweard, Beorhtric	ruled (not necessarily in this order) 794–855
Anna	? –654		
Aethelhere	654–15 Nov. 654	Edmund	855–20 Nov. 870
Ethelwold	late 654–? 663 or 664	Ethelred	(possibly Ethelred I of the West Saxons) ? 870
Aldwulf	663 or 664–713	Oswald	? *c.* 870
Alfwold	? 713–749		
Hun, Beonna, Alberht	reigning jointly 749		

After Oswald the East Angles came under Danish rule.

KINGS OF THE SOUTH SAXONS

Aelle	? 477–? 514	? Aethelstan	reigning jointly with Nunna in 714
? Cissa		Osmund	?
Aethelwalh	before 674–between 680 and 685	? Oswald	
Berhthun	? reigning jointly after	Oslac (dux)	reigning 780
Andhun	Aethelwalh till between 685 and 688	Aldwulf	late 8th cent.
Nothelm		? Aelhwald	reigning jointly with Aldwulf
Nunna [1]	reigning late 7th and early 8th centuries		
Wattus			

KINGS OF THE EAST SAXONS

Saeberht	before 604–616 or 617	Sebbi	c. 664–c. 694
Sexred	616 or 617–? c. 617	Sigeheard	c. 694–before 709
Saeweard		Swaefred	
Sigeberht I (Parvus)	? c. 617–653	Offa	after 694–709
Sigeberht II (Sanctus)	c. 653–before 664	Saelred	c. 709–746
		Swaefberht	d. 738
Swithelm	between 653 and 664	Swithred	c. 746–
Sighere	? c. 664–? 683 reigning jointly with Sebbi	Sigeric	? –? 799
		Sigered	? 799–? 825

From 825 the kingdom of the East Saxons, which had in Sigered's time been dependent on Mercia, was a dependency of the West Saxon kingdom.

KINGS OF THE WEST SAXONS

Cerdic	519–534	Cuthred	740–756
Cynric	534–560 possibly reigning jointly with Cerdic 519–534	Sigeberht	756–757
		Cynewulf	757–786
Ceawlin	560–591	Beorhtric	786–802
Ceol	591–597	Egbert	802–839
Ceolwulf	597–611	Ethelwulf	839–855
Cynegils	611–643	Ethelbald	855–860
Cenwalh	643–672	Ethelbert	860–866
Seaxburh (Queen)	? 672–? 674	Ethelred	866–April 871
? Cenfus	? 673–674	Alfred	April 871–26 Oct. 899
Aescwine	674–676	Edward the Elder	Oct. 899 (crowned 8 June 900)–17 July 925
Centwine	676–685	Athelstan	Summer 925 (crowned 4 Sept. 925)–27 Oct. 939
Caedwalla	685–688		
Ini	688–726	Edmund	Oct. 939–26 May 946
Aethelheard	726–? 740	Edred	May 946–23 Nov. 955

[1] Nunna is probably the short form of Nothelm.

RULERS OF ENGLAND

From the time of Egbert the West Saxon kings extended their authority over most of the Southern English, and Edward the Elder and his successors exercised a varying amount of control over the Scandinavian kingdoms of the north. From 954 the control is permanent, and the kings who follow Edred can claim to rule all England.

RULERS OF THE DANISH KINGDOM OF EAST ANGLIA

Guthrum (Æthelstan)	880–890	Eric (Eohric)	? 890–902

RULERS OF THE SCANDINAVIAN KINGDOM OF YORK

Halfdan	875 or 876–877 or 883	Anlaf Guthfrithson	late 939 or early 940–941
Guthfrith	? 883–24 Aug. 894	Anlaf Sihtricson (Cuaran)	941–Summer 943 (and see below)
Siefred			
? Cnut	? c. 894–? 899 or earlier	Ragnald Guthfrithson	Summer 943–944
Ethelwald	? 899–902		
Halfdan	? c. 902–910	Edmund (K. of the W. Saxons)	944–946
Eowils, (Ecwils, ? Eogils) Ivar	apparently reigned jointly with Halfdan ? –910	Edred (K. of the W. Saxons)	946–948
Ragnald	? 919–? 921	Eric Bloodaxe	948 (and see below)
Sihtric Caoch	921–927	Anlaf Sihtricson	949–952
Guthfrith	927	Eric Bloodaxe	952–954
Athelstan (K. of the W. Saxons)	927–27 Oct. 939		

Thereafter Northumbria was ruled by the kings of England.

RULERS OF ENGLAND

Edwy	Nov. 955–1 Oct. 959 (reigning in Wessex only after revolt of 957)
Edgar	959 (crowned 11 May 973)–8 July 975 (reigning in Mercia and the Danelaw 957–959)
Edward the Martyr	July (?) 975–18 March 979
Ethelred (Unraed)	March 979 (crowned 14 April 979)—Autumn 1013 (and see below)
Swegn Forkbeard (king of Denmark)	Autumn 1013–3 Feb. 1014 (uncrowned)
Ethelred (Unraed)	Feb. 1014–23 April 1016
Edmund Ironside	April 1016–30 Nov. 1016 (reigning in Wessex only from Summer 1016)
Cnut	Nov. 1016–12 Nov. 1035 (reigning in Mercia and the Danelaw from Summer 1016)

17

Harold Harefoot	late 1035–17 March 1040 (reigning jointly with Harthacnut until early 1037)	
Harthacnut	June 1040–8 June 1042 (reigning jointly with Harold Harefoot, late 1035–early 1037)	
Edward the Confessor	? June 1042 (crowned 3 April 1043)–5 Jan. 1066	
Harold Godwinson	6 Jan. 1066–14 Oct. 1066	
[Edgar Etheling	Oct. 1066—before Christmas 1066 (uncrowned)]	
William I (the Conqueror)	25 Dec. 1066–9 Sept. 1087	
William II (Rufus)	26 Sept. 1087–2 Aug. 1100	
Henry I	5 Aug. 1100–1 Dec. 1135	
Stephen	22 Dec. 1135–25 Oct. 1154	

HENRY II

Regnal year		Tables [1]	Regnal year		Tables
1	19 Dec. 1154–18 Dec. 1155	14, 6	19	19 Dec. 1172–18 Dec. 1173	26, 18
2	19 Dec. 1155–18 Dec. 1156	6, 25	20	19 Dec. 1173–18 Dec. 1174	18, 3
3	19 Dec. 1156–18 Dec. 1157	25, 10	21	19 Dec. 1174–18 Dec. 1175	3, 23
4	19 Dec. 1157–18 Dec. 1158	10, 30	22	19 Dec. 1175–18 Dec. 1176	23, 14
5	19 Dec. 1158–18 Dec. 1159	30, 22	23	19 Dec. 1176–18 Dec. 1177	14, 34
6	19 Dec. 1159–18 Dec. 1160	22, 6	24	19 Dec. 1177–18 Dec. 1178	34, 19
7	19 Dec. 1160–18 Dec. 1161	6, 26	25	19 Dec. 1178–18 Dec. 1179	19, 11
8	19 Dec. 1161–18 Dec. 1162	26, 18	26	19 Dec. 1179–18 Dec. 1180	11, 30
9	19 Dec. 1162–18 Dec. 1163	18, 3	27	19 Dec. 1180–18 Dec. 1181	30, 15
10	19 Dec. 1163–18 Dec. 1164	3, 22	28	19 Dec. 1181–18 Dec. 1182	15, 7
11	19 Dec. 1164–18 Dec. 1165	22, 14	29	19 Dec. 1182–18 Dec. 1183	7, 27
12	19 Dec. 1165–18 Dec. 1166	14, 34	30	19 Dec. 1183–18 Dec. 1184	27, 11
13	19 Dec. 1166–18 Dec. 1167	34, 19	31	19 Dec. 1184–18 Dec. 1185	11, 31
14	19 Dec. 1167–18 Dec. 1168	19, 10	32	19 Dec. 1185–18 Dec. 1186	31, 23
15	19 Dec. 1168–18 Dec. 1169	10, 30	33	19 Dec. 1186–18 Dec. 1187	23, 8
16	19 Dec. 1169–18 Dec. 1170	30, 15	34	19 Dec. 1187–18 Dec. 1188	8, 27
17	19 Dec. 1170–18 Dec. 1171	15, 7	35	19 Dec. 1188–6 July 1189	27, 19
18	19 Dec. 1171–18 Dec. 1172	7, 26			

RICHARD I

1	3 Sep. 1189–2 Sep. 1190	19, 4	6	3 Sep. 1194–2 Sep. 1195	20, 12
2	3 Sep. 1190–2 Sep. 1191	4, 24	7	3 Sep. 1195–2 Sep. 1196	12, 31
3	3 Sep. 1191–2 Sep. 1192	24, 15	8	3 Sep. 1196–2 Sep. 1197	31, 16
4	3 Sep. 1192–2 Sep. 1193	15, 7	9	3 Sep. 1197–2 Sep. 1198	16, 8
5	3 Sep. 1193–2 Sep. 1194	7, 20	10	3 Sep. 1198–6 Apr. 1199	8, 28

[1] The numbers under this heading refer to the tables on pp. 84–155 below, which provide calendars for each year. Thus, of Henry II's first regnal year the period 19–31 Dec. will be found in table 14, the period 1 Jan.–18 Dec. in table 6.

JOHN

Regnal year		Tables	Regnal year		Tables
1	27 May 1199–17 May 1200	28, 19	10	15 May 1208–6 May 1209	16, 8
2	18 May 1200–2 May 1201	19, 4	11	7 May 1209–26 May 1210	8, 28
3	3 May 1201–22 May 1202	4, 24	12	27 May 1210–11 May 1211	28, 13
4	23 May 1202–14 May 1203	24, 16	13	12 May 1211–2 May 1212	13, 4
5	15 May 1203–2 June 1204	16, 35	14	3 May 1212–22 May 1213	4, 24
6	3 June 1204–18 May 1205	35, 20	15	23 May 1213–7 May 1214	24, 9
7	19 May 1205–10 May 1206	20, 12	16	8 May 1214–27 May 1215	9, 29
8	11 May 1206–30 May 1207	12, 32	17	28 May 1215–18 May 1216	29, 20
9	31 May 1207–14 May 1208	32, 16	18	19 May 1216–19 Oct. 1216	20

HENRY III

Regnal year		Tables	Regnal year		Tables
1	28 Oct. 1216–27 Oct. 1217	20, 5	30	28 Oct. 1245–27 Oct. 1246	26, 18
2	28 Oct. 1217–27 Oct. 1218	5, 25	31	28 Oct. 1246–27 Oct. 1247	18, 10
3	28 Oct. 1218–27 Oct. 1219	25, 17	32	28 Oct. 1247–27 Oct. 1248	10, 29
4	28 Oct. 1219–27 Oct. 1220	17, 8	33	28 Oct. 1248–27 Oct. 1249	29, 14
5	28 Oct. 1220–27 Oct. 1221	8, 21	34	28 Oct. 1249–27 Oct. 1250	14, 6
6	28 Oct. 1221–27 Oct. 1222	21, 13	35	28 Oct. 1250–27 Oct. 1251	6, 26
7	28 Oct. 1222–27 Oct. 1223	13, 33	36	28 Oct. 1251–27 Oct. 1252	26, 10
8	28 Oct. 1223–27 Oct. 1224	33, 24	37	28 Oct. 1252–27 Oct. 1253	10, 30
9	28 Oct. 1224–27 Oct. 1225	24, 9	38	28 Oct. 1253–27 Oct. 1254	30, 22
10	28 Oct. 1225–27 Oct. 1226	9, 29	39	28 Oct. 1254–27 Oct. 1255	22, 7
11	28 Oct. 1226–27 Oct. 1227	29, 21	40	28 Oct. 1255–27 Oct. 1256	7, 26
12	28 Oct. 1227–27 Oct. 1228	21, 5	41	28 Oct. 1256–27 Oct. 1257	26, 18
13	28 Oct. 1228–27 Oct. 1229	5, 25	42	28 Oct. 1257–27 Oct. 1258	18, 3
14	28 Oct. 1229–27 Oct. 1230	25, 17	43	28 Oct. 1258–27 Oct. 1259	3, 23
15	28 Oct. 1230–27 Oct. 1231	17, 2	44	28 Oct. 1259–27 Oct. 1260	23, 14
16	28 Oct. 1231–27 Oct. 1232	2, 21	45	28 Oct. 1260–27 Oct. 1261	14, 34
17	28 Oct. 1232–27 Oct. 1233	21, 13	46	28 Oct. 1261–27 Oct. 1262	34, 19
18	28 Oct. 1233–27 Oct. 1234	13, 33	47	28 Oct. 1262–27 Oct. 1263	19, 11
19	28 Oct. 1234–27 Oct. 1235	33, 18	48	28 Oct. 1263–27 Oct. 1264	11, 30
20	28 Oct. 1235–27 Oct. 1236	18, 9	49	28 Oct. 1264–27 Oct. 1265	30, 15
21	28 Oct. 1236–27 Oct. 1237	9, 29	50	28 Oct. 1265–27 Oct. 1266	15, 7
22	28 Oct. 1237–27 Oct. 1238	29, 14	51	28 Oct. 1266–27 Oct. 1267	7, 27
23	28 Oct. 1238–27 Oct. 1239	14, 6	52	28 Oct. 1267–27 Oct. 1268	27, 18
24	28 Oct. 1239–27 Oct. 1240	6, 25	53	28 Oct. 1268–27 Oct. 1269	18, 3
25	28 Oct. 1240–27 Oct. 1241	25, 10	54	28 Oct. 1269–27 Oct. 1270	3, 23
26	28 Oct. 1241–27 Oct. 1242	10, 30	55	28 Oct. 1270–27 Oct. 1271	23, 15
27	28 Oct. 1242–27 Oct. 1243	30, 22	56	28 Oct. 1271–27 Oct. 1272	15, 34
28	28 Oct. 1243–27 Oct. 1244	22, 13	57	28 Oct. 1272–16 Nov. 1272	34
29	28 Oct. 1244–27 Oct. 1245	13, 26			

EDWARD I

Regnal year		Tables	Regnal year		Tables
1	20 Nov. 1272–19 Nov. 1273	34, 19	19	20 Nov. 1290–19 Nov. 1291	12, 32
2	20 Nov. 1273–19 Nov. 1274	19, 11	20	20 Nov. 1291–19 Nov. 1292	32, 16
3	20 Nov. 1274–19 Nov. 1275	11, 24	21	20 Nov. 1292–19 Nov. 1293	16, 8
4	20 Nov. 1275–19 Nov. 1276	24, 15	22	20 Nov. 1293–19 Nov. 1294	8, 28
5	20 Nov. 1276–19 Nov. 1277	15, 7	23	20 Nov. 1294–19 Nov. 1295	28, 13
6	20 Nov. 1277–19 Nov. 1278	7, 27	24	20 Nov. 1295–19 Nov. 1296	13, 4
7	20 Nov. 1278–19 Nov. 1279	27, 12	25	20 Nov. 1296–19 Nov. 1297	4, 24
8	20 Nov. 1279–19 Nov. 1280	12, 31	26	20 Nov. 1297–19 Nov. 1298	24, 16
9	20 Nov. 1280–19 Nov. 1281	31, 23	27	20 Nov. 1298–19 Nov. 1299	16, 29
10	20 Nov. 1281–19 Nov. 1282	23, 8	28	20 Nov. 1299–19 Nov. 1300	29, 20
11	20 Nov. 1282–19 Nov. 1283	8, 28	29	20 Nov. 1300–19 Nov. 1301	20, 12
12	20 Nov. 1283–19 Nov. 1284	28, 19	30	20 Nov. 1301–19 Nov. 1302	12, 32
13	20 Nov. 1284–19 Nov. 1285	19, 4	31	20 Nov. 1302–19 Nov. 1303	32, 17
14	20 Nov. 1285–19 Nov. 1286	4, 24	32	20 Nov. 1303–19 Nov. 1304	17, 8
15	20 Nov. 1286–19 Nov. 1287	24, 16	33	20 Nov. 1304–19 Nov. 1305	8, 28
16	20 Nov. 1287–19 Nov. 1288	16, 7	34	20 Nov. 1305–19 Nov. 1306	28, 13
17	20 Nov. 1288–19 Nov. 1289	7, 20	35	20 Nov. 1306–7 July 1307	13, 5
18	20 Nov. 1289–19 Nov. 1290	20, 12			

EDWARD II

1	8 July 1307–7 July 1308	5, 24	11	8 July 1317–7 July 1318	13, 33
2	8 July 1308–7 July 1309	24, 9	12	8 July 1318–7 July 1319	33, 18
3	8 July 1309–7 July 1310	9, 29	13	8 July 1319–7 July 1320	18, 9
4	8 July 1310–7 July 1311	29, 21	14	8 July 1320–7 July 1321	9, 29
5	8 July 1311–7 July 1312	21, 5	15	8 July 1321–7 July 1322	29, 21
6	8 July 1312–7 July 1313	5, 25	16	8 July 1322–7 July 1323	21, 6
7	8 July 1313–7 July 1314	25, 17	17	8 July 1323–7 July 1324	6, 25
8	8 July 1314–7 July 1315	17, 2	18	8 July 1324–7 July 1325	25, 17
9	8 July 1315–7 July 1316	2, 21	19	8 July 1325–7 July 1326	17, 2
10	8 July 1316–7 July 1317	21, 13	20	8 July 1326–20 Jan. 1327	2, 22

EDWARD III

1	25 Jan. 1327–24 Jan. 1328	22, 13	9	25 Jan. 1335–24 Jan. 1336	26, 10
2	25 Jan. 1328–24 Jan. 1329	13, 33	10	25 Jan. 1336–24 Jan. 1337	10, 30
3	25 Jan. 1329–24 Jan. 1330	33, 18	11	25 Jan. 1337–24 Jan. 1338	30, 22
4	25 Jan. 1330–24 Jan. 1331	18, 10	12	25 Jan. 1338–24 Jan. 1339	22, 7
5	25 Jan. 1331–24 Jan. 1332	10, 29	13	25 Jan. 1339–24 Jan. 1340	7, 26
6	25 Jan. 1332–24 Jan. 1333	29, 14	14 (F.1)[1]	25 Jan. 1340–24 Jan. 1341	26, 18
7	25 Jan. 1333–24 Jan. 1334	14, 6	15 (F.2)	25 Jan. 1341–24 Jan. 1342	18, 10
8	25 Jan. 1334–24 Jan. 1335	6, 26	16 (F.3)	25 Jan. 1342–24 Jan. 1343	10, 23

[1] I.e. Edward's fourteenth year as king of England, his first year as king of France.

EDWARD III—continued

Regnal year		Tables	Regnal year		Tables
17 (F.4)	25 Jan. 1343–24 Jan. 1344	23, 14	**35**	25 Jan. 1361–24 Jan. 1362	7, 27
18 (F.5)	25 Jan. 1344–24 Jan. 1345	14, 6	**36**	25 Jan. 1362–24 Jan. 1363	27, 12
19 (F.6)	25 Jan. 1345–24 Jan. 1346	6, 26	**37**	25 Jan. 1363–24 Jan. 1364	12, 3
20 (F.7)	25 Jan. 1346–24 Jan. 1347	26, 11	**38**	25 Jan. 1364–24 Jan. 1365	3, 23
21 (F.8)	25 Jan. 1347–24 Jan. 1348	11, 30	**39**	25 Jan. 1365–24 Jan. 1366	23, 15
22 (F.9)	25 Jan. 1348–24 Jan. 1349	30, 22	**40**	25 Jan. 1366–24 Jan. 1367	15, 28
23 (F.10)	25 Jan. 1349–24 Jan. 1350	22, 7	**41**	25 Jan. 1367–24 Jan. 1368	28, 19
24 (F.11)	25 Jan. 1350–24 Jan. 1351	7, 27	**42**	25 Jan. 1368–24 Jan. 1369	19, 11
25 (F.12)	25 Jan. 1351–24 Jau. 1352	27, 18	**43** (F.30)	25 Jan. 1369–24 Jan. 1370	11, 24
26 (F.13)	25 Jan. 1352–24 Jan. 1353	18, 3	**44** (F.31)	25 Jan. 1370–24 Jan. 1371	24, 16
27 (F.14)	25 Jan. 1353–24 Jan. 1354	3, 23	**45** (F.32)	25 Jan. 1371–24 Jan. 1372	16, 7
28 (F.15)	25 Jan. 1354–24 Jan. 1355	23, 15	**46** (F.33)	25 Jan. 1372–24 Jan. 1373	7, 27
29 (F.16)	25 Jan. 1355–24 Jan. 1356	15, 34	**47** (F.34)	25 Jan. 1373–24 Jan. 1374	27 ,12
30 (F.17)	25 Jan. 1356–24 Jan. 1357	34, 19	**48** (F.35)	25 Jan. 1374–24 Jan. 1375	12, 32
31 (F.18)	25 Jan. 1357–24 Jan. 1358	19, 11	**49** (F.36)	25 Jan. 1375–24 Jan. 1376	32, 23
32 (F.19)	25 Jan. 1358–24 Jan. 1359	11, 31	**50** (F.37)	25 Jan. 1376–24 Jan. 1377	23, 8
33 (F.20)	25 Jan. 1359–24 Jan. 1360	31, 15	**51** (F.38)	25 Jan. 1377–21 June 1377	8
34 (F.21)[1]	25 Jan. 1360–24 Jan. 1361	15, 7			

RICHARD II

		Tables			Tables
1	22 June 1377–21 June 1378	8, 28	**13**	22 June 1389–21 June 1390	28, 13
2	22 June 1378–21 June 1379	28, 20	**14**	22 June 1390–21 June 1391	13, 5
3	22 June 1379–21 June 1380	20, 4	**15**	22 June 1391–21 June 1392	5, 24
4	22 June 1380–21 June 1381	4, 24	**16**	22 June 1392–21 June 1393	24, 16
5	22 June 1381–21 June 1382	24, 16	**17**	22 June 1393–21 June 1394	16, 29
6	22 June 1382–21 June 1383	16, 1	**18**	22 June 1394–21 June 1395	29, 21
7	22 June 1383–21 June 1384	1, 20	**19**	22 June 1395–21 June 1396	21, 12
8	22 June 1384–21 June 1385	20, 12	**20**	22 June 1396–21 June 1397	12, 32
9	22 June 1385–21 June 1386	12, 32	**21**	22 June 1397–21 June 1398	32, 17
10	22 June 1386–21 June 1387	32, 17	**22**	22 June 1398–21 June 1399	17, 9
11	22 June 1387–21 June 1388	17, 8	**23**	22 June 1399–29 Sep. 1399	9
12	22 June 1388–21 June 1389	8, 28			

---

[1] Edward III undertook at Brétigny on 8 May 1360 to renounce the throne of France, but he continued to use the double form of dating (cf. *Fœdera*, III, i. 500). He repeated his undertaking at Calais on 24 Oct. 1360 and seems then to have dropped the double dating. His new seal omitted the French title. Formal renunciation was timed to take place at Bruges on 30 Nov. 1361, but this never occurred, and in June 1369 Edward III resumed his claim to the French throne, his former seal, and his system of double dating.

HENRY IV

Regnal year		Tables	Regnal year		Tables
1	30 Sep. 1399–29 Sep. 1400	9, 28	8	30 Sep. 1406–29 Sep. 1407	21, 6
2	30 Sep. 1400–29 Sep. 1401	28, 13	9	30 Sep. 1407–29 Sep. 1408	6, 25
3	30 Sep. 1401–29 Sep. 1402	13, 5	10	30 Sep. 1408–29 Sep. 1409	25, 17
4	30 Sep. 1402–29 Sep. 1403	5, 25	11	30 Sep. 1409–29 Sep. 1410	17, 2
5	30 Sep. 1403–29 Sep. 1404	25, 9	12	30 Sep. 1410–29 Sep. 1411	2, 22
6	30 Sep. 1404–29 Sep. 1405	9, 29	13	30 Sep. 1411–29 Sep. 1412	22, 13
7	30 Sep. 1405–29 Sep. 1406	29, 21	14	30 Sep. 1412–20 March 1413	13, 33

HENRY V

1	21 March 1413–20 March 1414	33, 18	6	21 March 1418–20 March 1419	6, 26
2	21 March 1414–20 March 1415	18, 10	7	21 March 1419–20 March 1420	26, 17
3	21 March 1415–20 March 1416	10, 29	8	21 March 1420–20 March 1421	17, 2
4	21 March 1416–20 March 1417	29, 21	9	21 March 1421–20 March 1422	2, 22
5	21 March 1417–20 March 1418	21, 6	10	21 March 1422–31 Aug. 1422	22

HENRY VI

1	1 Sep. 1422–31 Aug. 1423	22, 14	21	1 Sep. 1442–31 Aug. 1443	11, 31
2	1 Sep. 1423–31 Aug. 1424	14, 33	22	1 Sep. 1443–31 Aug. 1444	31, 22
3	1 Sep. 1424–31 Aug. 1425	33, 18	23	1 Sep. 1444–31 Aug. 1445	22, 7
4	1 Sep. 1425–31 Aug. 1426	18, 10	24	1 Sep. 1445–31 Aug. 1446	7, 27
5	1 Sep. 1426–31 Aug. 1427	10, 30	25	1 Sep. 1446–31 Aug. 1447	27, 19
6	1 Sep. 1427–31 Aug. 1428	30, 14	26	1 Sep. 1447–31 Aug. 1448	19, 3
7	1 Sep. 1428–31 Aug. 1429	14, 6	27	1 Sep. 1448–31 Aug. 1449	3, 23
8	1 Sep. 1429–31 Aug. 1430	6, 26	28	1 Sep. 1449–31 Aug. 1450	23, 15
9	1 Sep. 1430–31 Aug. 1431	26, 11	29	1 Sep. 1450–31 Aug. 1451	15, 35
10	1 Sep. 1431–31 Aug. 1432	11, 30	30	1 Sep. 1451–31 Aug. 1452	35, 19
11	1 Sep. 1432–31 Aug. 1433	30, 22	31	1 Sep. 1452–31 Aug. 1453	19, 11
12	1 Sep. 1433–31 Aug. 1434	22, 7	32	1 Sep. 1453–31 Aug. 1454	11, 31
13	1 Sep. 1434–31 Aug. 1435	7, 27	33	1 Sep. 1454–31 Aug. 1455	31, 16
14	1 Sep. 1435–31 Aug. 1436	27, 18	34	1 Sep. 1455–31 Aug. 1456	16, 7
15	1 Sep. 1436–31 Aug. 1437	18, 10	35	1 Sep. 1456–31 Aug. 1457	7, 27
16	1 Sep. 1437–31 Aug. 1438	10, 23	36	1 Sep. 1457–31 Aug. 1458	27, 12
17	1 Sep. 1438–31 Aug. 1439	23, 15	37	1 Sep. 1458–31 Aug. 1459	12, 4
18	1 Sep. 1439–31 Aug. 1440	15, 6	38	1 Sep. 1459–31 Aug. 1460	4, 23
19	1 Sep. 1440–31 Aug. 1441	6, 26	39	1 Sep. 1460–4 Mar. 1461	23, 15
20	1 Sep. 1441–31 Aug. 1442	26, 11	*and*		
			49 [1]	Sep.–Oct. 1470–11 Apr. 1471	32, 24

[1] Edward IV fled the country on 29 Sep. 1470 ; Henry VI was released on 3 Oct. and re-crowned on 13 Oct. ; letters patent and close in Henry VI's name are known from 9 Oct. onwards, dated in his 49th year ' et readeptionis nostre regie potestatis anno primo'. His restoration ended with his capture by Edward IV on 11 Apr. 1471.

EDWARD IV

Regnal year		Tables	Regnal year		Tables
1	4 March 1461–3 March 1462	15, 28	13	4 March 1473–3 March 1474	28, 20
2	4 March 1462–3 March 1463	28, 20	14	4 March 1474–3 March 1475	20, 5
3	4 March 1463–3 March 1464	20, 11	15	4 March 1475–3 March 1476	5, 24
4	4 March 1464–3 March 1465	11, 24	16	4 March 1476–3 March 1477	24, 16
5	4 March 1465–3 March 1466	24, 16	17	4 March 1477–3 March 1478	16, 1
6	4 March 1466–3 March 1467	16, 8	18	4 March 1478–3 March 1479	1, 21
7	4 March 1467–3 March 1468	8, 27	19	4 March 1479–3 March 1480	21, 12
8	4 March 1468–3 March 1469	27, 12	20	4 March 1480–3 March 1481	12, 32
9	4 March 1469–3 March 1470	12, 32	21	4 March 1481–3 March 1482	32, 17
10	4 March 1470–3 March 1471 [1]	32, 24	22	4 March 1482–3 March 1483	17, 9
11	4 March 1471–3 March 1472	24, 8	23	4 March 1483–9 April 1483	9
12	4 March 1472–3 March 1473	8, 28			

EDWARD V

1	9 April 1483–25 June 1483	9

RICHARD III

		Tables			Tables
1	26 June 1483–25 June 1484	9, 28	3	26 June 1485–22 Aug. 1485	13
2	26 June 1484–25 June 1485	28, 13			

HENRY VII

		Tables			Tables
1	22 Aug. 1485–21 Aug. 1486	13, 5	13	22 Aug. 1497–21 Aug. 1498	5, 25
2	22 Aug. 1486–21 Aug. 1487	5, 25	14	22 Aug. 1498–21 Aug. 1499	25, 10
3	22 Aug. 1487–21 Aug. 1488	25, 16	15	22 Aug. 1499–21 Aug. 1500	10, 29
4	22 Aug. 1488–21 Aug. 1489	16, 29	16	22 Aug. 1500–21 Aug. 1501	29, 21
5	22 Aug. 1489–21 Aug. 1490	29, 21	17	22 Aug. 1501–21 Aug. 1502	21, 6
6	22 Aug. 1490–21 Aug. 1491	21, 13	18	22 Aug. 1502–21 Aug. 1503	6, 26
7	22 Aug. 1491–21 Aug. 1492	13, 32	19	22 Aug. 1503–21 Aug. 1504	26, 17
8	22 Aug. 1492–21 Aug. 1493	32, 17	20	22 Aug. 1504–21 Aug. 1505	17, 2
9	22 Aug. 1493–21 Aug. 1494	17, 9	21	22 Aug. 1505–21 Aug. 1506	2, 22
10	22 Aug. 1494–21 Aug. 1495	9, 29	22	22 Aug. 1506–21 Aug. 1507	22, 14
11	22 Aug. 1495–21 Aug. 1496	29, 13	23	22 Aug. 1507–21 Aug. 1508	14, 33
12	22 Aug. 1496–21 Aug. 1497	13, 5	24	22 Aug. 1508–21 Apr. 1509	33, 18

[1] See p. 22, n. 1.

HENRY VIII

Regnal year		Tables	Regnal year		Tables
1	22 Apr. 1509–21 Apr. 1510	18, 10	20	22 Apr. 1528–21 Apr. 1529	22, 7
2	22 Apr. 1510–21 Apr. 1511	10, 30	21	22 Apr. 1529–21 Apr. 1530	7, 27
3	22 Apr. 1511–21 Apr. 1512	30, 21	22	22 Apr. 1530–21 Apr. 1531	27, 19
4	22 Apr. 1512–21 Apr. 1513	21, 6	23	22 Apr. 1531–21 Apr. 1532	19, 10
5	22 Apr. 1513–21 Apr. 1514	6, 26	24	22 Apr. 1532–21 Apr. 1533	10, 23
6	22 Apr. 1514–21 Apr. 1515	26, 18	25	22 Apr. 1533–21 Apr. 1534	23, 15
7	22 Apr. 1515–21 Apr. 1516	18, 2	26	22 Apr. 1534–21 Apr. 1535	15, 7
8	22 Apr. 1516–21 Apr. 1517	2, 22	27	22 Apr. 1535–21 Apr. 1536	7, 26
9	22 Apr. 1517–21 Apr. 1518	22, 14	28	22 Apr. 1536–21 Apr. 1537	26, 11
10	22 Apr. 1518–21 Apr. 1519	14, 34	29	22 Apr. 1537–21 Apr. 1538	11, 31
11	22 Apr. 1519–21 Apr. 1520	34, 18	30	22 Apr. 1538–21 Apr. 1539	31, 16
12	22 Apr. 1520–21 Apr. 1521	18, 10	31	22 Apr. 1539–21 Apr. 1540	16, 7
13	22 Apr. 1521–21 Apr. 1522	10, 30	32	22 Apr. 1540–21 Apr. 1541	7, 27
14	22 Apr. 1522–21 Apr. 1523	30, 15	33	22 Apr. 1541–21 Apr. 1542	27, 19
15	22 Apr. 1523–21 Apr. 1524	15, 6	34	22 Apr. 1542–21 Apr. 1543	19, 4
16	22 Apr. 1524–21 Apr. 1525	6, 26	35	22 Apr. 1543–21 Apr. 1544	4, 23
17	22 Apr. 1525–21 Apr. 1526	26, 11	36	22 Apr. 1544–21 Apr. 1545	23, 15
18	22 Apr. 1526–21 Apr. 1527	11, 31	37	22 Apr. 1545–21 Apr. 1546	15, 35
19	22 Apr. 1527–21 Apr. 1528	31, 22	38	22 Apr. 1546–28 Jan. 1547	35, 20

EDWARD VI

1	28 Jan. 1547–27 Jan. 1548	20, 11	5	28 Jan. 1551–27 Jan. 1552	8, 27
2	28 Jan. 1548–27 Jan. 1549	11, 31	6	28 Jan. 1552–27 Jan. 1553	27, 12
3	28 Jan. 1549–27 Jan. 1550	31, 16	7	28 Jan. 1553–6 July 1553	12
4	28 Jan. 1550–27 Jan. 1551	16, 8			

JANE

1	6 July 1553–19 July 1553	12

MARY

1	19 July 1553–5 July 1554	12, 4	2	6 July 1554 [1]–24 July 1554	4

PHILIP and MARY

1 & 2	25 July 1554–5 July 1555	4, 24	3 & 5	6 July 1557–24 July 1557	28
1 & 3	6 July 1555–24 July 1555	24	4 & 5	25 July 1557–5 July 1558	28, 20
2 & 3	25 July 1555–5 July 1556	24, 15	4 & 6	6 July 1558–24 July 1558	20
2 & 4	6 July 1556–24 July 1556	15	5 & 6	25 July 1558–17 Nov. 1558	20
3 & 4	25 July 1556–5 July 1557	15, 28			

[1] Mary dated her second year from 6 July, ignoring Jane's intrusion.

RULERS OF ENGLAND

ELIZABETH I

Regnal year		Tables	Regnal year		Tables
1	17 Nov. 1558–16 Nov. 1559	20 5	24	17 Nov. 1581–16 Nov. 1582	5, 25
2	17 Nov. 1559–16 Nov. 1560	5, 24	25	17 Nov. 1582–16 Nov. 1583	25, 10
3	17 Nov. 1560–16 Nov. 1561	24, 16	26	17 Nov. 1583–16 Nov. 1584	10, 29
4	17 Nov. 1561–16 Nov. 1562	16, 8	27	17 Nov. 1584–16 Nov. 1585	29, 21
5	17 Nov. 1562–16 Nov. 1563	8, 21	28	17 Nov. 1585–16 Nov. 1586	21, 13
6	17 Nov. 1563–16 Nov. 1564	21, 12	29	17 Nov. 1586–16 Nov. 1587	13, 26
7	17 Nov. 1564–16 Nov. 1565	12, 32	30	17 Nov. 1587–16 Nov. 1588	26, 17
8	17 Nov. 1565–16 Nov. 1566	32, 24	31	17 Nov. 1588–16 Nov. 1589	17, 9
9	17 Nov. 1566–16 Nov. 1567	24, 9	32	17 Nov. 1589–16 Nov. 1590	9, 29
10	17 Nov. 1567–16 Nov. 1568	9, 28	33	17 Nov. 1590–16 Nov. 1591	29, 14
11	17 Nov. 1568–16 Nov. 1569	28, 20	34	17 Nov. 1591–16 Nov. 1592	14, 5
12	17 Nov. 1569–16 Nov. 1570	20, 5	35	17 Nov. 1592–16 Nov. 1593	5, 25
13	17 Nov. 1570–16 Nov. 1571	5, 25	36	17 Nov. 1593–16 Nov. 1594	25, 10
14	17 Nov. 1571–16 Nov. 1572	25, 16	37	17 Nov. 1594–16 Nov. 1595	10, 30
15	17 Nov. 1572–16 Nov. 1573	16, 1	38	17 Nov. 1595–16 Nov. 1596	30, 21
16	17 Nov. 1573–16 Nov. 1574	1, 21	39	17 Nov. 1596–16 Nov. 1597	21, 6
17	17 Nov. 1574–16 Nov. 1575	21, 13	40	17 Nov. 1597–16 Nov. 1598	6, 26
18	17 Nov. 1575–16 Nov. 1576	13, 32	41	17 Nov. 1598–16 Nov. 1599	26, 18
19	17 Nov. 1576–16 Nov. 1577	32, 17	42	17 Nov. 1599–16 Nov. 1600	18, 2
20	17 Nov. 1577–16 Nov. 1578	17, 9	43	17 Nov. 1600–16 Nov. 1601	2, 22
21	17 Nov. 1578–16 Nov. 1579	9, 29	44	17 Nov. 1601–16 Nov. 1602	22, 14
22	17 Nov. 1579–16 Nov. 1580	29, 13	45	17 Nov. 1602–24 March 1603	14, 34
23	17 Nov. 1580–16 Nov. 1581	13, 5			

JAMES I[1]

		Tables			Tables
1	24 March 1603–23 March 1604	34, 18	13	24 March 1615–23 March 1616	19, 10
2	24 March 1604–23 March 1605	18, 10	14	24 March 1616–23 March 1617	10, 30
3	24 March 1605–23 March 1606	10, 30	15	24 March 1617–23 March 1618	30, 15
4	24 March 1606–23 March 1607	30, 15	16	24 March 1618–23 March 1619	15, 7
5	24 March 1607–23 March 1608	15, 6	17	24 March 1619–23 March 1620	7, 26
6	24 March 1608–23 March 1609	6, 26	18	24 March 1620–23 March 1621	26, 11
7	24 March 1609–23 March 1610	26, 18	19	24 March 1621–23 March 1622	11, 31
8	24 March 1610–23 March 1611	18, 3	20	24 March 1622–23 March 1623	31, 23
9	24 March 1611–23 March 1612	3, 22	21	24 March 1623–23 March 1624	23, 7
10	24 March 1612–23 March 1613	22, 14	22	24 March 1624–23 March 1625	7, 27
11	24 March 1613–23 March 1614	14, 34	23	24 March 1625–27 March 1625	27
12	24 March 1614–23 March 1615	34, 19			

[1] When James VI of Scotland became James I of England, he was in the thirty-sixth year of his reign in Scotland. He used the regnal years of England and Scotland in subsequent dating. As the 36th year of Scotland did not end till 23 July 1603, one may ascertain the year of Scotland by adding to the regnal year of England 35 for dates up to 23 July and 36 for dates after 23 July.

CHARLES I

Regnal year		Tables	Regnal year		Tables
1	27 March 1625–26 March 1626	27, 19	13	27 March 1637–26 March 1638	19, 4
2	27 March 1626–26 March 1627	19, 4	14	27 March 1638–26 March 1639	4, 24
3	27 March 1627–26 March 1628	4, 23	15	27 March 1639–26 March 1640	24, 15
4	27 March 1628–26 March 1629	23, 15	16	27 March 1640–26 March 1641	15, 35
5	27 March 1629–26 March 1630	15, 7	17	27 March 1641–26 March 1642	35, 20
6	27 March 1630–26 March 1631	7, 20	18	27 March 1642–26 March 1643	20, 12
7	27 March 1631–26 March 1632	20, 11	19	27 March 1643–26 March 1644	12, 31
8	27 March 1632–26 March 1633	11, 31	20	27 March 1644–26 March 1645	31, 16
9	27 March 1633–26 March 1634	31, 16	21	27 March 1645–26 March 1646	16, 8
10	27 March 1634–26 March 1635	16, 8	22	27 March 1646–26 March 1647	8, 28
11	27 March 1635–26 March 1636	8, 27	23	27 March 1647–26 March 1648	28, 12
12	27 March 1636–26 March 1637	27, 19	24	27 March 1648–30 Jan. 1649	12, 4

THE COMMONWEALTH

After the execution of King Charles I on 30 January 1649, the kingship was abolished (17 March 1649) and government by a Council of State was set up on 14 February 1649. The Council was dissolved on 20 April 1653 and replaced by another Council of State on 29 April 1653. Oliver Cromwell took the office of Lord Protector on 16 December 1653 and held it till his death on 3 September 1658. His son, Richard Cromwell, succeeded to the same office on the day of his father's death and abdicated on 24 May 1659. After a year of parliamentary government Charles II was proclaimed king on 5 May 1660 and arrived in London on 29 May 1660. During the whole of the period 1649–60 English official documents were dated by the year of grace. In proclaiming Charles II to be king, parliament declared that he had been *de jure* king since his father's death. Therefore Charles's establishment on the throne came in his twelfth regnal year, deemed to have begun on 30 January 1660. Before parliament proclaimed him, the king had already dated his declaration at Breda ' this $\frac{4}{14}$th day of April 1660 in the twelfth year of our reign '.

CHARLES II[1]

Regnal year		Tables	Regnal year		Tables
12	29 May 1660–29 Jan. 1661	32, 24	25	30 Jan. 1673–29 Jan. 1674	9, 29
13	30 Jan. 1661–29 Jan. 1662	24, 9	26	30 Jan. 1674–29 Jan. 1675	29, 14
14	30 Jan. 1662–29 Jan. 1663	9, 29	27	30 Jan. 1675–29 Jan. 1676	14, 5
15	30 Jan. 1663–29 Jan. 1664	29, 20	28	30 Jan. 1676–29 Jan. 1677	5, 25
16	30 Jan. 1664–29 Jan. 1665	20, 5	29	30 Jan. 1677–29 Jan. 1678	25, 10
17	30 Jan. 1665–29 Jan. 1666	5, 25	30	30 Jan. 1678–29 Jan. 1679	10, 30
18	30 Jan. 1666–29 Jan. 1667	25, 17	31	30 Jan. 1679–29 Jan. 1680	30, 21
19	30 Jan. 1667–29 Jan. 1668	17, 1	32	30 Jan. 1680–29 Jan. 1681	21, 13
20	30 Jan. 1668–29 Jan. 1669	1, 21	33	30 Jan. 1681–29 Jan. 1682	13, 26
21	30 Jan. 1669–29 Jan. 1670	21, 13	34	30 Jan. 1682–29 Jan. 1683	26, 18
22	30 Jan. 1670–29 Jan. 1671	13, 33	35	30 Jan. 1683–29 Jan. 1684	18, 9
23	30 Jan. 1671–29 Jan. 1672	33, 17	36	30 Jan. 1684–29 Jan. 1685	9, 29
24	30 Jan. 1672–29 Jan. 1673	17, 9	37	30 Jan. 1685–6 Feb. 1685	29

[1] Dating by Charles II's regnal year occurs very seldom until the Declaration of Breda. For an example, see *Eng. Hist. Rev.*, v (1890), 117–18 : ' Given at our Court at Worcester this six & twentieth daye of Augt in the third yeere of our reigne.'

JAMES II

Regnal year		Tables	Regnal year		Tables
1	6 Feb. 1685–5 Feb. 1686	29, 14	3	6 Feb. 1687–5 Feb. 1688	6, 25
2	6 Feb. 1686–5 Feb. 1687	14, 6	4	6 Feb. 1688–11 Dec. 1688	25

Interregnum   12 Dec. 1688–12 Feb. 1689 (Tables 25, 10)

WILLIAM and MARY

1	13 Feb. 1689–12 Feb. 1690	10, 30	4	13 Feb. 1692–12 Feb. 1693	6, 26
2	13 Feb. 1690–12 Feb. 1691	30, 22	5	13 Feb. 1693–12 Feb. 1694	26, 18
3	13 Feb. 1691–12 Feb. 1692	22, 6	6	13 Feb. 1694–27 Dec. 1694	18

WILLIAM III

6	28 Dec. 1694–12 Feb. 1695	18, 3	11	13 Feb. 1699–12 Feb. 1700	19, 10
7	13 Feb. 1695–12 Feb. 1696	3, 22	12	13 Feb. 1700–12 Feb. 1701	10, 30
8	13 Feb. 1696–12 Feb. 1697	22, 14	13	13 Feb. 1701–12 Feb. 1702	30, 15
9	13 Feb. 1697–12 Feb. 1698	14, 34	14	13 Feb. 1702–8 March 1702	15
10	13 Feb. 1698–12 Feb. 1699	34, 19			

ANNE

1	8 March 1702–7 March 1703	15, 7	8	8 March 1709–7 March 1710	34, 19
2	8 March 1703–7 March 1704	7, 26	9	8 March 1710–7 March 1711	19, 11
3	8 March 1704–7 March 1705	26, 18	10	8 March 1711–7 March 1712	11, 30
4	8 March 1705–7 March 1706	18, 3	11	8 March 1712–7 March 1713	30, 15
5	8 March 1706–7 March 1707	3, 23	12	8 March 1713–7 March 1714	15, 7
6	8 March 1707–7 March 1708	23, 14	13	8 March 1714–1 Aug. 1714	7
7	8 March 1708–7 March 1709	14, 34			

GEORGE I

1	1 Aug. 1714–31 July 1715	7, 27	8	1 Aug. 1721–31 July 1722	19, 4
2	1 Aug. 1715–31 July 1716	27, 11	9	1 Aug. 1722–31 July 1723	4, 24
3	1 Aug. 1716–31 July 1717	11, 31	10	1 Aug. 1723–31 July 1724	24, 15
4	1 Aug. 1717–31 July 1718	31, 23	11	1 Aug. 1724–31 July 1725	15, 7
5	1 Aug. 1718–31 July 1719	23, 8	12	1 Aug. 1725–31 July 1726	7, 20
6	1 Aug. 1719–31 July 1720	8, 27	13	1 Aug. 1726–11 June 1727	20, 12
7	1 Aug. 1720–31 July 1721	27, 19			

GEORGE II

Regnal year		Tables	Regnal year		Tables
1	11 June 1727–10 June 1728	12, 31	18	11 June 1744–10 June 1745	4, 24
2	11 June 1728–10 June 1729	31, 16	19	11 June 1745–10 June 1746	24, 9
3	11 June 1729–10 June 1730	16, 8	20	11 June 1746–10 June 1747	9, 29
4	11 June 1730–10 June 1731	8, 28	21	11 June 1747–10 June 1748	29, 20
5	11 June 1731–10 June 1732	28, 19	22	11 June 1748–10 June 1749	20, 5
6	11 June 1732–10 June 1733	19, 4	23	11 June 1749–10 June 1750	5, 25
7	11 June 1733–10 June 1734	4, 24	24	11 June 1750–10 June 1751	25, 17
8	11 June 1734–10 June 1735	24, 16	25	11 June 1751–10 June 1752	17, 36
9	11 June 1735–10 June 1736	16, 35	26[1]	11 June 1752–21 June 1753	36, 32
10	11 June 1736–10 June 1737	35, 20	27	22 June 1753–21 June 1754	32, 24
11	11 June 1737–10 June 1738	20, 12	28	22 June 1754–21 June 1755	24, 9
12	11 June 1738–10 June 1739	12, 32	29	22 June 1755–21 June 1756	9, 28
13	11 June 1739–10 June 1740	32, 16	30	22 June 1756–21 June 1757	28, 20
14	11 June 1740–10 June 1741	16, 8	31	22 June 1757–21 June 1758	20, 5
15	11 June 1741–10 June 1742	8, 28	32	22 June 1758–21 June 1759	5, 25
16	11 June 1742–10 June 1743	28, 13	33	22 June 1759–21 June 1760	25, 16
17	11 June 1743–10 June 1744	13, 4	34	22 June 1760–25 Oct. 1760	16

GEORGE III

Regnal year		Tables	Regnal year		Tables
1	25 Oct. 1760–24 Oct. 1761	16, 1	21	25 Oct. 1780–24 Oct. 1781	5, 25
2	25 Oct. 1761–24 Oct. 1762	1, 21	22	25 Oct. 1781–24 Oct. 1782	25, 10
3	25 Oct. 1762–24 Oct. 1763	21, 13	23	25 Oct. 1782–24 Oct. 1783	10, 30
4	25 Oct. 1763–24 Oct. 1764	13, 32	24	25 Oct. 1783–24 Oct. 1784	30, 21
5	25 Oct. 1764–24 Oct. 1765	32, 17	25	25 Oct. 1784–24 Oct. 1785	21, 6
6	25 Oct. 1765–24 Oct. 1766	17, 9	26	25 Oct. 1785–24 Oct. 1786	6, 26
7	25 Oct. 1766–24 Oct. 1767	9, 29	27	25 Oct. 1786–24 Oct. 1787	26, 18
8	25 Oct. 1767–24 Oct. 1768	29, 13	28	25 Oct. 1787–24 Oct. 1788	18, 2
9	25 Oct. 1768–24 Oct. 1769	13, 5	29	25 Oct. 1788–24 Oct. 1789	2, 22
10	25 Oct. 1769–24 Oct. 1770	5, 25	30	25 Oct. 1789–24 Oct. 1790	22, 14
11	25 Oct. 1770–24 Oct. 1771	25, 10	31	25 Oct. 1790–24 Oct. 1791	14, 34
12	25 Oct. 1771–24 Oct. 1772	10, 29	32	25 Oct. 1791–24 Oct. 1792	34, 18
13	25 Oct. 1772–24 Oct. 1773	29, 21	33	25 Oct. 1792–24 Oct. 1793	18, 10
14	25 Oct. 1773–24 Oct. 1774	21, 13	34	25 Oct. 1793–24 Oct. 1794	10, 30
15	25 Oct. 1774–24 Oct. 1775	13, 26	35	25 Oct. 1794–24 Oct. 1795	30, 15
16	25 Oct. 1775–24 Oct. 1776	26, 17	36	25 Oct. 1795–24 Oct. 1796	15, 6
17	25 Oct. 1776–24 Oct. 1777	17, 9	37	25 Oct. 1796–24 Oct. 1797	6, 26
18	25 Oct. 1777–24 Oct. 1778	9, 29	38	25 Oct. 1797–24 Oct. 1798	26, 18
19	25 Oct. 1778–24 Oct. 1779	29, 14	39	25 Oct. 1798–24 Oct. 1799	18, 3
20	25 Oct. 1779–24 Oct. 1780	14, 5	40	25 Oct. 1799–24 Oct. 1800	3, 23

[1] This regnal year was extended to 21 June 1753, so that it should consist of 365 days despite the omission of eleven days in Sep. 1752, when the New Style was adopted (above, p. 11).

GEORGE III—continued

Regnal year		Tables	Regnal year		Tables
41	25 Oct. 1800–24 Oct. 1801	23, 15	51	25 Oct. 1810–24 Oct. 1811	32, 24
42	25 Oct. 1801–24 Oct. 1802	15, 28	52	25 Oct. 1811–24 Oct. 1812	24, 8
43	25 Oct. 1802–24 Oct. 1803	28, 20	53	25 Oct. 1812–24 Oct. 1813	8, 28
44	25 Oct. 1803–24 Oct. 1804	20, 11	54	25 Oct. 1813–24 Oct. 1814	28, 20
45	25 Oct. 1804–24 Oct. 1805	11, 24	55	25 Oct. 1814–24 Oct. 1815	20, 5
46	25 Oct. 1805–24 Oct. 1806	24, 16	56	25 Oct. 1815–24 Oct. 1816	5, 24
47	25 Oct. 1806–24 Oct. 1807	16, 8	57	25 Oct. 1816–24 Oct. 1817	24, 16
48	25 Oct. 1807–24 Oct. 1808	8, 27	58	25 Oct. 1817–24 Oct. 1818	16, 1
49	25 Oct. 1808–24 Oct. 1809	27, 12	59	25 Oct. 1818–24 Oct. 1819	1, 21
50	25 Oct. 1809–24 Oct. 1810	12, 32	60	25 Oct. 1819–29 Jan. 1820	21, 12

GEORGE IV

		Tables			Tables
1	29 Jan. 1820–28 Jan. 1821	12, 32	7	29 Jan. 1826–28 Jan. 1827	5, 25
2	29 Jan. 1821–28 Jan. 1822	32, 17	8	29 Jan. 1827–28 Jan. 1828	25, 16
3	29 Jan. 1822–28 Jan. 1823	17, 9	9	29 Jan. 1828–28 Jan. 1829	16, 29
4	29 Jan. 1823–28 Jan. 1824	9, 28	10	29 Jan. 1829–28 Jan. 1830	29, 21
5	29 Jan. 1824–28 Jan. 1825	28, 13	11	29 Jan. 1830–26 June 1830	21
6	29 Jan. 1825–28 Jan. 1826	13, 5			

WILLIAM IV

		Tables			Tables
1	26 June 1830–25 June 1831	21, 13	5	26 June 1834–25 June 1835	9, 29
2	26 June 1831–25 June 1832	13, 32	6	26 June 1835–25 June 1836	29, 13
3	26 June 1832–25 June 1833	32, 17	7	26 June 1836–20 June 1837	13, 5
4	26 June 1833–25 June 1834	17, 9			

VICTORIA

		Tables			Tables
1	20 June 1837–19 June 1838	5, 25	15	20 June 1851–19 June 1852	30, 21
2	20 June 1838–19 June 1839	25, 10	16	20 June 1852–19 June 1853	21, 6
3	20 June 1839–19 June 1840	10, 29	17	20 June 1853–19 June 1854	6, 26
4	20 June 1840–19 June 1841	29, 21	18	20 June 1854–19 June 1855	26, 18
5	20 June 1841–19 June 1842	21, 6	19	20 June 1855–19 June 1856	18, 2
6	20 June 1842–19 June 1843	6, 26	20	20 June 1856–19 June 1857	2, 22
7	20 June 1843–19 June 1844	26, 17	21	20 June 1857–19 June 1858	22, 14
8	20 June 1844–19 June 1845	17, 2	22	20 June 1858–19 June 1859	14, 34
9	20 June 1845–19 June 1846	2, 22	23	20 June 1859–19 June 1860	34, 18
10	20 June 1846–19 June 1847	22, 14	24	20 June 1860–19 June 1861	18, 10
11	20 June 1847–19 June 1848	14, 33	25	20 June 1861–19 June 1862	10, 30
12	20 June 1848–19 June 1849	33, 18	26	20 June 1862–19 June 1863	30, 15
13	20 June 1849–19 June 1850	18, 10	27	20 June 1863–19 June 1864	15, 6
14	20 June 1850–19 June 1851	10, 30	28	20 June 1864–19 June 1865	6, 26

VICTORIA—continued

Regnal year		Tables	Regnal year		Tables
29	20 June 1865–19 June 1866	26, 11	47	20 June 1883–19 June 1884	4, 23
30	20 June 1866–19 June 1867	11, 31	48	20 June 1884–19 June 1885	23, 15
31	20 June 1867–19 June 1868	31, 22	49	20 June 1885–19 June 1886	15, 35
32	20 June 1868–19 June 1869	22, 7	50	20 June 1886–19 June 1887	35, 20
33	20 June 1869–19 June 1870	7, 27	51	20 June 1887–19 June 1888	20, 11
34	20 June 1870–19 June 1871	27, 19	52	20 June 1888–19 June 1889	11, 31
35	20 June 1871–19 June 1872	19, 10	53	20 June 1889–19 June 1890	31, 16
36	20 June 1872–19 June 1873	10, 23	54	20 June 1890–19 June 1891	16, 8
37	20 June 1873–19 June 1874	23, 15	55	20 June 1891–19 June 1892	8, 27
38	20 June 1874–19 June 1875	15, 7	56	20 June 1892–19 June 1893	27, 12
39	20 June 1875–19 June 1876	7, 26	57	20 June 1893–19 June 1894	12, 4
40	20 June 1876–19 June 1877	26, 11	58	20 June 1894–19 June 1895	4, 24
41	20 June 1877–19 June 1878	11, 31	59	20 June 1895–19 June 1896	24, 15
42	20 June 1878–19 June 1879	31, 23	60	20 June 1896–19 June 1897	15, 28
43	20 June 1879–19 June 1880	23, 7	61	20 June 1897–19 June 1898	28, 20
44	20 June 1880–19 June 1881	7, 27	62	20 June 1898–19 June 1899	20, 12
45	20 June 1881–19 June 1882	27, 19	63	20 June 1899–19 June 1900	12, 25
46	20 June 1882–19 June 1883	19, 4	64	20 June 1900–22 Jan. 1901	25, 17

EDWARD VII

		Tables			Tables
1	22 Jan. 1901–21 Jan. 1902	17, 9	6	22 Jan. 1906–21 Jan. 1907	25, 10
2	22 Jan. 1902–21 Jan. 1903	9, 22	7	22 Jan. 1907–21 Jan. 1908	10, 29
3	22 Jan. 1903–21 Jan. 1904	22, 13	8	22 Jan. 1908–21 Jan. 1909	29, 21
4	22 Jan. 1904–21 Jan. 1905	13, 33	9	22 Jan. 1909–21 Jan. 1910	21, 6
5	22 Jan. 1905–21 Jan. 1906	33, 25	10	22 Jan. 1910–6 May 1910	6

GEORGE V

		Tables			Tables
1	6 May 1910–5 May 1911	6, 26	14	6 May 1923–5 May 1924	11, 30
2	6 May 1911–5 May 1912	26, 17	15	6 May 1924–5 May 1925	30, 22
3	6 May 1912–5 May 1913	17, 2	16	6 May 1925–5 May 1926	22, 14
4	6 May 1913–5 May 1914	2, 22	17	6 May 1926–5 May 1927	14, 27
5	6 May 1914–5 May 1915	22, 14	18	6 May 1927–5 May 1928	27, 18
6	6 May 1915–5 May 1916	14, 33	19	6 May 1928–5 May 1929	18, 10
7	6 May 1916–5 May 1917	33, 18	20	6 May 1929–5 May 1930	10, 30
8	6 May 1917–5 May 1918	18, 10	21	6 May 1930–5 May 1931	30, 15
9	6 May 1918–5 May 1919	10, 30	22	6 May 1931–5 May 1932	15, 6
10	6 May 1919–5 May 1920	30, 14	23	6 May 1932–5 May 1933	6, 26
11	6 May 1920–5 May 1921	14, 6	24	6 May 1933–5 May 1934	26, 11
12	6 May 1921–5 May 1922	6, 26	25	6 May 1934–5 May 1935	11, 31
13	6 May 1922–5 May 1923	26, 11	26	6 May 1935–20 Jan. 1936	31, 22

EDWARD VIII

Regnal year		Tables
1	20 Jan. 1936–11 Dec. 1936	22

GEORGE VI

Regnal year		Tables	Regnal year		Tables
1	11 Dec. 1936–10 Dec. 1937	22, 7	9	11 Dec. 1944–10 Dec. 1945	19, 11
2	11 Dec. 1937–10 Dec. 1938	7, 27	10	11 Dec. 1945–10 Dec. 1946	11, 31
3	11 Dec. 1938–10 Dec. 1939	27, 19	11	11 Dec. 1946–10 Dec. 1947	31, 16
4	11 Dec. 1939–10 Dec. 1940	19, 3	12	11 Dec. 1947–10 Dec. 1948	16, 7
5	11 Dec. 1940–10 Dec. 1941	3, 23	13	11 Dec. 1948–10 Dec. 1949	7, 27
6	11 Dec. 1941–10 Dec. 1942	23, 15	14	11 Dec. 1949–10 Dec. 1950	27, 19
7	11 Dec. 1942–10 Dec. 1943	15, 35	15	11 Dec. 1950–10 Dec. 1951	19, 4
8	11 Dec. 1943–10 Dec. 1944	35, 19	16	11 Dec. 1951– 6 Feb. 1952	4, 23

ELIZABETH II

Regnal year		Tables
1	6 Feb. 1952–5 Feb. 1953	23, 15
2	6 Feb. 1953–5 Feb. 1954	15, 28
3	6 Feb. 1954–5 Feb. 1955	28, 20
4	6 Feb. 1955–5 Feb. 1956	20, 11
5	6 Feb. 1956–5 Feb. 1957	11, 31
6	6 Feb. 1957–5 Feb. 1958	31, 16
7	6 Feb. 1958–5 Feb. 1959	16, 8
8	6 Feb. 1959–5 Feb. 1960	8, 27
9	6 Feb. 1960–5 Feb. 1961	27, 12
10	6 Feb. 1961–5 Feb. 1962	12, 32
11	6 Feb. 1962–5 Feb. 1963	32, 24
12	6 Feb. 1963–5 Feb. 1964	24, 8
13	6 Feb. 1964–5 Feb. 1965	8, 28
14	6 Feb. 1965–5 Feb. 1966	28, 20
15	6 Feb. 1966–5 Feb. 1967	20, 5
16	6 Feb. 1967–5 Feb. 1968	5, 24
17	6 Feb. 1968–5 Feb. 1969	24, 16
18	6 Feb. 1969–5 Feb. 1970	16, 8
19	6 Feb. 1970–	8, 21

EXCHEQUER YEARS OF ENGLISH RULERS

Henry I	31st exchequer year ends 29 September 1130 [1]						
Henry II	2nd	,,	,,	,,	,,	,,	1156
Richard I	1st	,,	,,	,,	,,	,,	1189
John	,,	,,	,,	,,	,,	,,	1199
Henry III	2nd	,,	,,	,,	,,	,,	1218 [2]
Edward I	1st	,,	,,	,,	,,	,,	1273
Edward II	,,	,,	,,	,,	,,	,,	1308
Edward III	,,	,,	,,	,,	,,	,,	1327
Richard II	,,	,,	,,	,,	,,	,,	1378
Henry IV	,,	,,	,,	,,	,,	,,	1400
Henry V	,,	,,	,,	,,	,,	,,	1413
Henry VI	,,	,,	,,	,,	,,	,,	1423
Edward IV	,,	,,	,,	,,	,,	,,	1461
Richard III [3]	,,	,,	,,	,,	,,	,,	1483
Henry VII	,,	,,	,,	,,	,,	,,	1486
Henry VIII	,,	,,	,,	,,	,,	,,	1510
Edward VI	,,	,,	,,	,,	,,	,,	1548
Mary	,,	,,	,,	,,	,,	,,	1554
Philip and Mary	,,	,,	,,	,,	,,	,,	1555
Elizabeth	,,	,,	,,	,,	,,	,,	1560
James I	,,	,,	,,	,,	,,	,,	1604
Charles I	,,	,,	,,	,,	,,	,,	1626
Charles II	11th	,,	,,	,,	,,	,,	1660 [4]
James II	1st	,,	,,	,,	,,	,,	1686
William and Mary	,,	,,	,,	,,	,,	,,	1690
William III	,,	,,	,,	,,	,,	,,	1696
Anne	,,	,,	,,	,,	,,	,,	1703
George I	,,	,,	,,	,,	,,	,,	1715
George II	,,	,,	,,	,,	,,	,,	1728
George III	,,	,,	,,	,,	,,	,,	1762
George IV	,,	,,	,,	,,	,,	,,	1821
William IV	,,	,,	,,	,,	,,	,,	1831 [5]

[1] This may be inferred from the one surviving Pipe Roll of Henry I's reign, after which the next complete record to show the practice of the exchequer is the Pipe Roll of 2 Henry II.

[2] The accounts for the *tempus guerræ*, including the first year of Henry III, do not appear on the Pipe Rolls.

[3] The accounts for the reign of Edward V are included in the Pipe Roll for 1 Richard III.

[4] This is the year covered by the first Pipe Roll of Charles II.

[5] The last complete Pipe Roll is for 2 William IV.

LIST OF POPES FROM GREGORY THE GREAT TO PAUL VI

The earliest surviving papal documents to bear dates (A.D. 384–98) make no use of the pontifical year. Instead, the system of dating by the consulate, taken over from the Roman imperial chancery, is employed. To this the regnal year of the emperor and the year of the indiction were later added, in accordance with the edict of the Emperor Justinian (*Novellæ*, XLVII. i, A.D. 537). But the political change which brought the papacy under the protection of the Frankish ruler Charlemagne is marked clearly by the disappearance of the Eastern imperial dating from papal letters. From A.D. 800 the papal chancery uses the imperial year of the emperor in the West at certain periods up to the twelfth century, and from the latter part of the tenth century usually adds the year of grace. Another dating element, however, is more constant and more significant: the pontifical year is generally placed alongside of these other dates and often stands alone.

The year of pontificate came to be used as an element in the dating of papal documents late in the eighth century. The earliest known document to show this usage is dated on the calends of December in the tenth year of Pope Adrian I (1 December 781). Thereafter the pontifical year frequently appears, and from the eleventh century becomes a regular element, in the dating clause of solemn papal privileges. Its use was extended in February 1188 to other products of the papal chancery. Even outside the Curia, documents were sometimes dated by the pontifical year, but this practice was never common in England.

For purposes of dating official documents, the papal clerks of the twelfth century sometimes calculated the pontifical year from the day of the pope's election. Materials are not sufficiently abundant to prove that this had always been the case in earlier centuries or, indeed, that it was regular in the twelfth century. But from the time of Innocent III onwards, the day of the pope's coronation,[1] not his election, is the determining date. This conforms to the diplomatic practice of issuing only *dimidiæ bullæ* between election and coronation.[2] It is necessary to insist on this system of reckoning because, for the purpose of reckoning the *duration* of a pontificate, it has been usual since the eleventh century to reckon from the day of election,[3] and it is an established principle of canon law that the pope exercises full jurisdiction from that day.[4] At the same time, the reader must be warned that he may encounter dates in papal documents which are inconsistent with this rule. In the first place, the pope sometimes issued letters before coronation, using either

---

[1] Not, as Bresslau says, from his consecration (*Handbuch*, ii. 422), for in the rare cases when coronation did not take place on the day of consecration (as with Leo X), the later date marks the beginning of the pontifical year.

[2] These 'half seals' bore the effigies of St. Peter and St. Paul, but not the name of the new pope. See P. M. Baumgarten, *Aus Kanzlei und Kammer* (Freiburg, 1907), pp. 163–74 and G. Battelli, *Acta pontificum* (Exempla scripturarum, fasc. iii, Vatican, 1933), nos. 13, 17, 28.

[3] Poole, *Studies*, pp. 154–5.

[4] P. Hinschius, *System des kath. Kirchenrechts*, i. 291.

the usual formula *pontificatus nostri anno primo* or a special one such as *suscepti a nobis apostolatus officii anno primo*; but the first anniversary of his coronation became the beginning of his second pontifical year, and thereafter the reckoning was normal. More serious divergences from the rule occur, but they may probably be accounted for on the supposition that the papal clerks of the fifteenth century and later sometimes lapsed into error; the inconsistency of letters dated 7 October 1647, *anno 4*, and 9 October 1647, *anno 3*, can hardly be otherwise explained.[1] In this period carelessness was perhaps the more likely to be condoned because the dating clause of all letters and briefs recorded the year of grace as well as the pontifical year.

In the following list the letter *e* indicates the date of election. There is occasionally a difference of a day or two between this date and the date of publishing the election (e.g. of Leo X, Julius III, Paul V); but in these cases only the earlier date is recorded here. The letter *c* introduces the date of coronation, which is also usually that of consecration or benediction. If the pope-elect has not been chosen from the episcopate, consecration (= *ordinatio*) precedes his coronation. If the elect is already a bishop, the ceremony of benediction precedes the crowning. These ceremonies have usually been reserved for a Sunday or some important festival.

The list has been compiled from the various sources cited in the bibliographical note, since none of the complete lists (in Gams, Grotefend, etc.) is entirely satisfactory. Even now, as the plentiful marks of interrogation show, many of the dates assigned to pontificates earlier than the twelfth century are conjectural. The indented, bracketed entries concern persons whose claim to be included in the list of popes is doubtful or who have definitely been stigmatized as anti-popes by the Roman Church. Some of these were included in the numeration of genuine popes, some were not. Their precise status in certain instances admits of doubt, but that is of no importance for the chronological purposes which this list serves.

Gregory I. *e.* ? Feb. 590; *c.* 3 Sep. 590; *d.* 12 March 604
Sabinian. *c.* 13 Sep. 604; *d.* 22 Feb. 606
Boniface III. *c.* 19 Feb. 607; *d.* 12 Nov. 607
Boniface IV. *c.* 15 Sep. 608; *d.* 25 May 615
Deusdedit. *c.* 19 Oct. 615; *d.* 8 Nov. 618
Boniface V. *c.* 23 Dec. 619; *d.* 25 Oct. 625
Honorius I. *c.* ? 27 Oct. 625; *d.* 12 Oct. 638
Severinus. *e.* ? Oct. 638; *c.* 28 May 640; *d.* 2 Aug. 640
John IV. *c.* 24 Dec. 640; *d.* 12 Oct. 642
Theodore I. *c.* 24 Nov. 642; *d.* 14 May 649
Martin I. *c.* 5 July 649; *exiled* 17 June 653; *d.* 26 Sep. 655
Eugenius I. *c.* 10 Aug. 654; *d.* 2 June 657
Vitalian. *c.* 30 July 657; *d.* 27 Jan. 672
Adeodatus. *c.* 11 Apr. 672; *d.* 17 June 676
Donus. *e.* Aug. 676; *c.* 2 Nov. 676; *d.* 11 Apr. 678
Agatho. *c.* 27 June 678; *d.* 10 Jan. 681

---

[1] *Bullarium romanum, sub anno.* Cf. the letter of Pope Paul III, dated 31 Oct. 1537 *anno 4* (*ibid., s.a.*), with his letter dated 22 Oct. 1537 *anno 3* (Battelli, *op. cit.*, no. 29). For still earlier errors see *Calendar of papal letters*, ix, pp. xxix–xxx.

Leo II. *e.* before Dec. 681 ; *c.* 17 Aug. 682 ; *d.* 3 July 683
Benedict II. *e.* Summer 683 ; *c.* 26 June 684 ; *d.* 8 May 685
John V. *c.* 23 July 685 ; *d.* 2 Aug. 686
Conon. *c.* 21 Oct. 686 ; *d.* 21 Sep. 687
    [Theodore. *e.* after 21 Sep. 687 ; *resigned* Oct.–Dec. 687]
    [Paschal. *e.* after 21 Sep. 687 ; *deposed* after 15 Dec. 687 ; *d.* ? 692]
Sergius I. *e.* Oct.–Dec. 687 ; *c.* 15 Dec. 687 ; *d.* 8 Sep. 701
John VI. *c.* 30 Oct. 701 ; *d.* 11 Jan. 705
John VII. *c.* 1 March 705 ; *d.* 18 Oct. 707
Sisinnius. *c.* 15 Jan. 708 ; *d.* 4 Feb. 708
Constantine I. *c.* 25 March 708 ; *d.* 9 Apr. 715
Gregory II. *c.* 19 May 715 ; *d.* 11 Feb. 731
Gregory III. *e.* 11 Feb. 731 ; *c.* 18 March 731 ; *d.* 29 Nov. 741
Zacharias. *c.* 10 Dec. 741 ; *d.* 15 March 752
Stephen (II).[1] *e.* 15–22 March 752 ; *d.* 18–25 March 752
Stephen II (III). *e.* 18–25 March 752 ; *c.* 26 March 752 ; *d.* ? 26 Apr. 757
Paul I. *e.* ? 26 Apr. 757 ; *c.* 29 May 757 ; *d.* 28 June 767
Constantine II. *e.* 28 June 767 ; *c.* 5 July 767 ; *deposed* 6 Aug. 768
    [Philip. *e.* 31 July 768 ; *deposed* 31 July 768]
Stephen III (IV). *e.* 1 Aug. 768 ; *c.* 7 Aug. 768 ; *d.* 24 Jan. 772
Adrian I. *e.* 1 Feb. 772 ; *c.* 9 Feb. 772 ; *d.* 25 Dec. 795
Leo III. *e.* 26 Dec. 795 ; *c.* 27 Dec. 795 ; *d.* 12 June 816
Stephen IV (V). *c.* 22 June 816 ; *d.* 24 Jan. 817
Paschal I. *c.* 25 Jan. 817 ; *d.* ? 11 Feb. 824
Eugenius II. *c.* before 6 June 824 ; *d.* Aug. 827
Valentine. *c.* ? Aug. 827 ; *d.* ? Sep. 827
Gregory IV. *e.* Dec. 827 ; *c.* 5 Jan. 828 ; *d.* 25 Jan. 844
    [John. ? Jan. 844]
Sergius II. *c.* ? Jan. 844 ; *d. before* 27 Jan. 847
Leo IV. *c.* 10 Apr. 847 ; *d.* 17 July 855
Benedict III. *e.* 17 July 855 ; *c.* ? 6 Oct. 855 ; *d.* ? 17 Apr. 858
    [Anastasius. *e.* Aug. 855 ; *expelled* 24 Sep. 855]
Nicholas I. *c.* 24 Apr. 858 ; *d.* 13 Nov. 867
Adrian II. *c.* 14 Dec. 867 ; *d.* ? 14 Dec. 872
John VIII. *c.* 14 Dec. 872 ; *d.* 15 Dec. 882
Marinus I (called Martin II). *c.* Dec. 882 ; *d.* 15 May 884
Adrian III. *c.* 17 May 884 ; *d.* Sep. 885
Stephen V (VI). *c.* ? Sep. 885 ; *d.* 14 Sep. 891
Formosus. *e.* ? late Sep. 891 ; *c.* ? 6 Oct. 891 ; *d.* 4 Apr. 896
    [Boniface VI. *e.* Apr. 896 ; *d.* ? May 896]
Stephen VI (VII). *e.* ? May 896 ; *expelled* ? July 897
Romanus. *c.* ? early Aug. 897 ; *d.* ? Nov. 897
Theodore II. *c.* ? Nov. 897 ; *d.* ? Dec. 897
John IX. *c.* ? June 898 ; *d.* ? May 900

[1] This Stephen was not reckoned in the numeration of popes of this name in the Middle Ages. The more recent numbering of the later Stephens, which includes him, has no old authority and is not now regularly employed. Cf. R. L. Poole, *Studies*, pp. 168–70.

Benedict IV. *c.* 900 ; *d.* ? late July 903
Leo V. *e.* ? late July 903 ; *d.* ? Sep. 903
Christopher. *c.* ? Sep. 903 ; *expelled* Jan. 904
Sergius III. *c.* 29 Jan. 904 ; *d.* 14 Apr. 911
Anastasius III. *c.* ? Apr. 911 ; *d.* ? June 913
Lando. *c.* ? late July 913 ; *d.* ? Feb. 914
John X. *c.* March 914 ; *deposed* ? May 928
Leo VI. *c.* ? May 928 ; *d.* ? Dec. 928
Stephen VII (VIII). *c.* ? Jan. 929 ; *d.* ? Feb. 931
John XI. *c.* Feb.–Mar. 931 ; *d.* Dec. 935–Jan. 936
Leo VII. *c.* ? 3 Jan. 936 ; *d.* July 939
Stephen VIII (IX). *c.* ? 14 July 939 ; *d.* ? late Oct. 942
Marinus II (called Martin III). *c.* ? 30 Oct. 942 ; *d.* early May 946
Agapitus II. *c.* 10 May 946 ; *d.* Dec. 955
John XII. *c.* ? 16 Dec. 955 ; *deposed* 4 Dec. 963 ; *d.* 14 May 964
Leo VIII. *e.* 4 Dec. 963 ; *c.* 6 Dec. 963 ; *d.* ? March 965
Benedict V. *c.* ? 22 May 964 ; *deposed* 23 June 964 ; *d.* 4 July 966
John XIII. *c.* 1 Oct. 965 ; *d.* 6 Sep. 972
Benedict VI. *c.* 19 Jan. 973 ; *d.* ? June 974
   [Boniface VII. *e.* ? June 974 ; *expelled* ? July 974]
Benedict VII. *c.* Oct. 974 ; *d.* 10 July 983
John XIV.[1] *c.* ? Aug. or Dec. 983 ; *deposed* Apr. 984 ; *d.* 20 Aug. 984
   [Boniface VII. *returned* Aug. 984 ; *d.* July 985]
John XV. *c.* ? Aug. 985 ; *d.* ? Apr. 996
Gregory V. *c.* 3 May 996 ; *d.* 18 Feb. 999
   [John XVI. *c.* ? Apr. 997 ; *deposed* ? Feb. 998]
Silvester II. *e.* ? early Apr. 999 ; *c.* ? 2 or 9 Apr. 999 ; *d.* 12 May 1003
John XVII. *c.* ? June 1003 ; *d.* ? Dec. 1003
John XVIII. *c.* ? Jan. 1004 ; *d.* ? July 1009
Sergius IV. *c.* ? 31 July 1009 ; *d.* 12 May 1012
Benedict VIII. *e.* ? 17 May 1012 ; *c.* 18 May 1012 ; *d.* 7 or 9 Apr. 1024
   [Gregory. *e.* ? May 1012 ; *expelled* late 1012]
John XIX. *c.* Apr.–May 1024 ; *d.* ? 6 Nov. 1032
Benedict IX. *e.* ? 12 Dec. 1032 ; *c.* ? 17 Dec. 1032 ; *resigned* 1 May 1045 ; *deposed*
   20 Dec. 1046
   [Silvester III. *e.* 10 Jan. 1045 ; *c.* 13 or 20 Jan. 1045 ; *deposed* 10 March
   1045]
Gregory VI. *e.* 1 May 1045 ; *c.* ? 5 May 1045 ; *deposed* 20 Dec. 1046
Clement II. *e.* 24 Dec. 1046 ; *c.* 25 Dec. 1046 ; *d.* 9 Oct. 1047
Benedict IX. *returned* 8 Nov. 1047 ; *expelled* 17 July 1048
Damasus II. *e.* Dec. 1047 ; *c.* 17 July 1048 ; *d.* 9 Aug. 1048
Leo IX. *e.* Dec. 1048 ; *c.* 12 Feb. 1049 ; *d.* 19 Apr. 1054
Victor II. *e.* late 1054 ; *c.* 16 Apr. 1055 ; *d.* 28 July 1057

---

[1] Owing to a corrupt text, the period of this pontificate was in the thirteenth century assigned to two popes, John XIV and John XV ; in consequence, the real John XV was reckoned as John XVI, and so on to John XIX, who was called John XX in some late lists. When in 1276 another pope took the name of John, he was called John XXI. Cf. R. L. Poole, *Studies*, pp. 166–7.

Stephen IX (X). *e.* 2 Aug. 1057 ; *c.* 3 Aug. 1057 ; *d.* 29 March 1058
Benedict X. *e.* 4 or 5 Apr. 1058 ; *c.* 5 Apr. 1058 ; *deposed* 24 Jan. 1059
Nicholas II. *e.* late Dec. 1058 ; *c.* 24 Jan. 1059 ; *d.* ? 22 July 1061
Alexander II. *e.* 29 or 30 Sep. 1061 ; *c.* 30 Sep. 1061 ; 21 Apr. 1073
    [Honorius II. *c.* 28 Oct. 1061 ; *d.* late 1072]
Gregory VII. *e.* 22 Apr. 1073 ; *c.* 29 or 30 June 1073 ; *d.* 25 May 1085
    [Clement III. *e.* 25 June 1080 ; *c.* 24 March 1084 ; *d.* Sep. 1100]
Victor III. *e.* 24 May 1086 ; *c.* 9 May 1087 ; *d.* 16 Sep. 1087
Urban II. *e.* and *c.* 12 March 1088 ; *d.* 29 July 1099
Paschal II. *e.* 13 Aug. 1099 ; *c.* 14 Aug. 1099 ; *d.* 21 Jan. 1118
    [Theodoric. *c.* Sep. 1100 ; *expelled* late 1100]
    [Albert. *e.* and *deposed* Feb.–March 1102]
    [Silvester IV. *e.* 18 Nov. 1105 ; *deposed* 13 Apr. 1111]
Gelasius II. *e.* 24 Jan. 1118 ; *c.* 10 March 1118 ; *d.* 29 Jan. 1119
    [Gregory VIII. *e.* and *c.* 8 March 1118 ; *deposed* Apr. 1121]
Calixtus II. *e.* 2 Feb. 1119 ; *c.* 9 Feb. 1119 ; *d.* 13 Dec. 1124
Honorius II. *e.* 16 Dec. 1124 ; *c.* 21 Dec. 1124 ; *d.* 13 or 14 Feb. 1130
Innocent II. *e.* 14 Feb. 1130 ; *c.* 23 Feb. 1130 ; *d.* 24 Sep. 1143
    [Anacletus II. *e.* 14 Feb. 1130 ; *c.* 23 Feb. 1130 ; *d.* 25 Jan. 1138]
    [Victor IV. *e.* ? 15 March 1138 ; *resigned* 29 May 1138]
Celestine II. *e.* and *c.* 26 Sep. 1143 ; 8 March 1144
Lucius II. *e.* 12 March 1144 ; *d.* 15 Feb. 1145
Eugenius III. *e.* 15 Feb. 1145 ; *c.* 18 Feb. 1145 ; *d.* 8 July 1153
Anastasius IV. *e.* or *c.* 12 July 1153 ; *d.* 3 Dec. 1154
Adrian IV. *e.* 4 Dec. 1154 ; *c.* 5 Dec. 1154 ; *d.* 1 Sep. 1159
Alexander III. *e.* 7 Sep. 1159 ; *c.* 20 Sep. 1159 ; *d.* 30 Aug. 1181
    [Victor IV. *e.* 7 Sep. 1159 ; *c.* 4 Oct. 1159 ; *d.* 20 Apr. 1164]
    [Paschal III. *e.* 22 Apr. 1164 ; *c.* 26 Apr. 1164 ; *d.* Sep. 1168]
    [Calixtus III. *e.* ? Sep. 1168 ; *resigned* 29 Aug. 1178]
    [Innocent III. *e.* ? 29 Sep. 1179 ; *deposed* Jan. 1180]
Lucius III. *e.* 1 Sep. 1181 ; *c.* 6 Sep. 1181 ; *d.* 25 Nov. 1185
Urban III. *e.* 25 Nov. 1185 ; *c.* 1 Dec. 1185 ; *d.* 20 Oct. 1187
Gregory VIII. *e.* 21 Oct. 1187 ; *c.* 25 Oct. 1187 ; *d.* 17 Dec. 1187
Clement III. *e.* 19 Dec. 1187 ; *c.* 20 Dec. 1187 ; *d.* late March 1191
Celestine III. *e.* 30 March 1191 ; *c.* 14 Apr. 1191 ; *d.* 8 Jan. 1198
Innocent III. *e.* 8 Jan. 1198 ; *c.* 22 Feb. 1198 ; *d.* 16 July 1216
Honorius III. *e.* 18 July 1216 ; *c.* 24 July 1216 ; *d.* 18 March 1227
Gregory IX. *e.* 19 March 1227 ; *c.* 21 March 1227 ; *d.* 22 Aug. 1241
Celestine IV. *e.* 25 Oct. 1241 ; *c.* ? 27 Oct. 1241 ; *d.* 10 Nov. 1241
Innocent IV. *e.* 25 June 1243 ; *c.* 28 June 1243 ; *d.* 7 Dec. 1254
Alexander IV. *e.* 12 Dec. 1254 ; *c.* 20 Dec. 1254 ; *d.* 25 May 1261
Urban IV. *e.* 29 Aug. 1261 ; *c.* 4 Sep. 1261 ; *d.* 2 Oct. 1264
Clement IV. *e.* 5 Feb. 1265 ; *c.* 15 Feb. 1265 ; *d.* 29 Nov. 1268
Gregory X. *e.* 1 Sep. 1271 ; *c.* 27 March 1272 ; *d.* 10 Jan. 1276
Innocent V. *e.* 21 Jan. 1276 ; *c.* 22 Feb. 1276 ; *d.* 22 June 1276
Adrian V. *e.* 11 July 1276 ; *d.* 18 Aug. 1276
John XXI. *e.* ? 8 Sep. 1276 ; *c.* 20 Sep. 1276 ; *d.* 20 May 1277

Nicholas III. *e.* 25 Nov. 1277 ; *c.* 26 Dec. 1277 ; *d.* 22 Aug. 1280
Martin IV. *e.* 22 Feb. 1281 ; *c.* 23 March 1281 ; *d.* 28 March 1285
Honorius IV. *e.* 2 Apr. 1285 ; *c.* 20 May 1285 ; *d.* 3 Apr. 1287
Nicholas IV. *e.* 15–22 Feb. 1288 ; *c.* 22 Feb. 1288 ; *d.* 4 Apr. 1292
Celestine V. *e.* 5 July 1294 ; *c.* 29 Aug. 1294 ; *resigned* 13 Dec. 1294
Boniface VIII. *e.* 24 Dec. 1294 ; *c.* 23 Jan. 1295 ; *d.* 12 Oct. 1303
Benedict XI. *e.* 22 Oct. 1303 ; *c.* 27 Oct. 1303 ; *d.* 7 July 1304
Clement V. *e.* 5 June 1305 ; *c.* 14 Nov. 1305 ; *d.* 20 Apr. 1314
John XXII. *e.* 7 Aug. 1316 ; *c.* 5 Sep. 1316 ; *d.* 4 Dec. 1334
    [Nicholas V. *e.* 12 May 1328 ; *c.* 22 May 1328 ; *resigned* 25 July 1330]
Benedict XII. *e.* 20 Dec. 1334 ; *c.* 8 Jan. 1335 ; *d.* 25 Apr. 1342
Clement VI. *e.* 7 May 1342 ; *c.* 19 May 1342 ; *d.* 6 Dec. 1352
Innocent VI. *e.* 18 Dec. 1352 ; *c.* 30 Dec. 1352 ; *d.* 12 Sep. 1362
Urban V. *e.* 28 Sep. 1362 ; *c.* 6 Nov. 1362 ; *d.* 19 Dec. 1370
Gregory XI. *e.* 30 Dec. 1370 ; *c.* 5 Jan. 1371 ; *d.* 27 March 1378
Urban VI. *e.* 8 Apr. 1378 ; *c.* 18 Apr. 1378 ; *d.* 15 Oct. 1389
    [Clement VII. *e.* 20 Sep. 1378 ; *c.* 31 Oct. 1378 ; *d.* 16 Sep. 1394]
Boniface IX. *e.* 2 Nov. 1389 ; *c.* 9 Nov. 1389 ; *d.* 1 Oct. 1404
    [Benedict XIII. *e.* 28 Sep. 1394 ; *c.* 11 Oct. 1394 ; *deposed by Council of Pisa*
        5 June 1409 *and by Council of Constance* 26 July 1417 ; *d.* 29 Nov. 1422]
Innocent VII. *e.* 17 Oct. 1404 ; *c.* 11 Nov. 1404 ; *d.* 6 Nov. 1406
Gregory XII. *e.* 30 Nov. 1406 ; *c.* 19 Dec. 1406 ; *deposed by Council of Pisa* 5 June
        1409 ; *resigned* 4 July 1415
Alexander V. *e.* 26 June 1409 ; *c.* 7 July 1409 ; *d.* 3 May 1410
John XXIII. *e.* 17 May 1410 ; *c.* 25 May 1410 ; *deposed by Council of Constance*
        29 May 1415 ; *d.* 22 Nov. 1419
Martin V. *e.* 11 Nov. 1417 ; *c.* 21 Nov. 1417 ; *d.* 20 Feb. 1431
    [Clement VIII. *e.* 10 June 1423 ; *resigned* 26 July 1429]
Eugenius IV. *e.* 3 March 1431 ; *c.* 11 March 1431 ; *suspended by Council of Basel*
        24 Jan. 1438 *and deposed by the Council* 25 June 1439 ; *d.* 23 Feb. 1447
    [Felix V. *e.* 5 Nov. 1439 ; *c.* 24 July 1440 ; *resigned* 7 Apr. 1449]
Nicholas V. *e.* 6 March 1447 ; *c.* 19 March 1447 ; *d.* 24 March 1455
Calixtus III. *e.* 8 Apr. 1455 ; *c.* 20 Apr. 1455 ; *d.* 6 Aug. 1458
Pius II. *e.* 19 Aug. 1458 ; *c.* 3 Sep. 1458 ; *d.* 15 Aug. 1464
Paul II. *e.* 30 Aug. 1464 ; *c.* 16 Sep. 1464 ; *d.* 26 July 1471
Sixtus IV. *e.* 9 Aug. 1471 ; *c.* 25 Aug. 1471 ; *d.* 12 Aug. 1484
Innocent VIII. *e.* 29 Aug. 1484 ; *c.* 12 Sep. 1484 ; *d.* 25 July 1492
Alexander VI. *e.* 11 Aug. 1492 ; *c.* 26 Aug. 1492 ; *d.* 18 Aug. 1503
Pius III. *e.* 22 Sep. 1503 ; *cons.* 1 Oct. 1503 ; *c.* 8 Oct. 1503 ; *d.* 18 Oct. 1503
Julius II. *e.* 1 Nov. 1503 ; *c.* 26 Nov. 1503 ; *d.* 20–21 Feb. 1513
Leo X. *e.* 9 March 1513 ; *cons.* 17 March 1513 ; *c.* 19 March 1513 ; *d.* 1 Dec. 1521
Adrian VI. *e.* 9 Jan. 1522 ; *c.* 31 Aug. 1522 ; *d.* 14 Sep. 1523
Clement VII. *e.* 19 Nov. 1523 ; *c.* 26 Nov. 1523 ; *d.* 25 Sep. 1534
Paul III. *e.* 13 Oct. 1534 ; *c.* 1 Nov. 1534 ; *d.* 10 Nov. 1549
Julius III. *e.* 7 Feb. 1550 ; *c.* 22 Feb. 1550 ; *d.* 23 March 1555
Marcellus II. *e.* 9 Apr. 1555 ; *c.* 10 Apr. 1555 ; *d.* 1 May 1555
Paul IV. *e.* 23 May 1555 ; *c.* 26 May 1555 ; *d.* 18 Aug. 1559

LIST OF POPES

Pius IV. *e.* 25 Dec. 1559; *c.* 6 Jan. 1560; *d.* 9 Dec. 1565
Pius V. *e.* 7 Jan. 1566; *c.* 17 Jan. 1566; *d.* 1 May 1572
Gregory XIII. *e.* 13 May 1572; *c.* 25 May 1572; *d.* 10 Apr. 1585 [1]
Sixtus V. *e.* 24 Apr. 1585; *c.* 1 May 1585; *d.* 27 Aug. 1590
Urban VII. *e.* 15 Sep. 1590; *d.* 27 Sep. 1590
Gregory XIV. *e.* 5 Dec. 1590; *c.* 8 Dec. 1590; *d.* 16 Oct. 1591
Innocent IX. *e.* 29 Oct. 1591; *c.* 3 Nov. 1591; *d.* 30 Dec. 1591
Clement VIII. *e.* 30 Jan. 1592; *c.* 9 Feb. 1592; *d.* 3 March 1605
Leo XI. *e.* 1 Apr. 1605; *c.* 10 Apr. 1605; *d.* 27 Apr. 1605
Paul V. *e.* 16 May 1605; *c.* 29 May 1605; *d.* 28 Jan. 1621
Gregory XV. *e.* 9 Feb. 1621; *c.* 14 Feb. 1621; *d.* 8 July 1623
Urban VIII. *e.* 6 Aug. 1623; *c.* 29 Sep. 1623; *d.* 29 July 1644
Innocent X. *e.* 15 Sep. 1644; *c.* 4 Oct. 1644; *d.* 7 Jan. 1655
Alexander VII. *e.* 7 Apr. 1655; *c.* 18 Apr. 1655; *d.* 22 May 1667
Clement IX. *e.* 20 June 1667; *c.* 26 June 1667; *d.* 9 Dec. 1669
Clement X. *e.* 29 Apr. 1670; *c.* 11 May 1670; *d.* 22 July 1676
Innocent XI. *e.* 21 Sep. 1676; *c.* 4 Oct. 1676; *d.* 12 Aug. 1689
Alexander VIII. *e.* 6 Oct. 1689; *c.* 16 Oct. 1689; *d.* 1 Feb. 1691
Innocent XII. *e* 12 July 1691; *c.* 15 July 1691; *d.* 27 Sep. 1700
Clement XI. *e.* 23 Nov. 1700; *cons.* 30 Nov. 1700; *c.* 8 Dec. 1700; *d.* 19 Mar. 1721
Innocent XIII. *e.* 8 May 1721; *c.* 18 May 1721; *d.* 7 March 1724
Benedict XIII. *e.* 29 May 1724; *c.* 4 June 1724; *d.* 21 Feb. 1730
Clement XII. *e.* 12 July 1730; *c.* 16 July 1730; *d.* 6 Feb. 1740
Benedict XIV. *e.* 17 Aug. 1740; *c.* 22 Aug. 1740; *d.* 3 May 1758
Clement XIII. *e.* 6 July 1758; *c.* 16 July 1758; *d.* 2 Feb. 1769
Clement XIV. *e.* 19 May 1769; *cons.* 28 May 1769; *c.* 4 June 1769; *d.* 22 Sep. 1774
Pius VI. *e.* 15 Feb. 1775; *c.* 22 Feb. 1775; *d.* 29 Aug. 1799
Pius VII. *e.* 14 March 1800; *c.* 21 March 1800; *d.* 20 Aug. 1823
Leo XII. *e.* 28 Sep. 1823; *c.* 5 Oct. 1823; *d.* 10 Feb. 1829
Pius VIII. *e.* 31 March 1829; *c.* 5 Apr. 1829; *d.* 30 Nov. 1830
Gregory XVI. *e.* 2 Feb. 1831; *c.* 6 Feb. 1831; *d.* 1 June 1846
Pius IX. *e.* 16 June 1846; *c.* 21 June 1846; *d.* 7 Feb. 1878
Leo XIII. *e.* 20 Feb. 1878; *c.* 3 March 1878; *d.* 20 July 1903
Pius X. *e.* 4 Aug. 1903; *c.* 9 Aug. 1903; *d.* 20 Aug. 1914
Benedict XV. *e.* 3 Sep. 1914; *c.* 6 Sep. 1914; *d.* 22 Jan. 1922
Pius XI. *e.* 6 Feb. 1922; *c.* 12 Feb. 1922; *d.* 10 Feb. 1939
Pius XII. *e.* 2 March 1939; *c.* 12 March 1939; *d.* 9 Oct. 1958
John XXIII. *e.* 28 Oct. 1958; *c.* 4 Nov. 1958; *d.* 3 June 1963
Paul VI. *e.* 21 June 1963; *c.* 30 June 1963

[1] This date, and all succeeding ones in this table, are given in the New Style introduced by Pope Gregory XIII's reformed calendar in 1582. For the adjustments necessary for turning these dates into the Old Style of reckoning, see p. 11.

SAINTS' DAYS AND FESTIVALS USED IN DATING

Reference has been made (above, p. 7) to the widespread practice of dating by the nearest festival of the Church. Sometimes this is additional to the dating by the Roman calendar, as when the Anglo-Saxon chronicler writes, *sub anno* 1122: 'Siððons on þaes daei vi Idus Sept. þet was on Sancte Marie messedaei'. At other times one observes in a single class of medieval records, or in a single chronicle, the use of either method indifferently. In the annals of Tewkesbury, for example, the abbot of Pershore and the Emperor Frederick II expire in adjacent sentences, the one on 'iii non. Martii' and the other 'in vigilia Sancti Lucæ'. A glance through any long series of letters of identical nature, such as the excuses sent by bishops, abbots, and others unable to attend parliament, preserved in the Public Record Office files of parliamentary proxies, illustrates the variety of methods in use. But in general it may be said that the method of dating by festivals was early in favour with chroniclers and only in the thirteenth century became usual in dating letters and other documents. It was also used very early for specifying the days of markets and fairs, or those on which rents or other payments were due: of some such we are reminded in modern times by the fact that our English quarter-days still correspond with four Church festivals (Christmas, the Annunciation, the Nativity of St. John the Baptist, and Michaelmas), and other days were similarly used, such as the Conversion of St. Paul and the feast of St. James the Apostle.[1] Hocktide, the second Monday and Tuesday after Easter, was a movable feast often specified for the payment of rents.

A list of saints' days and festivals, in order to be of assistance in problems of dating, must be based on the material and the usage of the country concerned. The list given below is an attempt to help specially the student of English history indicating to him whence each entry is derived and where he may expect to find a particular observance in use. The form of the list is dictated by the nature of its sources, and this must next be explained.

The medieval calendars, upon which such lists as this are naturally based, were themselves highly individual. It was not merely a question of what one might call geographical variation—between the use of Sarum, the use of York, and so on; between Scotland, Ireland, and Wales; between saints of giant ecclesiastical stature, universally honoured, and others who, though pigmies to the general vision, were in their own localities themselves giants. There was further variation due to emulation or tradition or prejudice of many kinds; between abbeys and churches in close geographical proximity; between (for a while) the Norman conqueror and the English he had conquered. The Abingdon chronicler tells us that the first Norman abbot forbade 'that any memorial or commemoration should be made of St. Ethelwold or of St. Edward, for he said they were English boors'.

---

[1] The Scottish quarter-days are the Purification, or Candlemas (2 February), Whit-Sunday (fixed at 15 May), Lammas (1 August), and Martinmas (11 November).

Eadmer tells us how doubtful Lanfranc was as to the claims of certain saints venerated by the English, and how Anselm convinced him that Alphege was indeed ' a great and glorious martyr '.   All three saints, of course, retained their place in the affections of medieval England, despite these early dangers.[1] Similarly, whereas in the calendar prefixed to the psalter written by Eadwine, monk of Christ Church, Canterbury, about the middle of the twelfth century, ' very little notice is taken . . . either of Augustine or his early successors ',[2] because of the feud between the monastery and the adjacent abbey of St. Augustine's, where the first ten archbishops lay buried, that too was a distinction which rightly disappeared in later Christ Church calendars.

It is not easy for the historian to bear always in mind the background which explains the dating peculiarities of the documents he is using.   An example may illustrate the kind of problem which may arise.   Two famous saints of the same name were St. Thomas the Apostle and St. Thomas of Canterbury.   The feast of the former was observed on 21 December, his translation on 3 July; the feast of the latter was 29 December, his translation 7 July.   In both cases, the dates are so near each other that the historian may be at a loss to know which is meant if no distinguishing epithet is given.   Thus, when an exchequer ordinance of 1324 directed that the year of account for the royal wardrobe should end ' a la feste de la Translacion Seynt Thomas ', even so practised a medievalist as the late Professor Tout was caught napping.   He commented : ' The regnal year of Edward II ended on 7 July.   The wardrobe year, according to the ordinance, ended on 3 July.   I do not understand why there was this difference of four days.'[3] The translation referred to, however, was that of St. Thomas of Canterbury, exactly coincident in date with the close of Edward II's regnal year.   An exchequer clerk would take that for granted, for in calendars used for reference in his office, such as that prefixed to the thirteenth-century Black Book of the Exchequer,[4] he would see for St. Thomas the Apostle merely his feast on 21 December, whereas there appeared for St. Thomas of Canterbury his feast, its octave, and his translation.

It is of course impossible, in a mere hand-list for ready reference, to treat exhaustively problems of origin and variation.   It is hoped, however, that the appended list may at any rate draw attention to some important categories in which individuality of dating may be expected.   Each entry bears a superior letter showing the source from which it was derived.   Thus a superior e (^{e}), indicating that the entry came from an exchequer source, marks the translation of St. Thomas of Canterbury, but not that of his namesake, so that our list would give a hint towards the solution of the apparent discrepancy described above.   It must be clearly understood, however, that while the superior letter gives a guarantee that the feast so marked was in use in the category indicated, the inference must not be made that its use was exclusive to that category.

Three main groups of original sources were used in the compilation of the list :

(1) Its nucleus consists of 168 entries taken from the Black Book calendar mentioned above, which was probably first written between 1252 and 1260, with

[1] Both incidents are cited by G. G. Coulton, *Five centuries of religion*, iii. 4.

[2] M. R. James, *The Canterbury psalter*, Introduction.

[3] T. F. Tout, *The place of Edward II in history*. (2nd ed., 1936), p. 179, n. 1.

[4] A Public Record Office MS. (T. R. Misc. Books, no. 266) ; see Giuseppi, *Guide to the public records*, i. 210.   It is not to be confused with the earlier ' liber niger parvus ' (K. R. Misc. Books, series i, vol. 12), printed by Thomas Hearne (1728) under the title *Liber niger scaccarii.*

many additions inserted as time went on. This calendar was chosen as starting-point, partly because of its chronological position in the heart of the Middle Ages, partly because the ramifications of a financial department so old and so important produced innumerable records and influenced innumerable datings. The resultant list was then tested from an official source of a different kind and half a century later in date, namely, three rolls, covering the period from November 1299 to November 1302,[1] in which Edward I's almoner set down each day the number of poor fed at the king's expense as the court travelled about the country, and the name of the saint thus honoured. Only seven fresh names were thus obtained, so that it is evident that the Black Book calendar might still serve at that date as a good guide to the saints most frequently quoted in court and official circles.

(2) It seemed desirable next to examine some source which presented a different range of interests and covered a wider period. This was found in the *Index et concordantia festorum*, compiled by Canon Christopher Wordsworth, from six calendars of the universities of Oxford, Cambridge, and Paris, varying in date from the fourteenth to late in the fifteenth century, together with the *Compotus manualis ad usum Oxoniensium* printed in 1519–20, from which he himself constructed a calendar.[2] The ninety entries added to our list from this source are of considerable interest. They bring in such saints as St. Anne, whose commemoration was not introduced until late in the fourteenth century, scholastic philosophers or famous religious (St. Thomas Aquinas, St. Dominic, St. Gilbert of Sempringham, St. Anthony of Padua), and also names reflecting the varied origins of university students (St. William of York, St. Peter of Milan, St. Patrick).

(3) The augmented list was next compared with calendars originating from Canterbury, Salisbury, Hereford, and York,[3] with the result that some ninety entries were added. Not many additions came from Sarum, since that Use was the foundation of several calendars which had already been utilized. The Canterbury group, which ranged from the twelfth to the fifteenth century, included a secular specimen from the Black Book of the Archdeacon, as well as monastic examples from Christ Church and St. Augustine's. The printed edition of the thirteenth-century Hereford breviary includes also a fifteenth-century Worcester small breviary ; both sources provide additions. This section of the list was completed by a few entries of a miscellaneous kind (and therefore in most cases not marked in the list by any special indication), coming either from local uses (e.g., Glastonbury, Winchester, and Durham), or found in use in chronicles or other sources when a number of these were examined in order to test the usefulness of the list at the point now reached. Feasts of the dedication of churches have not been included.

The remainder of the list consists of a selection from the ordinary works of reference of special names, local, liturgical, or traditional, given to certain days and seasons, particularly in England. These have been included alphabetically in the general list of festivals in the hope that this will prove more convenient for reference than the usual method of printing them in a separate glossary.

[1] P.R.O., Exchequer Accts., K.R., 357/29, 359/15, 361/21.
[2] The *Index* occupies pp. 257–64 of Wordsworth's *Ancient kalendar of the university of Oxford*; the other texts are printed in the same volume. Entries which appear in the Paris calendar only have not been included in the present list.
[3] Examined in the texts listed in the bibliography, above, p. xiv.

SAINTS' DAYS AND FESTIVALS USED IN DATING

Most of the abbreviations used below are obvious—*m.*, martyr, *reg.*, regina, etc. *Presbyter* is shortened to *pr.* and *papa* to *p.*   The description used is not necessarily in every case that given in the calendar from which the entry was taken.
Sources are indicated by superior letters as follows :

a = alms rolls	**sa** = Sarum gradual
ca = Canterbury calendars	**u** = University calendars
e = Black Book of the Exchequer	**w** = Worcester breviary
h = Hereford breviary	**win** = Winchester calendar
hw = Hereford and Worcester breviaries	**y** = York breviary

A

Abdon et Sennes, *mm.*e	30 July
Achilleus	*see* Nereus et Achilleus
Ad te levavi	1st Sun. in Advent
Adam creatus est	23 March
Adauctus	*see* Felix et Adauctus
Adelburga	*see* Ethelburga
Adeldreda	*see* Etheldreda
Adorate dominum	3rd Sun. after Epiphany
Adrianus, *abb.*ca	9 Jan.
Adrianus, *m.*[1]	4 March
Adrianus, Hadrianus, *m.*sa . . .	8 Sep.
Advent Sunday	nearest Sun. to feast of St. Andrew
Adventus domini	the 4 weeks preceding Christmas
Adventus spiritus sancti super discipulos ca .	15 May
Aedburga	*see* Eadburga
Aeluric, *archiep. etc.*ca . . .	16 Nov.
Agapitus, *m.*	6 Aug.u, 18 Aug.e
Agatha, *v. et m.*e	5 Feb.
Agnes, *v. et m.*e	21 Jan.
—— secundo e	28 Jan.[2]
Aidan, *ep et c.*y	31 Aug.
Albanus, *m.*e	22 June
Albinus, *ep.*u	1 March
Aldelmus, Aldhelmus, *ep. et c.*e . .	25 May
Alexander, *p.*u	3 May
All Hallows, All Saints' Day . . .	1 Nov.
All Souls' Day	2 Nov.
Alphegus, *archiep. et m.*e . . .	19 April
—— translatio	8 June ca
—— ordinatio	16 Nov.ca

[1] Sometimes described as *miles*.
[2] Viz. her nativity. Sometimes entered in calendars as octave (e.g. in thirteenth-century calendar of St. Augustine's, Canterbury ; *see* Feltoe, pp. 8, 9).

Amandus	*see* Vedastus et Amandus
Ambrosius, *ep. et c.*[e] . . .	4 April
Anastasius, *ep.*[u]	27 April
Andreas, *ap.*[e]	30 Nov.
Angarie	Ember Weeks
Anianus, *ep. et c.*[e] . . .	17 Nov.
Animarum commemoratio . . .	*see* Commemoratio fidelium
Anna, mater b. Marie [u] . . .	26 July
Annunciatio dominica [u] . . .	25 March
Anselmus, *archiep.*[ca] . . .	21 April
Antoninus, *m.*[ca]	2 Sep.
Antonius, *m. et c.*[sa] . . .	17 Jan.
Antonius cordigerius [u] [1] . .	13 June
Apollinaris, *m.*[e]	23 July
Apollinaris et Timotheus . . .	*see* Timotheus et Apollinaris
Apparitio domini	6 Jan.
Apuleius et Marcellus . . .	*see* Marcellus et Apuleius
Arnulfus, *ep. et m.*[e] . . .	18 July
Ascensio, Ascensa, domini in celum . .	Thursday following Rogation Sunday
Ash Wednesday	1st day of Lent
Aspiciens a longe	1st Sun. in Advent
Assumptio domini, Christi . .	old name of Ascension Day
Audactus	*see* Felix et Adauctus
Audoenus, *ep. et c.* . . .	24 Aug.[e], 25 Aug.[ca]
Audrey	*see* Etheldreda
Augustinus, *Anglorum ap., archiep.*[e] .	26 May
—— translatio [ca]	13 Sep.
Augustinus (magnus), *ep. et doct.*[e] .	28 Aug.
—— translatio	11 Oct.
Austreberta, Austroberta, *v.* . .	10 Feb.[ca], 20 Oct.[y]
Aves incipiunt cantare [2] . .	12 Feb.

B

Babillus, Babylas, *ep.*, et soc.[y] .	24 Jan.
Balthilides	*see* Batilda
Barbara, *v.*[ca]	4 Dec.[3]
Barbara, *v.*[ca]	15 Dec.[3]
Barnabas, *ap.*[e]	11 June
Bartholomew, *ap.*[e] . . .	24 Aug.
Basilides, Curinus (Cirinus, Cyrinus), et Nabor,	
mm.	12 June

[1] i.e. Anthony of Padua, the Franciscan.
[2] This occurs in three Durham calendars (twelfth and fourteenth century).
[3] 4 Dec. in archdeacon of Canterbury's Black Book (early fifteenth century); 15 Dec. in a Christchurch calendar, *c.* 1286. There are two different saints of the same name, and it is odd that the calendars should differ as to which was to be commemorated at Christchurch. The commemoration is on 16 Dec. in Whytford's *Martiloge* (H. Bradshaw Soc. Publ., iii, 1893).

Basilius, *ep. et c.*e	14 June
Batilda, Balthilides, Bathildis, *reg. et v.*e .	30 Jan.
Bavo	*see* Remigius, Germanus, Vedastus, et Bavo
Beatrix, *v. et. m.*e	29 July
Benedicta	Trinity Sunday
Benedictus, *abb.*a	21 March
—— translatio e	11 July
Benedictus, *abb.*e (Benedict Biscop). .	12 Jan.
Berchtinus	*see* Bertinus
Bernardus, *abb.*u	21 Aug.[1]
Bertelinus Staffordie u	9 Sep.
Bertinus, Berchtinus, *abb.*e . . .	5 Sep.
Birinus, *ep. et c.*	3 Dec.
—— translatio	4 Sep.
Black Monday	Easter Monday [2]
Blasius, *ep. et m.*e	3 Feb.[3]
Bonefacius et soc., *mm.*e . . .	5 June
Borae	*see Brandones*
Botulfus, *abb. et c.*e	17 June
Brancheria	Palm Sunday
Brandones, Borae, Burae, Bules . .	1st Sun. in Lent and week following
Bregwinus, *archiep.*ca	26 Aug.
Bricius, Briccius, *ep. et c.* . . .	13 Nov.e, 14 Nov.sa
Brigida, *v.*e	1 Feb.
Bules, Burae	*see Brandones*
Byrnstanus, *ep.*win	4 Nov.

C

Caesarius, *m.*sa	1 Nov.
Calixtus, Calestus, Kalixtus, *p. et m.*e .	14 Oct.
Candelaria, candelatio, candlemas . .	2 Feb.
Canite tuba or *Canite*	4th Sun. in Advent
Cantate domino	4th Sun. after Easter
Canutus, Cnutus,[4] *r.*	10 July
Capitiluvium	Palm Sunday
Caput jejunii	Ash Wednesday
Cara cognatio	22 Feb.
Caramentranum, Caremprenium . .	Shrove Tuesday

[1] 20 Aug. in fourteenth-century calendar of university of Paris (*Chart. univ. paris.*, ii. 709–16).

[2] For various early examples of the use of 'Black Monday' for Easter Monday, see *Oxford English Dictionary*, *s.v.* Monday.

[3] 14 June, in fifteenth-century calendar of university of Cambridge.

[4] Found at Evesham only (Bodl. Lib., MS. Barlow 41). Mr. Wormald points out that the Chnutus substituted for Gundonis in a later hand under 11 Nov. in a thirteenth-century calendar of St. Augustine's (Feltoe, p. 28) is merely an obit.

Caristia	22 Feb.
Caritas dei	Sat. in Ember Week of Pentecost
Carle *or* Carling Sunday	5th Sun. in Lent
Carnibrevium	Shrove Tuesday
Carniprivium, Carnisprivium, Privicarnium [1] .	*either (a)* first days of Lent *or (b)* Septuagesima Sunday *or (c)* Sexagesima Sunday
Carniprivium novum	Quinquagesima Sunday
Carniprivium sacerdotum . . .	Septuagesima Sunday
Carniprivium vetus	Quadragesima Sunday [2]
Carnivora	Shrove Tuesday
Cathedra sancti Petri	22 Feb.
Catherina	*see* Katherina
Ceci nati	Wed. of 4th week in Lent
Cecilia, *v. et m.*[e]	22 Nov.
Cedda, Chad, *ep. et c.*[u]	2 March
Cena domini ⎫	⎧Maundy Thursday
Chare Thursday ⎭	⎩
Childermas Day	28 Dec.
Christina, Cristina, *v. et m.*[u] . . .	24 July
Christoforus et Cucufas, *mm.* . . .	25 July
Chrysogonus, Grisogonus, *m.*[e] . . .	24 Nov.
Ciprianus	*see* Cyprianus
Circumcisio domini	1 Jan.
Circumdederunt	Septuagesima Sunday
Ciriacus, *m.*[e].	8 Aug.
Ciricus et Julitta, *mm.*[e]	16 June
Cirinus, Cyrinus	*see* Basilides, Curinus, et Nabor
Clara, *v.*	12 Aug.
Clausum Pasche	Sun. after Easter
Clausum Pentecostes	Trinity Sunday
Clean Lent	the days of Lent reckoned from Ash Wednesday [3]
Clemens, *p. et m.*[e]	23 Nov.
Cletus, *p. et m.*[hw]	12 July
Cnutus, Chnutus	*see* Canutus
Collop Monday	Mon. before Shrove Tuesday
Commemoratio fidelium defunctorum, Animarum commemoratio	2 Nov.
Commovisti terram et conturbasti eam .	Sexagesima Sunday
Cornelius et Cyprianus, *mm.*[u] . . .	14 Sept.
Corpus Christi	Thurs. after Trinity Sunday

[1] For an example of an important historical point turning upon the variant uses of this term *see* 'The parliament of Lincoln of 1316' (*Eng. Hist. Rev.*, xxxvi. 53–7, 480).
[2] Till the ninth century, in the Latin church, Lenten abstinence did not begin till this day. *Inter duo carnisprivia* is used for the days of Quinquagesima week.
[3] So that the 1st Mon. in Clean Lent will be the Monday after Quadragesima Sunday.

Cosmas et Damianus, *mm.*ᵉ	27 Sep.
Crescentius	*see* Vitus, Modestus, et Crescentius
Crisanthus et Daria, *mm.*ʸ	1 Dec.
Crisogonus	*see* Chrysogonus
Crispinus et Crispinianus, *mm.*ᵉ . .	25 Oct.
Cristina	*see* Christina
Cross Week	Rogation Week
Crouchmas, Crowchemesse Day . .	14 Sep.
Cruces nigre	25 April
Crucis, Adoratio (or *dies sancte crucis adorate, dies crucis adorande, veneris dies adoratus*) . .	Good Friday
Crucis, Exaltatio sancte ᵉ . . .	14 Sep.
Crucis, Inventio sancte ᵉ	3 May
Cucufas	*see* Christoforus et Cucufas
Curinus, Cyrinus	*see* Basilides, Curinus, et Nabor
Cuthberga, Cuthburga, *v.*ᵉ . . .	31 Aug.
Cuthbertus, *ep. et c.*ᵉ	20 March
—— translatio	4 Sep.
Cuthlac	*see* Guthlac
Cyprianus et Cornelius, *mm.*ᵘ . .	14 Sep.
Cyprianus et Justina, *mm.*ᵉ . . .	26 Sep.
Cyriacus	*see* Ciriacus

D

Da pacem	18th Sun. after Pentecost
Daemon mutus	3rd Sun. in Lent
Damasus, *p.*	11 Dec.
Damianus	*see* Cosmas et Damianus
David, *ep. et c.*ᵃ	1 March
Deductio Christi in Egyptum . . .	9 Jan.
Denis	*see* Dionysius
Depositio	day of death of a saint who is not a martyr
Deus in adjutorium	12th Sun. after Pentecost
Deus in loco sancto	11th Sun. after Pentecost
Deus qui errantibus	3rd Sun. after Easter
*Deusdedit, archiep.*ᶜᵃ ¹	15 July
Diabolus recessit a domino . . .	15 Feb.
Dicit dominus	23rd and 24th Sun. after Pentecost
Dies absolutionis	Thurs. before Good Friday
Dies adoratus	Good Friday
Dies animarum	2 Nov.
Dies burarum	1st Sun. in Lent
Dies cinerum	Ash Wednesday
Dies crucis adorande, adorate . . .	Good Friday

¹ Frithona of Wessex, the first archbishop of English birth (Feltoe, p. 21).

E

Dies dominica, dominicus	*either* (*a*) Sunday *or* (*b*) Easter Day
Dies felicissimus	Easter Day
Dies florum	Palm Sunday
Dies focorum	1st Sun. in Lent
Dies jovis	Thursday
Dies jovis absoluti	*see Dies absolutionis*
Dies lune	Monday
Dies lune periurata [1]	? Hock Monday
Dies mandati	Maundy Thursday
Dies martis	Tuesday
Dies mercurii, mercurinus, mercoris . . .	Wednesday
Dies neophytorum	the six days between Easter Day and Quasimodo Sunday
Dies osanne ⎫	
Dies palmarum ⎬	Palm Sunday
Dies ramorum ⎭	
Dies sabbati	Saturday
Dies veneris	Friday
Dies veneris adoratus	Good Friday
Dies viginti	the twenty days between Christmas and the octave of Epiphany
Dionysius (Denis) et soc., *mm.*ᵉ . .	9 Oct.
Distaff Day	7 Jan.
Divisio apostolorum	15 July
Domine, in tua misericordia . . .	1st Sun. after Pentecost
Domine, ne longe	Palm Sunday
Dominica in albis, in albis depositis, post albas .	1st Sun. after Easter
Dominica ante litanias	5th Sun. after Easter
Dominica Cananee	2nd Sun. in Lent
Dominica ad carnes levandas . . .	Quinquagesima Sunday
Dominica duplex	Trinity Sunday
Dominica indulgentie	Palm Sunday
Dominica mapparum albarum . . .	2nd Sun. after Easter
Dominica mediana	Passion Sunday (5th in Lent)
Dominica olivarum . . . ⎫	
Dominica osanna . . . . ⎬ .	Palm Sunday
Dominica ad palmas, in ramis palmarum ⎭	
Dominica in passione domini . . .	Passion Sunday
Dominica post focos, post ignes . . .	2nd Sun. in Lent
Dominica post strenas	Sun. next after 1 Jan.
Dominica quintana	1st Sun. in Lent
Dominica refectionis	Mid-Lent Sunday

[1] On day thus described, in a rental of 1185, a ward-penny was due from Rivenhall, Essex ; a later rental speaks of payment due from Rivenhall *die ropemoneday* and from Cressing *ad hokeday.* The three expressions probably indicate the same day, Hocktide being a favourite time for spring payments. *See* B. A. Lees, *Records of the Templars in England*, p. lxxviii *and* n.

Dominica rogationum	5th Sun. after Easter
Dominica de rosa, de rosis	Sun. in octave of Ascension
Dominica rose, rosata	4th Sun. in Lent
Dominica samaritani	4th Sun. after Easter
Dominica sancta	Easter Sunday
Dominica sancte trinitatis	Trinity Sunday
Dominica de transfiguratione . . .	2nd Sun. in Lent
Dominica trium septimanarum Pasche .	3rd Sun. after Easter
Dominicus, *c.*u	4 Aug.[1]
—— translatio[u]	24 May
Dominus fortitudo	6th Sun. after Pentecost
Dominus illuminatio mea	4th Sun. after Pentecost
Donatianus, *ep. et c.*ca	15 Oct.
Donatus, *ep. et m.*e	7 Aug.
Dormitio sancte Marie	15 Aug.[2]
Dum clamarem	10th Sun. after Pentecost
Dum medium silentium	*either* (*a*) Sun. in octave of Christmas *or* (*b*) Sun. after 1 Jan., if this Sun. falls on eve of Epiphany
Dunstanus, *archiep. et c.*e . . .	19 May
—— ordinatio [3]	21 Oct.ca
—— translatio	7 Sep.ca

E

Eadburga, Edburga, Aedburga, *v. et abb.*ca [4] .	12 *or* 13 July
Eadburga, *v.*wln	15 June
Eadburga, *v.*wln	18 July
Eanswitha, *v.*ca	31 Aug.[5]
Easter	*see* Pascha
Ebdomada	*see* Hebdomada
Ecce Deus adjuvat	9th Sun. after Pentecost
Edburga	*see* Eadburga
Editha, *v.*e	16 Sep.
Edmundus, *archiep. et c.*e . . .	16 Nov.
—— translatio [e]	9 June
Edmundus, *r. et. m.*e	20 Nov.
—— translatio [u]	29 April
Edwardus, *r. et c., depositio* [e] . . .	5 Jan.
—— translatio [e]	13 Oct.
Edwardus, *r. et m.*e	18 March

[1] 5 Aug. at Paris. [2] 18 Jan. in some ancient calendars.

[3] Translation and ordination occur in Christchurch calendars only; when the saint's feast is found elsewhere the deposition is intended.

[4] Abbess of Thanet.

[5] In thirteenth-century calendar of St. Augustine's, Canterbury, and in Jesus Coll., Cambridge, MS., Q 6 (twelfth-century psalter).

Edwardus, *r. et m.*, translatio prima [e] . .	18 Feb.
—— translatio secunda [e] . . .	20 June
Egg Saturday	Sat. before Shrove Tuesday
Egidius, *abb.*[e]	1 Sep.
Ego sum pastor bonus	2nd Sun. after Easter
Egressus, Egressio, Noe de archa [u] . .	29 April
Eligius, *ep. Noviomensis, c.*[u] . . .	25 June
Ember Days	*see Quatuor tempora*
Emerentiana, *v. et m.*[ca] . . .	23 Jan.
Epimachus	*see Gordianus et Epimachus*
Epiphania domini, Theophania . .	Epiphany, 6 Jan.
Erconwaldus, Erkenwaldus, *ep. London., c.,* depositio [e]	30 April
—— translatio [e]	14 Nov.
Ermenhilda, *v.*[win] [1]	13 Feb.
Esto mihi	Quinquagesima Sunday
Ethelbert, *r. et m.*.	20 May
Ethelburga, *v. et abb.*	11 Oct.
Etheldreda, Adeldreda, Audrey, *v.*[e] . .	23 June
—— translatio [u]	17 Oct.
Ethelfleda, *v.*[win]	27 Jan.
Ethelgarus, *archiep.*[ca] . . .	11 Feb.
Ethelred, *r. et c.*.	4 May
Ethelredus et Ethelbrictus, *mm.*[ca] . .	17 Oct.
Ethelwoldus, *ep. et c.*[win] . . .	1 Aug.
Eucharistia, Sancta	Corpus Christi
Eufemia, Lucianus, et Geminianus, *mm.*[e]	16 Sep.
Eugenia, *v.*[ca]	16 March
Eulalia, *v.*[ca]	12 Feb.
Eusebius, *pr. et c.*[ur]	14 Aug.
Eustachius et soc.[e]	2 Nov.
Eventius, *m.*[u]	3 May
Everilda, *v.*[y].	9 July
Evurcius, *ep. et c.*[y] [2]	7 Sep.
Exaudi domine	*either* (a) Sun. in the octave of Ascension *or* (b) 6th Sun. after Easter
Expectatio beate Marie	16 Dec. *or* 18 Dec.
Exsurge domine	Sexagesima Sunday

F

Fabianus et Sebastianus, *mm.*[e] . .	20 Jan.
Factus est dominus	2nd Sun. after Pentecost
Fastmas, Fastren's Eve . . .	Shrove Tuesday
Fastyngong	Shrovetide

[1] She is really an Ely saint.

[2] In James I's prayer-book of 1604, this saint appears, owing to a misreading, as ' Enurchus '.

Faustinus, Faustus . . .	*see* Felix et Faustinus
Felicianus	*see* Primus et Felicianus
Felicissimus et Agapitus, *mm.*ᵉ . .	6 Aug.
Felicitas, *v.*ᵉ	23 Nov.
Felicitas et Perpetua, *vv. et mm.*ᵉ	7 March
Felix, *ep. et c.*[1] . . .	8 March
Felix (*in pincis*), *c.*ᵉ . . .	14 Jan.
Felix et Adauctus (Audactus), *mm.*ᵉ .	30 Aug.
Felix et Faustinus, Faustus, *mm.*ᵉ .	29 July
Feria ad angelum	Wed. in Ember Week of Advent
Feria magni scrutinii . . .	Wed. in 4th week in Lent
Feria prima	Sunday
Feria secunda major or *magna* [2] .	Mon. of Passion Week
Festum animarum	*see* Commemoratio fidelium
Festum apostolorum . . .	1 May
Festum architriclini . . .	2nd Sun. after Epiphany
Festum azymorum . . .	Easter Day
Festum candelarum . . .	*see* Candelaria
Festum Christi	Christmas
Festum luminum	*see* Candelaria
Festum ovorum	*see* Egg Saturday
Festum primitiarum . . .	1 Aug.
Festum stelle	6 Jan.
Festum stultorum . . .	1 Jan.
Fides, *v. et m.*ᵉ . . .	6 Oct.
Firminus, *ep. et. m.*ᵉ . . .	25 Sep.
Franciscus, *c.*ᵃ	4 Oct.
—— translatio ᵘ . . .	25 May
Frideswida, Fredeswida, *v. et reg.*ᵉ .	19 Oct.
—— inventio ᵘ . . .	15 May
—— translatio ᵘ . . .	11 Feb.
Furseus, *c.*ᶜᵃ	16 Jan.

G

Gamaliel ᶜᵃ	4 Aug.
Gang Days	Rogation Days
Gaudete in domino . . .	3rd Sun. in Advent
Geminianus	*see* Lucianus et Geminianus
Georgius, *m.*ᵉ	23 April [3]
Gereon, Ieron, et soc., *mm.*ᵘ . .	10 Oct.
Germanicus, *m.*ʸ . . .	19 Jan.
Germanus, *c.*	*see* Remigius, Germanus, Vedastus, et Bavo

[1] The apostle of East Anglia.
[2] And similarly *tertia major, quarta major*, etc., for the remaining days of this week.
[3] Entered both on 21 April and 23 April in thirteenth-century calendar of St. Augustine's, Canterbury (Feltoe, p. 14).

Germanus, *ep. et c.* [Auxerre] e . . . 31 July
Germanus, *ep. et c.* [Capua] y . . . . 30 Oct.
Germanus, *ep. et c.* [Paris] e . . . . 28 May ; 21 May u
Gervasius et Prothasius, *mm.*e . . . 19 June
Gilbertus [de Sempringham], *c.*u . . . 4 Feb.
—— translatio . . . . . 13 Oct.
Gildardus . . . . *see* Medardus et Gildardus
Giles . . . . *see* Egidius
Good Friday . . . . . Friday next before Easter
Gordianus et Epimachus, *mm.*e . . . 10 May
Gorgonius, *m.*e . . . . . 9 Sep.
Gorgonius, *m.*u . . . . . 24 Nov.
Grass Week . . . . . . Rogation Week
Great Week . . . . . . week before Easter Day
Gregorius, *p.*e . . . . . 12 March
—— ordinatio . . . . . 3 Sep.
Grimbaldus, Grumbaldus, Grimbambus, *c.*ca 1 . 8 July
Grisogonus . . . . . . *see* Chrysogonus
Gula Augusti . . . . . 1 Aug.
Gunpowder Plot . . . . . 5 Nov.
Guthlac, Cuthlac, *c.*u . . . . 11 April

H

Hadrianus . . . . . . *see* Adrianus
Hallowmas . . . . . . 1 Nov.
Hebdomada, ebdomada . . . . a week
Hebdomada authentica ⎱
Hebdomada crucis ⎰ . . . Holy Week
Hebdomada duplex or *trinitatis* . . . Week after Trinity Sunday
Hebdomada expectationis . . . Week after Ascension
Hebdomada indulgentie . . . . Holy Week
Hebdomada magna . . . . . *either* (*a*) Holy Week *or* (*b*) week
  before Pentecost
Hebdomada mediana quadragesime . . 4th week in Lent
Hebdomada muta . . . . . Holy Week
Hebdomada penalis, penosa . . . Holy Week
Hebdomada sacra . . . . . (*a*) week before Easter, (*b*) week
  before Pentecost
Hermes, *m.*ca . . . . . 28 Aug
Hieronymus . . . . . . *see* Jeronimus
Hilarion, *c.* . . . . . 21 Oct.
Hilarius, Hillarius, *ep.*a . . . . 13 Jan.
Hilda, *v. et ab.*y . . . . 25 Aug., elsewhere 17 Nov.
Hipolitus . . . . . . *see* Hypolitus
Hock Day, Hoke Day . . . . 2nd Tues. after Easter
Hocktide, Hoketide . . . . 2nd Mon. and Tues. after Easter.

1 Described in one Christchurch calendar as *c. et anchorita.*

Hogmanay	31 Dec.
Holy Friday	Good Friday
Holymas Day	1 Nov.
Holy Monday [1]	Mon. in Holy Week
Holy Rood Day	*see* Crucis, Exaltatio sancte
Holy Thursday	Ascension Day
Holy Week	the week before Easter
Honorina, *v.*[ca]	27 Feb.
Honorius, *archiep.*[ca]	30 Sep.
Hugo, *ep. Linc. et c.*[e] . . .	17 Nov.
—— translatio	6 Oct.[u], 7 Oct.[a]
Hyacinthus, Iacinctus . . .	*see* Prothus et Hyacinthus
Hypapante, Hypapanti, Hypante . .	2 Feb.
Hypolitus, Ypolitus, *m.* et soc.[e] .	13 Aug.
Hyreneus	*see* Ireneus

I

Iacinctus	*see* Prothus et Hyacinthus
Ieron	*see* Gereon
In excelso throno	1st Sun. after Epiphany
In voluntate tua	21st Sun. after Pentecost
Incarnatio domini	25 Dec.
Inclina aurem tuam . . .	15th Sun. after Pentecost
Innocentes, *mm.*[e]	28 Dec.
Introitus Noe in archam [u] . .	17 March
Invocavit me	1st Sun. in Lent
Ireneus, Hyreneus et soc.[ca] . .	5 July
Isidorus, *ep.*[ca]	2 Jan.
Isti sunt dies	Passion Sunday
Ivo, *ep. et c.*	24 April

J

Jacobus, *ap.*[e]	25 July
Jambertus, *archiep.*[ca] . . .	12 Aug.
Jejunia temporalia . . .	*see* Quatuor tempora
Jejunium autumnale or *septimi mensis* .	Ember Days of Sep.
Jejunium estivale or *quarti mensis* .	Ember Days of Pentecost
Jejunium hiemale or *decimi mensis* .	Ember Days of Advent
Jejunium vernale or *primi mensis* .	Ember Days of Lent
Jeronimus, Hieronymus, *pr. et doc.*[e] .	30 Sep.
Jesu nomen dulcissimum [u] . .	7 Aug.
Johannes, *ap. et evan.*[e] . .	27 Dec.
Johannes albus	24 June
Johannes ante portam latinam [e] .	6 May
Johannes Bapt., decollatio or natalis [e] .	29 Aug.
—— Nativitas [e]	24 June

[1] And similarly Holy Tuesday, Wednesday, and Saturday.

Johannes de Beverlaco [u]	7 May
—— translatio [a]	25 Oct.
Johannes de Bridlington, translatio . .	11 May
Johannes et Paulus, *mm.*[e]	26 June
Jubilate omnis terra	3rd Sun. after Easter
Judas	*see* Simon et Judas
Judica me	Passion Sunday
Judocus, *c.*[ca]	13 Dec.
—— translatio [win]	9 Jan.
Juliana, *v. et m.*[e]	16 Feb.
Juliana, *v.*[u]	23 Feb.
Julianus, *ep. et c.*[e]	27 Jan.
Julitta	*see* Ciricus et Julitta
Justin [sa]	28 Aug.[1]
Justina	*see* Cyprianus et Justina
Justus, *archiep.*[ca]	10 Nov.
Justus [sa]	18 Oct.
Justus es Domine	17th Sun. after Pentecost

K

Kalixtus	*see* Calixtus
Katerina, Catherina, *v. et m.*[e] . . .	25 Nov.
Kenelmus, Kynelmus, *r. et m.*[e] . .	17 July

L

Lady Day	25 March
Lambertus, Lanbertus, Landberhtus, *ep. et m.*[e]	17 Sep.
Lamfrancus, Lanfrancus, *archiep.*[ca] . .	28 May
Lammas Day	1 Aug.
Laurentius, *m.*[e]	10 Aug.
Laurentius, *archiep.*[ca]	3 Feb.
Lent	*see* Quadragesima
Leo, *p.*[e]	28 June
Leodegarius, *ep. et m.*[e]	2 Oct.
Leonardus, *abb.*	6 Nov.
Letardus, *ep.*[ca] [2]	7 May
Letare Hierusalem	4th Sun. in Lent
Leufredus, Leothfredus, *abb.*[ca] . .	21 June
Lex Moysi data est	15 May
Linus, *p. et m.*[e]	26 Nov.
Litania major	25 April
Little Easter	Pentecost
Livinus, *ep. et m.*[ca]	12 Nov.

[1] Displacing Hermes.
[2] Local. Liudhard, bishop of Senlis, who came to England with Queen Bertha (Feltoe, p. 17).

Long Friday	Friday next before Easter Day
Low Sunday	Sunday next after Easter Day
Lucas, *ev.*e	18 Oct.
Lucia, *v. et m.*e	13 Dec.
Lucianus, *pr. et m.*u	8 Jan.
Lucianus et Geminianus, *mm.*e . . .	16 Sep.

M

Maccabaei, *mm.*ca	1 Aug.
Machutus, *ep. et c.*e	15 Nov.
Maglorius, *ep. et c.*u	24 Oct.
Magnus, *m.*e	19 Aug.
Mamertus, *ep. et c.*	11 May
Marcellianus	*see* Marcus et Marcellianus
Marcellinus et Petrus, *mm.*e . . .	2 June
Marcellus, *p. et m.*e	16 Jan.
Marcellus, *m.*u	4 Sep.
Marcellus et Apuleius, *mm.*e 1 . . .	7 Oct.
Marcus, *ev.*e	25 April
Marcus et Marcellianus, *mm.*e . . .	18 June
Margareta, *reg.*2	8 July
Margareta, *v. et m.*e	20 July
Maria, *B.V.*, annunciatio,e Maria in Marcio 3 .	25 March
—— ascensio, assumptio e . . .	15 Aug.4
—— conceptio e	8 Dec.
—— nativitas e	8 Sep.
—— oblatio ca	21 Nov.
—— pausatio	15 Aug.
—— presentatio u	21 Nov.
—— purificatio e	2 Feb.
—— salutatio	25 June
—— visitatio sa	2 July
Maria Egyptiaca u	2 April
Maria Magdalena e	22 July
Maria ad nives	5 Aug.
Maria Salome u	22 Oct.
Martha, *v.*y	27 July
Martinianus	*see* Processus et Martinianus
Martinus, *ep. et c.* (in hyeme) e . .	11 Nov.
—— ordinatio et translatio e (Martinus calidus)	4 July
Martinus, *p. et c.*y	10 Nov.5
Mass-day	*see* Missa

1 Entered as Marcus, Marcellus, et Apuleius in calendar of Black Book of the Exchequer.
2 Margaret, queen of Scotland.
3 Cf. *Reg. antiquissimum Linc.*, iii. 643, l. 18.
4 'Betwixt the two St. Mary's masses' (*Anglo-Saxon Chron.*, R.S., i. 343) is between the Assumption and the Nativity.
5 12 Nov. is given as the date in most works of reference.

Mathias, *ap.*^e	24 Feb.[1]
Mattheus, *ap. et ev.*	21 Sep.
Maundy Thursday	Thurs. before Good Friday
Mauricius et soc., *mm.*^e	22 Sep.
Maurilius, *ep. et c.*^y	13 Sep.
Maurus, *abb.*^e	15 Jan.
Medardus et Gildardus, *epp. et cc.*^e	8 June
Meliorus, *m.*^a	1 Oct.
Mellitus, *archiep.*^{ca}	24 April
Memento mei [2]	4th Sun. in Advent
Menna, *m.*^e	11 Nov.
Mensis fenalis	July
Mensis imbrium	April
Mensis magnus	June
Mensis messionum	August
Mensis novarum	April
Mensis Pasche	Month or *quindena* of Easter
Mensis purgatorius	2 Feb.
Michael, *archang.*^e	29 Sep.
—— *in Monte Tumba* ^e	16 Oct.
Mid-Lent Sunday	4th Sun. in Lent
Midsummer Day	24 June
Midwinter Day	25 Dec.
Milburga, Mulburga, *v.*^{ca}	23 Feb.
Mildreda, Mildritha, *v.*^u	13 July
Mille martyres apud Lichefeld	2 Jan.
Miserere mei domine, Misericordia domini	2nd Sun. after Easter
Missa, Mass-day	Feast-day of a saint
Misse domini Alleluia	*Quasimodo* Sunday
Modestus	*see* Vitus et Modestus
Mothering Sunday	4th Sun. in Lent
Mulburga	*see* Milburga

N

Nabor	*see* Basilides, Curinus, et Nabor
Natalis Calicis	Holy Thursday
Natalis S. Johannis Baptiste	*see* Joh. Bapt. decollatio
Nativitas, natale, domini	25 Dec.
Negasius	*see* Nigasius
Neot, *abb.*^{ca}	31 July
Nereus et Achilleus, *mm.*^e	12 May
Nicasius	*see* Nigasius
Nichodemus, Nicodemus ^{ca}	4 Aug.
Nicholas, *ep. et c.*^e	6 Dec.
—— translatio ^u	9 May

[1] This festival is observed on 25 Feb. in leap years.
[2] Former introit. Now *Rorate celi.*

Nichomedes, Nicomedes, *m.*	1 June,[e] 15 Sep.[ca] [1]
Nigasius et soc., *mm.*[e]	11 Oct.
Nothelmus, *archiep.*[ca]	17 Oct.
Nouvel Caresme	Quinquagesima Sunday

O

O sapientia	16 Dec.[2]
Octava infantium	Sun. in octave of Easter
Octave	the 8th day after any feast, the feast-day itself being counted
Oculi	3rd Sun. in Lent
Odo, *archiep.*[ca]	2 June
Olavus, r. et m.	29 July
Omnes gentes	7th Sun. after Pentecost
Omnia que fecisti	20th Sun. after Pentecost
Omnis terra	2nd Sun. after Epiphany
Omnium sanctorum festivitas[e]	1 Nov.
Osanna	Palm Sunday
Ositha[ca]	7 Oct.
Osmundus, *ep. et c.*[u]	4 Dec.
—— translatio[u]	16 July
Oswaldus, *ep. et c.*[ca]	28 Feb.
Oswaldus, *r. et m.*[e]	5 Aug.
Oswinus, Oswynus, *r. et m.*	20 Aug.
—— translatio	11 March
Owen	*see* Audoenus

P

Palm Sunday	6th Sun. in Lent
Pancake Tuesday	Shrove Tuesday
Pancratius, *m.*	12 May
Pantaleon, *m.*[e]	28 July
Parasceve	Good Friday
Pardon Sunday	Palm Sunday
Pascha	*either* (*a*) Easter Day, i.e. Sun. after full moon on or next after 21 March *or* (*b*) Easter Week
Pascha competentium ⎱ —— *floridum, florum* ⎰	Palm Sunday
—— *primum*	22 March [3]
—— *rosarum*	Pentecost
Passionis dies	Good Friday

[1] 1 June is the dedication of his church, 15 Sep. the day of his death.

[2] On this day and each of the octave the anthem sung at vespers begins with O. Cf. in French *les oleries, la feste des Os*.

[3] Because this is the earliest date upon which Easter can fall.

Passio sanctorum XL militum ca . . .	9 March
Passion Sunday	5th Sun. in Lent
Passion Week	week before Easter
Patricius, *ep.*ᵘ	17 March
Paulinus, *ep. et. c.*ca	10 Oct.
Paulus, *ap.*, conversio ᵃ	25 Jan.
—— decollatio ca	30 June
—— translatio ¹	25 Jan.
Paulus, *er.*ca	10 Jan.
Paulus et Johannes, *mm.*e . . .	26 June
Paulus et Petrus, *app.*e . . .	29 June
—— commemoratio	30 June
Pelagia ʸ	8 Oct.
Pentecost (Whit-Sunday) . . .	7th Sun. after Easter Day
Perdon Sunday	*see* Pardon Sunday
Pernella	*see* Petronilla
Perpetua et Felicitas, *vv. et mm.*e . .	7 March
Petrocus, *c.*ʸ	4 June
Petronilla, Pernella, *v.*e . . .	31 May
Petrus ad vincula e	1 Aug.
Petrus in cathedra in Antiochia e . .	22 Feb.
Petrus Mediolanus, *predic. et m.*e . .	29 April
Petrus et Marcellinus	*see* Marcellinus et Petrus
Petrus et Paulus, *app.*e . . .	29 June
Philippus et Jacobus, *app.*e . . .	1 May
Piranus, *ep.*ʰʷ	5 March
Plough Monday	Mon. after 6 Jan.
Policarpus, *ep. et m.*ʸ	26 Jan.
Populus Sion	2nd Sun. in Advent
Potentiana, Pudentiana, *v. et m.*ᵘ . .	19 May
Powder Plot	5 Nov.
Praxedes, Praxedis, *v.*e	21 July
Prejectus, *m.*e	25 Jan.
Presentatio domini	2 Feb.
Preteriens Jesus	Wed. after *Letare Hierusalem*
Primus et Felicianus, *mm.*ᵉ . . .	9 June
Prisca, *v.*e	18 Jan.
Priscus, *m.*ʷ	28 March
Priscus, *m.*e	1 Sep.
Privicarnium	*see Carniprivium*
Procession Week	Rogation Week
Processus et Martinianus, *mm.*e . .	2 July
Protector noster	14th Sun. after Pentecost
Prothasius	*see* Gervasius et Prothasius
Prothus et Hyacinthus (Iacinctus), *mm.*e .	11 Sep.
Pudentiana	*see* Potentiana

¹ Rare. But cf. *Reg. palat. dunelmense*, iii. 426, and *Acta sanctorum*, vii. 428, 431–2.

Q

Quadragesima, Quadringesima	.	.	.	Lent, the 40 week-days preceding Easter [1]
Quadragesima intrans	.	.	.	*either* (*a*) opening of Lent *or* (*b*) 1st Sun. in Lent
Quadragesima major	.	.	.	the Lent of Easter
Quadragesima pura	.	.	.	*see* Clean Lent
Quadragesima Sunday	.	.	.	1st Sun. in Lent
Quadraginta .	.	.	.	Quinquagesima Sunday [2]
Quasimodo .	.	.	.	1st Sun. after Easter
Quatuor coronati martyres [e]	.	.	.	8 Nov.
Quatuor tempora, jejunia temporalia	.			Ember days at the four seasons, viz. the Wed., Fri. and Sat. after (*a*) 1st Sun. in Lent, (*b*) Pentecost, (*c*) Holy Rood Day, (*d*) St. Lucy's Day. If (*c*) and (*d*) fall on a Wed., the Ember Days begin on the Wed. following
Queen's Day	.	.	.	17 Nov. [3]
Quindena, quinzaine	.	.	.	quindene, 15th day after any feast, the date of the feast itself being included in the reckoning
Quinquagesima	.	.	.	Usually Quinquagesima Sunday. Also used for (*a*) the 50 days from Easter to Pentecost, (*b*) the day of Pentecost
Quinquagesima Sunday	.	.	.	Sun. before Ash Wednesday
Quintana	.	.	.	1st Sun. in Lent
Quintinus, *m.*[e]	.	.	.	31 Oct.
Quinzaine, quindisme, quinsime	.	.	*see Quindena*

R

Radegonda, reg.[ca] .	.	.	.	13 Aug.
Ramispalma .	.	.	.	Palm Sunday
Reddite que sunt Caesaris Caesari	.	.	23rd Sun. after Pentecost
Regressio de exilio .	.	.	.	*see* Thomas, *archiep. et m.*
Relatio pueri Jesu de Egypto	.	.	.	7 Jan.
Relic Sunday [4]	.	.	.	1st Sun. after 7 July

[1] But formerly the Latin Church also observed the Lent of Pentecost (40 days succeeding Pentecost) and the Lent of Christmas (40 days preceding Christmas).

[2] Because the first response at Matins is ' Quadraginta dies et noctes ', etc.

[3] Date of accession of Queen Elizabeth.

[4] This name almost certainly relates to the feast of Sarum relics. At Salisbury in the twelfth century the appointed day was 17 Sep., but it was changed in 1319 to the first Sun. after the feast of St. Thomas of Canterbury. Thereafter it was widely used in dioceses where the Sarum

Remigius, *ep. et c.*[y]	13 Jan.
Remigius,[1] Germanus, Vedastus, et Bavo, *epp.*[e]	1 Oct.
Reminiscere	2nd Sun. in Lent
Respice domino	13th Sun. after Pentecost
Resurrectio domini [e]	27 March
Ricardus, *ep. et c.*[a] (Chichester) . .	3 April
—— translatio [u]	16 June
Rochus, *c.*[u]	16 Aug.
Rock Day	7 Jan.
Rogation Days	Mon., Tues., Wed., before Ascension Day
Rogation Sunday	5th Sun. after Easter Day
Roi des Dimanches	Trinity Sunday
Romanus, *m.*[e]	9 Aug.
Romanus, *archiep. et c.*[e] . . .	23 Oct.
Ronanus, *ep. et c.*[ca]	19 Nov.
Rope Monday	2nd Mon. after Easter Day
Rorate celi [2]	4th Sun. in Advent.
Rosary, feast of the	1 Oct.
Royal Oak Day	29 May
Rufus, *m.*[e]	27 Aug.
Rushbearing	Often *either* (*a*) St. Bartholomew's day, viz. 24 Aug. *or* (*b*) feast of the dedication of a particular church.[3]

S

Sabbata duodecim lectionum . . .	the 4 Sats. of Ember Weeks
Sabbatum	Usually Sat.; sometimes used of whole week.[4]
Sabbatum in albis	Sat. before 1st Sun. after Easter
Sabbatum Alleluia *Sabbatum luminum* *Sabbatum magnum* *Sabbatum Pasche* *Sabbatum sanctum*	Sat. before Easter Day
Sabina [8a]	29 Aug.

Use was followed. It is also found at Hereford. Some churches had their own days, e.g. St. Albans, 27 Jan.; Exeter, 23 May, later (mid xiv cent.), Mon. after Ascension; Lincoln, 10 July; Westminster, 16 July; Durham, 31 Aug.; Norwich, 16 Sep.; Glastonbury, 8 Oct.; Chichester, 13 Oct.; Wells, 14 Oct.; Worcester, 15 Oct.; Ely, 16 Oct.; York, 19 Oct.

    [1] 'Remedius' in *Bosworth psalter.*
    [2] Introit. Formerly *Memento mei.*
    [3] Thus at Warton, Lancs., dedicated to St. Oswald, rushbearing was 5 Aug.; on the other hand at Altcar, Lancs., dedicated to St. Michael, rushbearing was in July (Hampson, *Kalendarium,* i. 341).
    [4] Thus *una* or *prima Sabbati* would be Sunday; *dua Sabbati* Monday; and so on.

Salus populi	19th Sun. after Pentecost
Salvator [sa]	24 May
Salvius, *ep.*[ca]	26 June
Salvius, *ep. et m.*[ca] . . .	11 Jan.
Sampson, Samson, *ep.*[e] . .	28 July
Saturninus, *m.*[e]	29 Nov.
Saturninus et Sisinnius, *mm.*[u] .	29 Nov.
Scholastica, *v.*[e]	10 Feb.
Sebastianus	*see* Fabianus et Sebastianus
Sennes	*see* Abdon et Sennes
Septem dormientes [e] . . .	27 July
Septem fratres martyres [e] . .	10 July
Septimana	a week ; *see also* Hebdomada
Septimana communis . . .	week beginning Sun. after Michaelmas Day
Septimana media jejuniorum paschalium [1]	3rd week in Lent
Septimana penosa	*see Hebdomada penosa*
Septuagesima Sunday . . .	3rd Sun. before Ash Wednesday
Sexagesima Sunday . . .	2nd Sun. before Ash Wednesday
Sexburga, *v.*[ca]	6 July
Sexburga, *v.*[u]	8 April
Shere or Shrive Thursday . .	Thurs. in Holy Week
Shrove Monday	Mon. before Shrove Tuesday
Shrove Sunday	Sun. before Shrove Tuesday
Shrove Thursday	Thurs. after Shrove Tuesday
Shrove Tuesday	Tues. next after Quinquagesima Sunday
Si iniquitates	22nd Sun. after Pentecost
Sicut oculi servorum . . .	Mon. after 1st Sun. in Lent
Silvester, *p. et. c.*[e] . . .	31 Dec.
Simon et Judas, *app.*[e] . .	28 Oct.
Simplicius [e]	29 July
Sisinnius	*see* Saturninus et Sisinnius
Sitientes	Sat. before Passion Sunday
Sixtus, Xystus, *ep.*[u] . . .	6 April
Sixtus, *p. et m.*[e] . . .	6 Aug.
Solemnitas solemnitatum . .	Easter Day
Sowlemas Day	2 Nov.
Stephanus, *p. et m.*[a] . . .	2 Aug.
Stephanus, *protom.*[e] . . .	26 Dec.
—— inventio [e]	3 Aug. ; 4 Aug.[ca]
Sulpicius, *ep. et c.*[e] . . .	17 Jan.
Suscepimus deus	8th Sun. after Pentecost
Swithinus, *ep. et c.*[e] . . .	2 July

---

[1] Not to be confused with *Hebdomada mediana Quadragesime* (*q.v.*).

Swithinus, *ep. et c.*, translatio [e]	. . .	15 July
Symphorianus	. . . . .	*see* Timotheus et Symphorianus
Sytha (Zita of Lucca), *v.*[ca]	. . .	27 April

T

Tathwinus, Tatwyn, *archiep. et c.*[ca] .	. .	31 July
Taurinus, *c.*[hw]	. . . .	11 Aug.
Tecla, Thecla, *v. et m.*[e]	. . .	23 Sep.
Theodorus, *archiep.*[ca]	. . .	19 Sep.
—— ordinacio [ca]	. . .	26 March
Theodorus, *m.*[e]	. . . .	9 Nov.
Theophania .	. . . .	Epiphany
Theophilus [ca]	. . . .	28 Feb.
Thomas, *ap.*[e]	. . . .	21 Dec.
—— translatio	. . . .	3 July
Thomas de Aquino [u]	. . .	7 March
Thomas, *archiep. Cantuar. et m.*[e]	. .	29 Dec.
—— translatio [e]	. . .	7 July
—— regressio de exilio [ca]	. . .	2 Dec.
Thomas Herefordensis, *ep. et c.*[u]	. .	2 Oct.
Thousand martyrs at Lichfield	. .	*see* Mille martyres
Tiburtius, *m.*[e]	. . . .	11 Aug.
Tiburtius et Valerianus, *mm.*[e]	. .	14 April
Timotheus et Apollinaris, *mm.*[e]	. .	23 Aug.
Timotheus et Symphorianus, *mm.*[e] .	.	22 Aug.
Transfiguratio domini [u] .	. .	6 Aug.
Tres septimane	. . .	The three weeks beginning with Easter Day, Pentecost, Christmas, and St. John Bapt., distinguished as Paschales, Pentecostes, Nativitatis, et Sancti Johannis Baptiste [1]
Trinitas estivalis .	. . . .	Trinity Sunday
Trinity Sunday .	. . .	Sunday next after Pentecost [2]
Trium magorum (regum) dies	. .	Epiphany
Twelfth Day .	. . .	Epiphany
Typhayne .	. . . .	Epiphany

U

Undecim millia virgines [e]	. . .	21 Oct.[e] ; 22 Aug.[u]
Urbanus, *p. et m.*[sa]	. . .	25 May
Utas .	. . . .	The octave of any feast

[1] In many places these great festivals had three consecutive octaves, in others only two.
[2] Kept on this date in England by order of Thomas Becket when consecrated archbishop (3 June 1162). English usage was extended to the whole western Church by Pope John XXII (1333).

V

Valentinus, *ep. et m.*[e]	14 Feb.
Valerianus, *ep. et m.*[u]	15 Dec.
Valerianus, *m.*	*see* Tiburtius et Valerianus
Vandregisilus, Wandregisilus, *abb.*[ca] .	22 July
Vedastus et Amandus, *app.*[e] . . .	6 Feb.
Vedastus, *ep.*	*see* Remigius, Germanus, Vedastus, et Bavo
Vigilia	the day before any feast
Vincentius, *m.*[e]	22 Jan.
Viri Galilei	Ascension Day
Vitalis, *m.*[e]	28 April
Vitus, Modestus, et Crescentius, *mm.*[e] .	15 June
Vocem jucunditatis	5th Sun. after Easter
Vuilfridus	*see* Wilfridus
Vulganius, *c.*[ca]	3 Nov.
Vulmarus, *c.*[ca]	20 July

W

Wandregisilus	*see* Vandregisilus
Wenefrida, Winifreda, *v. et m.*[u] . .	3 Nov.
Werburga, *v.*[ca]	3 Feb.
—— translatio	21 June
Whit-Monday	Mon. following Whit-Sunday
Whit-Sunday (Pentecost) . . .	7th Sun. after Easter Day
Whitsuntide	Whit-Sunday, -Monday, -Tuesday
Whit-Tuesday	Tues. following Whit-Sunday
Wilfridus, Vuilfridus, *archiep. et c.*[ca] .	12 Oct.
—— translatio [y] [1]	24 April
Willebrordus, *ep. et c.*[y] . . .	7 Nov.
Willelmus, *archiep. Ebor.*[e] . . .	8 June
—— translatio [u]	Sun. after Epiphany
Winifreda	*see* Wenefrida
Winwalocus, Wynewaldus . . .	3 March
Withburga, *v.*[u]	17 March, 8 July
Wives' Feast Day	2 Feb.
Wulfranus, *ep.*[e]	15 Oct.
Wulfstanus, Wolstanus, Wulstanus, *ep. et c.*[e]	19 Jan.
—— translatio [e]	7 June
Wulganus, *c.*[ca]	3 Nov.
Wynewaldus [u]	*see* Winwalocus

[1] 24 April was the day of Wilfrid's death, and the primitive feast recorded in the Old English Martyrology. In the south it was displaced by the feast of St. Mellitus of Canterbury, but survived at York, where, however, it was kept as a *translatio* (Gasquet and Bishop, *Bosworth psalter*, p. 159).

X

Xystus . . . . *see* Sixtus

Y

Ypolitus . . . . *see* Hypolitus

Z

Zita of Lucca . . . . . . *see* Sytha

LEGAL CHRONOLOGY

THE LIMIT OF LEGAL MEMORY

The limit of legal memory is 3 September 1189. Edward I compromised the disputes over his *quo warranto* proceedings by agreeing not to contest the rights of holders of franchises who had exercised them ever since ' the time of King Richard ' (Statute of Quo Warranto, 1290). This was construed as meaning since the commencement of his reign on 3 September 1189.[1]

LIMITATION OF ACTIONS

The limitation of writs of right had already been fixed at 3 September 1189 by statute in 1275 (Westminster I, c. 39) ; the limit had originally been the death of Henry I and, since 1237 (Merton, c. 8), the coronation of Henry II. The limit of novel disseisin was more frequently changed, and since the date was an integral part of the writ, it is possible to deduce approximately the age of early registers of writs by consulting the data in Pollock and Maitland's *History of English law*, ii. 51, and in Maitland's *Collected papers*, ii. 110. There was no change between 1275 and 1540, in spite of some attempts.[2]

THE LAW TERMS

The law terms were necessarily situated in those portions of the year which remained available for legal business after certain days and seasons had been excluded for one reason or another. The excluded days were a fairly constant list. Within the ecclesiastical province of Canterbury they were defined in a constitution of Archbishop Simon Islip of 1362 [3] thus : all Sundays ; Christmas ; St. Stephen (26 Dec.) ; St. John Evangelist (27 Dec.) ; Holy Innocents (28 Dec.) ; St. Thomas the Martyr (29 Dec.) ; Circumcision (1 Jan.) ; Epiphany (6 Jan.) ; Purification of the B.V.M. (2 Feb.) ; St. Matthias (24 or 25 Feb.) ; Annunciation of the B.V.M. (25 March) ; Easter and the three following days ; St. Mark (25 Apr.) ; Sts. Philip and James (1 May) ; Invention of the Holy Cross (3 May) ; Ascension ; Whit-Sunday and the three following days ; Corpus Christi ; Nativity of St. John the Baptist (24 June) ; Sts. Peter and Paul (29 June) ; Transl. of St. Thomas the Martyr (7 July) ; St. Mary Magdalene (22 July) ; St. James (25 July) ; St. Lawrence (10 Aug.) ; Assumption of the B.V.M. (15 Aug.) ; St. Bartholomew (24 Aug.) ; Nativity of the B.V.M. (8 Sep.) ; Exaltation of the Cross (14 Sep.) ; St. Matthew (21 Sep.) ; St. Michael (29 Sep.) ; St. Luke (18 Oct.) ; Sts. Simon and Jude (28 Oct.) ; All Saints (1 Nov.) ; St. Andrew (30 Nov.) ; St. Nicholas (6 Dec.) ; Conception of the B.V.M. (8 Dec.) ; and St. Thomas the Apostle (21 Dec.).[4] On all these days there was to be abstention ' ab universis popularium operibus eciam rei publice

[1] Cf. Pollock and Maitland, *Hist. of Eng. law*, i. 168.
[2] W. S. Holdsworth, *Hist. of Eng. law*, iv. 484 ; *Rotuli parl.*, ii. 300/16, 341/119.
[3] W. Lyndwood, *Provinciale* (Oxford, 1679), pp. 101–2.
[4] To these Chichele added the feast of St. George (23 Apr.) *Ibid.*, p. 103.

utilibus '.[1] These prohibited works are defined by Lyndwood as including litigation, whether as a principal or on behalf of another, subject to the exception of ' reasonable necessity '.[2] If one of these days fell within a law term, the court ought therefore to suspend business, and probably did so as a rule ; when pressed for time, however, the king's bench would sit on a Sunday,[3] and so did the exchequer. The observance long survived the Reformation and in the early seventeenth century certain feasts which fell within term (as then fixed) were regarded as *dies non juridici* ; according to Coke, *Institutes*, i. 135a, they were (besides Sundays) All Saints and All Souls (in Michaelmas term) ; Purification (in Hilary term) ; Ascension (in Easter term) ; and St. John the Baptist (in Trinity term). A cluster of such days falling close together naturally made the whole period between them impracticable.

The excluded seasons were, as to two of them, those periods during which the Church had forbidden certain types of oath to be taken. Before the Norman Conquest these periods were from Advent to the octave of Epiphany, and from Septuagesima to the quindene of Easter (VI Aethelred 25 ; I Canute 17). The prohibition was long observed.[4] The statute of Westminster I (1275), c. 51, concludes with a prayer from the king to the bishops for a relaxation of the rule in the particularly urgent matter of the petty assizes, their whole object being to avoid delays. The bishops declined to make any general concession, and assizes continued to be suspended during these seasons.[5] Individual bishops sometimes made temporary dispensations.[6] After the Reformation the matter seems to have been settled by the simple device of mistranslating the statute and corrupting the text [7] by inserting ' it is provided '. The third excluded season was due to the harvest and fear of plague during the hot season in town. Lawyers, jurors, and litigants alike could not leave their estates during harvest nor during the period of stocktaking, rent-collecting and accounting which centred on Michaelmas. In practice this rules out August and September ; in later times the heavy work of quartersessions ruled out October as well.

The combined effect of all this is to leave four main periods during which fairly continuous legal business was possible, and those periods became the law terms. Michaelmas necessarily began some few days after that feast, and had to end before Advent. The Advent break was prolonged by the cluster of great feasts following Christmas until the octave of Epiphany (which coincides with St. Hilary) ; St. Hilary is therefore the earliest date for resuming business, but how long the term lasts (a week or a month) will depend upon the divagations of Septuagesima which may fall as early as 19 Jan. or as late as 22 Feb. In the long stretch from the quindene of Easter to harvest-tide, there is clearly a break caused by the cluster of great feasts of Ascension, Whitsuntide, Trinity, and Corpus Christi. The octave of Trinity

---

[1] This is apparently the original reading of the constitution, as recorded in the registers of Islip and of Simon Sudbury, bishop of London. Lyndwood reads ' servilibus ' for ' popularium ', thus bringing the text into line with other canonistic references to *opera servilia*.

[2] *Op. cit.*, p. 57, gloss on *canonicis institutis*.

[3] Sayles, *Sel. cases in the court of king's bench*, II. lxxvi.

[4] *Curia regis rolls*, vi. 105, 108–9, 111.

[5] Sayles, *op. cit.*, I. cxlv ; R. Stewart-Brown, *Chester county court rolls* (Chetham Society), p. 91, no. 130.

[6] Cf. *Register of R. Baldock* (London), p. 42 ; *Register of W. de Stapeldon* (Exeter), p. 36 ; for a bishop who refused, see *Foedera*, II. ii. 1151–2.

[7] Coke, *Institutes*, ii. 265–6 and *Statutes of the realm*, i. 39.

is therefore the first normally practicable date for resuming business, which will have to be suspended again at harvest time.

It must further be observed that the old books of practice do not conceive a term as being an even flow of time between the first and the last day, but rather as being a succession of procedural crises called 'return days' which normally occur at intervals of about a week; thus they describe a term not as lasting from one date to another, but as containing so many returns. Every return day consisted in fact of four calendar days, the later theory being that the first was for casting essoins, the second for laying exceptions, the third for the return of writs by the sheriff, and the fourth for the appearance of parties and jurors in the court of common pleas.[1] The pseudo-statute *Dies communes in banco* (*Statutes of the realm*, i. 208) is primarily concerned with continuances from one day to another, but from it a list of return days can be constructed, as follows; the date seems to be mid-thirteenth century:

Michaelmas	*Hilary*	*Easter*	*Trinity*
octave	octave	quindene	octave
quindene	quindene	three weeks	quindene
three weeks	cras. Purification	month	cras. (or octave)
month	octave Purif.	five weeks	John Baptist
cras. Animarum			quindene John
cras. Martini			Baptist
octave Martini			
quindene Martini			

It is the existence of these return days which in fact determined the duration of the terms. The system of continuance from one day to another, as described in the *Dies communes*, is explained by Reeves and Holdsworth.[2] Certain actions moved more swiftly: Dower,[3] Darrein presentment and Quare impedit,[4] and Attaint.[5] This rigid system of return days was part of the law of actions and so did not obtain in courts of equity, nor in proceedings upon Bills of Middlesex.[6]

The king's bench was concerned with many proceedings besides the common law actions, and although it kept terms and return days, it seems to have taken some liberties with the system. Its sessions for thirty-four years have been tabulated by Dr. G. O. Sayles,[7] and the following results appear:

Michaelmas invariably began on the octave (6 Oct.), and extended generally to the quindene of St. Martin (25 Nov.); in 1274 it ran on to three weeks from Martinmas (2 Dec., which was also Advent Sunday).

Hilary almost always began on the octave (20 Jan.) the single exception being in 14 Edw. I when it began on the Sunday after Christmas. It closed at various dates: the morrow, the octave, or the quindene of Purification. Several times it

---

[1] Arthur Hopton, *Concordancy of yeeres* (1612), p. 240; Thomas Powell, *Attorneys academy* (1630), sig. Pp.
[2] John Reeves, *Hist. Eng. law* (ed. Finlason), i. 232, 499; Holdsworth, *Hist. Eng. law*, iii. 675.
[3] *Dies communes in dote*, which is possibly connected with a document of 1259 printed in E. F. Jacob, *Studies in the period of baronial reform and rebellion*, 368.
[4] *Statute of Marlborough*, c. 12.
[5] 5 Edw. III, c. 6.
[6] Hopton, *Concordancy*, 240–1.
[7] *Op. cit.*, II. cxviii–cxxi.

extended into the week following Septuagesima, Sexagesima, and even Quinquagesima. It would therefore seem that the king's bench confined its observance to Lent, but that within the above limits the length of Hilary term varied for reasons independent of the calendar from two to three or four weeks.

Easter invariably began on the quindene. Normally that should mean the second Sunday after Easter, but later books [1] explain that it means seventeen days after Easter, and therefore a Wednesday. Very generally it ended on the morrow of Ascension, nearly four weeks later; on a few occasions it ended five weeks or even a month from Easter, thus lasting less than three weeks.

Trinity usually ran from the octave of Trinity to the quindene of St. John the Baptist (8 July). Twice it ran from the morrow of Trinity to the octave of St. John. The duration thus varied from a fortnight (in 1291 and 1302) to five weeks (in 1285 and 1296) according to the incidence of Trinity.

To the scanty medieval legislation already mentioned we may add a statute defining the effect of leap year in 1256.[2] Later statutes dealt with the terms as follows :

32 Henry VIII, c. 21. Trinity term in 1541 and for the future shall begin the morrow of Trinity for formal matters, and full term on the following Friday. The return days shall be Crastino trinitatis, octave, quindene and three weeks (tres septimanas) ; the act abolishes the returns of the morrow, octave and quindene of St. John the Baptist. (The result is to begin term a week earlier and to fix its duration, hitherto variable, at three weeks.)

16 Charles I, c. 6. Michaelmas term (which conflicts with quarter sessions, causing great inconvenience) shall begin in and after 1641 three weeks from Michaelmas (full term four days later). The first two (octave and quindene of Michaelmas) of its eight traditional returns are abolished, the other six retained. (The result is to cut off two weeks at the commencement of term.)

24 George II, c. 48. The early part of Michaelmas term being much interrupted by saints' days, term shall begin in 1752 and thenceforward on the morrow of All Souls, thus leaving only the last four of the traditional eight returns. The dates of naming sheriffs and swearing the Lord Mayor of London no longer falling within the shortened term, new dates are ordained (and further amended by 25 Geo. II, c. 30).

11 George IV & 1 William IV, c. 70. In and after 1831 the dates of terms were fixed as follows: Hilary, 11–31 Jan.; Easter, 15 April–8 May; Trinity, 22 May–12 June; Michaelmas, 2–25 November. The connection with movable feasts was thus severed. An amending act (1 William IV, c. 3) provided for the incidence of Sunday in the above scheme, and for the suspension of sittings from Thursday before Easter to the Wednesday after, if those days should fall within term.

2 & 3 William IV, c. 39. By s. 11 of this Uniformity of Process Act (1832), return days were abolished together with the procedures of which they formed a part.

36 & 37 Victoria, c. 66. By s. 26 of this Judicature Act (1873) terms were abolished. The sittings are now governed by the Rules of the Supreme Court, and have no procedural significance.

[1] Such as Finch, *Law*, p. 236, and Powell, *op. cit.*, sig. Pp.
[2] *Statutes of the realm*, i. 7 ; Maitland, *Bracton's note book*, i. 43.

The above material should be sufficient to date legal proceedings with sufficient accuracy for most purposes. Minor points of difficulty abound, however. It has not been possible to get access to the early almanacks; those of the seventeenth century cited above contain some discrepancies in detail. Thus the four days which constitute a return are sometimes included in the term, and sometimes not. Nor was it unusual for the dates to be altered by proclamation, especially in time of plague.[1] There was also a certain element of fiction, as when judgements were deemed to take effect from the first day of term; that rule was abolished in 1677 by the Statute of Frauds (29 Charles II, c. 3).

In using the Plea Rolls, Year Books, and early reports it will be observed that in certain reigns the regnal year changes in the course of a term; in strict practice that term ought to be ascribed to both years, and that is done in the Plea Rolls. Thus Michaelmas 18 & 19 Edw. I would be described as *anno xviii finiente*, or *anno xviii, incipiente xix*.[2] The Year Books frequently omit the precaution, and thus leave it to be conjectured whether the term which they report is the one at the beginning or the end of the regnal year. The double year is often needed for John's Easter term, and always for the following:

Henry III: Michaelmas

Edward I: Michaelmas (Year Books treat it as the last term of the year, neglecting the five days which technically belong to the beginning of the next year).

Edward II: Trinity (the year changed on 8 July which was the quindene of St. John and the last return day; the Year Books treat it as the last term of the year).

Richard II: Trinity (as far as has been ascertained, the Year Books always regard the regnal year as beginning with Trinity term irrespective of the actual incidence of the term).

Richard III: Trinity (there is no printed Year Book for Trin. in any year of this king).

The position next occurs in Edward VI (Hilary) and Elizabeth (Michaelmas); by this time the reporters and their editors generally take care to use the double regnal year.

The Exchequer of Pleas

The reckoning of the exchequer's fiscal year is explained elsewhere. It seems to have influenced the dating of exchequer Plea Rolls although they do not actually use the fiscal dates. The medieval rolls are annual, not terminal; each roll contains a year's business, but divided according to the four terms and ascribed to the sessions within the term. Under Henry III the annual rolls begin with Michaelmas and generally bear a double year since the regnal year changes at mid-term. Thus the first extant roll contains a year's business beginning *in crastino sancti Michaelis anno xx incipiente xxi*—a period corresponding with the twenty-first exchequer year. Under Edward I the situation was similar, save that the year turned almost at the end of term; the exchequer of pleas continued, however, to begin its annual roll with Michaelmas under the double date (the Year Books would treat that same term as the last of the preceding year). The accident of the accession date in these

[1] Leadam, *Court of requests* (Selden Society), xxxvi. no. 7.
[2] Cf. *List of Plea Rolls*.

two reigns was thus utilized in keeping the Plea Rolls in step with the fiscal year. The same chance allowed the Plea Rolls of Edward II's exchequer to begin with Michaelmas. But Edward III's accession in January made a double date again necessary; thus the roll 1 & 2 Edw. III contains the Michaelmas of the first year and Hilary, Easter, and Trinity of the second.

The terms had less procedural significance than in the common pleas. Within the term certain days became habitual as sitting days rather than as return days. Thus in 1236–7 the sessions were:

the morrow, octave and three weeks of Michaelmas; octave of All Saints; quindene of St. Martin; morrow and octave of St. Andrew;

the morrow and octave of Hilary; the octave and quindene of the Purification; morrow of Ash Wednesday;

the morrow of the close of Easter, the quindene and the month; morrow of the Ascension;

the morrow and octave of Trinity; three weeks of St. John.

In 52 Henry III a rule of the court attempted to check its growing encroachment upon common pleas jurisdiction by shortening this list, thus leaving more time for revenue cases, but apparently without success. It will be observed from these dates that the court sat within the first week of Advent and Lent. The exchequer of account sat as late as mid-Lent, and not infrequently on Sundays.

The material in this section is based largely upon *Select cases in the exchequer of pleas*, which ends at 1307. There is little subsequent material in print from which to reconstruct the court's chronology. One feature which may have remained characteristic for centuries is the fact that the court's terms began on the morrow of Trinity, Michaelmas, Hilary and the close of Easter, while the common pleas began on the octaves and quindene (and thus a week later). We still find in 1612 that ' the exchequer always opens eight days before any term, only excepting Trinity and then it openeth but four days before '.[1]

CHANCERY AND STAR CHAMBER

The old tradition that ' the chancery is always open '[2] means that the court's procedure was not fettered by the common law system of terms and return days. Both chancery and star chamber, however, held their sessions, and to some extent organized their work, according to the common law terms.

PARLIAMENT AND STATUTES

The chronological and procedural unit of parliamentary business is the session, and it has long been the rule that work (not being judicial or quasi-judicial) left incomplete in one session cannot be finished in the next, but must be re-commenced *de novo*, if at all.[3] The normal mode of terminating a session and beginning a new one is by prorogation. The matter is confused, however, by the fact that in former times some prorogations (especially those occasioned by Christmas or Easter) were regarded by contemporaries as merely adjournments and consequently as not

[1] Hopton, *Concordancy*, p. 245.
[2] William Tothill, *Transactions of the high court of chancery*, (1649) 9
[3] M. Hale, *Jurisdiction of the Lords' House*, p. 167; Blackstone, *Commentaries*, i. 186; *Report of the joint committee on the suspension of bills*, 1929, H.C. 105.

'discontinuing' business; it will further be observed that Hale (writing between 1674 and 1676) uses the words 'prorogation' and 'adjournment' interchangeably. In the sixteenth century, moreover, there was an opinion (*Commons' Journal*, 21 Nov. 1554) that a session was automatically determined by the royal assent to a bill (which for centuries past had normally taken place on the last day of the parliament). We find in consequence that even after the Restoration it was sometimes felt necessary to include a clause saying that the royal assent to this act shall not be held to have determined the session.

The construction of a chronological list of sessions, meaning thereby sittings whose uncompleted work was held by contemporary officials to have been 'discontinued', is therefore rendered difficult since the meaning of the words 'prorogation' and 'adjournment' is known to have varied, and the detailed history of the idea of a 'session' still awaits investigation.[1] The list in the *Interim report of the committee on House of Commons personnel*, 1932 (Cmd. 4130) is of great utility, but it does not fulfil these requirements since it seems to be based upon the assumption that a prorogation always ended a session. The list thus introduces some discrepancies: it discerns eight sessions in the Reformation Parliament, where the older books (based on the parliament roll) found only seven; on the other hand it enumerates sixteen sessions of the Cavalier Parliament, although the parliament roll as printed in the *Statutes of the realm* tells of seventeen. Other instances will be mentioned shortly. For historical reference, therefore, we need a list of the periods over which parliament actually sat, accompanied by an indication of how those periods were grouped into sessions for the purpose of parliamentary procedure. The dates in such a list should be in regnal as well as calendar years, since the resulting statutes are cited by the regnal years.

The dating and citing of statutes presents a number of problems, which are in no way simplified by the fact that the citation consists partly of a date.

In one sense the date of a statute is the date when it comes into force. There is no difficulty when there is an 'appointed day' in the body of the act, but, failing that, recourse was made to the fiction that the whole of a parliamentary session was one day, and that the first day (which was of course normally well known through the writs of summons and election). This proposition, or something like it, appears in *Pilkington's Case* in 1455 (Y.B. 33 Hen. VI, Pasch. no. 8). In a well-known essay, Maitland [2] questioned whether this doctrine was still held in 1559; but he seems to have overlooked the case of *Partridge* v. *Strange* [3] which had just reiterated the principle in 1553. Thus an act which received the royal assent at the end of a long session was deemed to have been in force ever since the first day. This retrospective operation resulting from the fictitious date caused great injustice, especially when the statute imposed penalties, but the principle was rigorously applied in the seventeenth and eighteenth centuries [4] until 1793, when the act of 33 Geo. III, c. 13, required that the date of the royal assent be endorsed upon the act, and that the act come into force on that day, unless otherwise provided. If the date of the making (as distinct from the commencement) of a statute is required,

[1] Cf. A. F. Pollard in *The Times* newspaper of 11 Jan. 1940.
[2] *Collected papers*, iii. 195.
[3] Edmund Plowden, *Les comentaires, ou les reportes* (1571), 77.
[4] Cf. the cases collected in Kent, *Commentaries*, i. 454 *sqq.*

the only sure method is to trace the stages of its progress through the *Journals* down to the royal assent in the *Lords' Journal*. It must be remembered that the *Journals*, like *Rotuli parliamentorum* and the *Statutes of the realm* all begin the year of grace on 25 March, until 1752.

The citation of a statute consists of a date and a chapter number. The present system is the result of the practices of the parliamentary officials, the printers of the session laws, the editors of various collections of statutes, and the increasingly strict requirements of the law courts in the pleading of statutes. The lack of uniformity, especially for the older statutes, is due to the fact that as the system slowly took shape, older statutes were reprinted with citations conformable to the newer fashion. The regnal year in the citation is the year of the session (or at least of the sitting) in which the statute was passed. Every act of a session forms a chapter, but their order is not strictly chronological (thus in 33 Geo. III, cc. 26 and 28 received the royal assent on 30 April, c. 27 on 7 May). By a useful but modern convention public acts have the chapter number in arabic numerals, private acts are numbered separately in roman numerals. The following situations may occur:

(*a*) If there was but one session in the regnal year, and if that session lay wholly within the year, there is generally little difficulty and the statute will be cited by that year. Thus 12 Charles II, c. 1 (the 'Convention' Parliament sat April–December 1660, wholly within the regnal year; the parliament roll as printed in the *Statutes of the realm* treats this period as one session, but the *Interim report* finds two sessions there).

(*b*) If there were two sessions both wholly within the same regnal year, their acts are usually distinguished as 'statute I' and 'statute II' (or 'session I' and 'session II'). Thus 13 Charles II, stat. I, c. 1, is the Treason Act of 1661, and 13 Charles II, stat. II, c. 1, is the Corporations Act, 1661 (the 'Cavalier' Parliament sat May–July and November–December 1661 and the thirteenth regnal year ran from 30 Jan. 1661; the parliament roll groups the two sets of statutes separately, but the *Interim report* regards both of these two periods as forming a single session with the one next following).

(*c*) If one session extends over two regnal years, its acts must be cited by both years. Thus 13 & 14 Charles II, c. 23, reorganized the Insurance Court (the Cavalier Parliament reassembled on 7 Jan. 1662, 13 Charles II, and sat until 19 May 1662, 14 Charles II; the double citation is used in Ruffhead's *Statutes at large* but not in the *Statutes of the realm*. As an example of the confusion possible see the general index to Holdsworth, who, having used different citations for this statute in different volumes, listed them separately as though they were two different statutes).

(*d*) Occasional oddities occur such as the Long Parliament, which seems never to have been prorogued or adjourned by the king, with the result that all its legitimate acts bear the date 16 Charles I.

The above examples illustrate the application to old statutes of the modern system whose present working is explained by Sir Cecil Carr, 'The citation of statutes', in *Cambridge legal essays*. In the interests of uniformity it is desirable that acts down to 1713 should be cited as in the *Statutes of the realm* (but *not* by volume and page only). Since that work is not easily accessible it is worth remembering that the *Chronological table and index of statutes* issued annually since 1870 by the Stationery Office reproduces its citations, and also contains a table of differences between the *Statutes of the realm* and Ruffhead's *Statutes at large*.

COUNTY COURT DAYS

These days are of more than local interest since they determine the dates of (*a*) outlawry proceedings, and (*b*) parliamentary elections. Data from which they can be calculated will be found in J. J. Alexander's note on ' The dates of county days ' (see above, p. xv).

THE TERMS OF THE COURT OF ARCHES

There is very little material accessible on the terms kept by English ecclesiastical courts in the Middle Ages. There is, however, a *Kalendare commune cum diebus non sessionis in curia de arcubus et obituus episcoporum Cicestr'* in the Bodleian MS. Ashmole 1146, fos. 1v–7r. It was written in 1369–70, and it would seem that at that time the court of arches kept three sessions, thus :

(*a*) Prima dies sessionis : 14 Jan.

Dies non sessionis : St. Wulfstan (19 Jan., dedication of the church of St. Mary de arcubus) ; St. Vincent (22 Jan.) ; Conversion of St. Paul (25 Jan.) ; Purification of the B.V.M. (2 Feb.) ; St. Blasius (3 Feb.) ; Cathedra Petri (22 Feb.) ; St. Matthias (24 Feb.) ; Ash Wednesday and the two preceding days ; St. Gregory (12 March) ; Annunciation of the B.V.M. (25 March) ; St. Ambrose (4 April) ; St. Mark (25 April) ;

—ultima dies sessionis : vigilia passionis dominice.

(*b*) Prima dies sessionis : dies lune proxima post dominicam qua cantatur officium ' Misericordia domini ' [i.e. Monday after the second Sunday after Easter ; hence 6 April is the earliest possible date].

Dies non sessionis : Sts. Philip and James (1 May) ; Holy Cross (3 May) ; St. John ante portam latinam (6 May) ; St. Dunstan (19 May) ; St. Augustine (26 May) ; three rogation days and the vigil of Pentecost ; Transl. St. Edmund (9 June) ; St. Barnabas (11 June) ; St. Etheldreda (23 June) ; St. John the Baptist (24 June) ; Sts. Peter and Paul (29 June) ; Conversion of St. Paul (30 June) ; Transl. St. Thomas the Martyr (7 July) ; St. Margaret (20 July) ; St. Mary Magdalene (22 July) ; St. James (25 July) ;

—ultima dies sessionis : 31 July.

(*c*) Prima dies sessionis : 7 Oct.

Dies non sessionis : Transl. St. Edward the king (13 Oct.) ; St. Luke (18 Oct.) ; Sts. Simon and Jude (28 Oct.) ; All Saints (1 Nov.) ; All Souls (2 Nov.) ; St. Martin (11 Nov.) ; St. Edmund the abp. (16 Nov.) ; St. Edmund the king (20 Nov.) ; St. Clement the pope (23 Nov.) ; St. Katherine (25 Nov.) ; St. Andrew (30 Nov.) ; St. Nicholas (6 Dec.) ; Conception of the B.V.M. (8 Dec.) ;

—ultima dies sessionis : 16 December.

This scheme of apparently three sessions easily breaks into four terms, and had done so before Arthur Hopton published *Concordancy of yeeres* (1612). In his day Hilary term began on the morrow of Hilary (14 Jan.), Easter term on the fifteenth day after Easter, Trinity term on Trinity Monday, and Michaelmas term on the morrow of St. Faith (7 Oct.). This closely corresponds with the Chichester calendar summarized above, save for the new term at Trinitytide. His list of holy days is similar but shorter, and he says that the court may dispense with those later in the term if pressed for time. Substantially the same scheme with minor variants will be found in T. Powell, *Attorneys academy* (1630). Thomas Oughton, *Ordo judiciorum*, title III, gives the commencement of the terms as above with some notes on earlier practice. In his day the official of the court named all days of business according to need, the only fixed days being the first day of every term.

Other Ecclesiastical and Civilian Courts

Practitioners in the court of arches were also generally concerned with many other ecclesiastical courts, and also with the court of admiralty. There was a curious working arrangement which enabled them to conduct their multifarious business, described by both Hopton and Oughton. When business began on the first day of term, or was resumed after a holy day, the morning of the first day was devoted to the arches, and the afternoon to the admiralty; the morning of the second day was for the audience court of Canterbury, and the afternoon for the prerogative court of Canterbury; the morning of the third day was for the bishop of London's consistory court and the afternoon for the high court of delegates and commissioners of appeals.

THE ROMAN CALENDAR

The Middle Ages inherited from the Roman world not only its system of reckoning the years (see above, p. 1), but also its method of describing the months and days. The Romans divided the year into twelve months, and each month into the periods of Calends, Nones, and Ides, reckoning the days after the Ides in relation to the Calends of the ensuing month. The following table sets this out at large. In leap years the extra day, or *dies bissextus*, preceded *vi kal. Mar.* In these years, therefore, 24 February became *bis vi kal. Mar.* and 25 February became *vi kal. Mar.*, and the feast of St. Matthias (with any other ceremonies commonly observed on the 24th) was transferred to 25 February.[1] While the Roman calendar of days was commonly used, particularly by ecclesiastical authorities, throughout the Middle Ages, and lingered on in the use of the papal curia until the nineteenth century, it was in competition, from the early Middle Ages onwards, with the modern system of reckoning the days of the month and with dating by reference to the feasts of the Church.

The table reproduced below gives the Julian calendar as modified by Augustus. It is well to remember that the medieval clerk or chronicler, while using the Roman calendar, occasionally departed from its classical form. In the first place, he sometimes described *pridie kal.* as *ii kal.* Secondly, instead of reckoning the calends, etc., in retrograde order, he sometimes reckoned them in direct order and described the fourteenth day of January as *prima die kalendarum Feb.* (or *in capite kalendarum Feb.*) instead of *xix kal. Feb.*, and so on. Finally, he might exclude from his reckoning the actual day of the calends, nones, or ides, so that 14 January became *xviii kal. Feb.* instead of *xix kal. Feb.* But it is, in the nature of things, extremely unusual for the historian to be able to detect these peculiarities or to be sure that they are not simply errors of calculation or copying; the student should certainly not be in a hurry to assume aberrations of this kind without good evidence.

---

[1] This was the medieval reckoning. Ancient authorities are not clear about the position of the extra day, before or after *vi kal. Mar.*, in classical times. See the discussion of sources in Pauly-Wissowa, *Real-Encyclopädie d. class. Altertumswissenschaft* (1893–), III. i. 503 (*s.v.* Bissextum).

JANUARY

	Kalendæ	Jan.	1	January
IV	Non.	Jan.	2	,,
III	Non.	Jan.	3	,,
Prid.	Non.	Jan.	4	,,
	Nonæ	Jan.	5	,,
VIII	Id.	Jan.	6	,,
VII	Id.	Jan.	7	,,
VI	Id.	Jan.	8	,,
V	Id.	Jan.	9	,,
IV	Id.	Jan.	10	,,
III	Id.	Jan.	11	,,
Prid.	Id.	Jan.	12	,,
	Idus	Jan.	13	,,
XIX	Kal.	Feb.	14	,,
XVIII	Kal.	Feb.	15	,,
XVII	Kal.	Feb.	16	,,
XVI	Kal.	Feb.	17	,,
XV	Kal.	Feb.	18	,,
XIV	Kal.	Feb.	19	,,
XIII	Kal.	Feb.	20	,,
XII	Kal.	Feb.	21	,,
XI	Kal.	Feb.	22	,,
X	Kal.	Feb.	23	,,
IX	Kal.	Feb.	24	,,
VIII	Kal.	Feb.	25	,,
VII	Kal.	Feb.	26	,,
VI	Kal.	Feb.	27	,,
V	Kal.	Feb.	28	,,
IV	Kal.	Feb.	29	,,
III	Kal.	Feb.	30	,,
Prid.	Kal.	Feb.	31	,,

FEBRUARY

	Kalendæ	Feb.	1	February
IV	Non.	Feb.	2	,,
III	Non.	Feb.	3	,,
Prid.	Non.	Feb.	4	,,
	Nonæ	Feb.	5	,,
VIII	Id.	Feb.	6	,,
VII	Id.	Feb.	7	,,
VI	Id.	Feb.	8	,,
V	Id.	Feb.	9	,,
IV	Id.	Feb.	10	,,
III	Id.	Feb.	11	,,
Prid.	Id.	Feb.	12	,,
	Idus	Feb.	13	,,
XVI	Kal.	Mar.	14	,,
XV	Kal.	Mar.	15	,,
XIV	Kal.	Mar.	16	,,
XIII	Kal.	Mar.	17	,,
XII	Kal.	Mar.	18	,,
XI	Kal.	Mar.	19	,,
X	Kal.	Mar.	20	,,
IX	Kal.	Mar.	21	,,
VIII	Kal.	Mar.	22	,,
VII	Kal.	Mar.	23	,,

Common years

VI	Kal.	Mar.	24	February
V	Kal.	Mar.	25	,,
IV	Kal.	Mar.	26	,,
III	Kal.	Mar.	27	,,
Prid.	Kal.	Mar.	28	,,

Leap years [1]

Bis VI	Kal.	Mar.	24	February
VI	Kal.	Mar.	25	,,
V	Kal.	Mar.	26	,,
IV	Kal.	Mar.	27	,,
III	Kal.	Mar.	28	,,
Prid.	Kal.	Mar.	29	,,

[1] Cf. p. 75, footnote 1.

MARCH				APRIL			
Kalendæ	Mar.		1 March	Kalendæ	Apr.		1 April
VI	Non.	Mar.	2 ,,	IV	Non.	Apr.	2 ,,
V	Non.	Mar.	3 ,,	III	Non.	Apr.	3 ,,
IV	Non.	Mar	4 ,,	Prid.	Non.	Apr.	4 ,,
III	Non.	Mar.	5 ,,		Nonæ	Apr.	5 ,,
Prid.	Non.	Mar.	6 ,,	VIII	Id.	Apr.	6 ,,
	Nonæ	Mar.	7 ,,	VII	Id.	Apr.	7 ,,
VIII	Id.	Mar.	8 ,,	VI	Id.	Apr.	8 ,,
VII	Id.	Mar.	9 ,,	V	Id.	Apr.	9 ,,
VI	Id.	Mar.	10 ,,	IV	Id.	Apr.	10 ,,
V	Id.	Mar.	11 ,,	III	Id.	Apr.	11 ,,
IV	Id.	Mar.	12 ,,	Prid.	Id.	Apr.	12 ,,
III	Id.	Mar.	13 ,,		Idus	Apr.	13 ,,
Prid.	Id.	Mar.	14 ,,	XVIII	Kal.	Mai.	14 ,,
	Idus	Mar.	15 ,,	XVII	Kal.	Mai.	15 ,,
XVII	Kal.	Apr.	16 ,,	XVI	Kal.	Mai.	16 ,,
XVI	Kal.	Apr.	17 ,,	XV	Kal.	Mai.	17 ,,
XV	Kal.	Apr.	18 ,,	XIV	Kal.	Mai.	18 ,,
XIV	Kal.	Apr.	19 ,,	XIII	Kal.	Mai.	19 ,,
XIII	Kal.	Apr.	20 ,,	XII	Kal.	Mai.	20 ,,
XII	Kal.	Apr.	21 ,,	XI	Kal.	Mai.	21 ,,
XI	Kal.	Apr.	22 ,,	X	Kal.	Mai.	22 ,,
X	Kal.	Apr.	23 ,,	IX	Kal.	Mai.	23 ,,
IX	Kal.	Apr.	24 ,,	VIII	Kal.	Mai.	24 ,,
VIII	Kal.	Apr.	25 ,,	VII	Kal.	Mai.	25 ,,
VII	Kal.	Apr.	26 ,,	VI	Kal.	Mai.	26 ,,
VI	Kal.	Apr.	27 ,,	V	Kal.	Mai.	27 ,,
V	Kal.	Apr.	28 ,,	IV	Kal.	Mai.	28 ,,
IV	Kal.	Apr.	29 ,,	III	Kal.	Mai.	29 ,,
III	Kal.	Apr.	30 ,,	Prid.	Kal.	Mai.	30 ,,
Prid.	Kal.	Apr.	31 ,,				

MAY				JUNE			
Kalendæ Mai.		1	May	Kalendæ Jun.		1	June
VI	Non. Mai.	2	,,	IV	Non. Jun.	2	,,
V	Non. Mai.	3	,,	III	Non. Jun.	3	,,
IV	Non. Mai.	4	,,	Prid.	Non. Jun.	4	,,
III	Non. Mai.	5	,,		Nonæ Jun.	5	,,
Prid.	Non. Mai.	6	,,	VIII	Id. Jun.	6	,,
	Nonæ Mai.	7	,,	VII	Id. Jun.	7	,,
VIII	Id. Mai.	8	,,	VI	Id. Jun.	8	,,
VII	Id. Mai.	9	,,	V	Id. Jun.	9	,,
VI	Id. Mai.	10	,,	IV	Id. Jun.	10	,,
V	Id. Mai.	11	,,	III	Id. Jun.	11	,,
IV	Id. Mai.	12	,,	Prid.	Id. Jun.	12	,,
III	Id. Mai.	13	,,		Idus Jun.	13	,,
Prid.	Id. Mai.	14	,,	XVIII	Kal. Jul.	14	,,
	Idus Mai.	15	,,	XVII	Kal. Jul.	15	,,
XVII	Kal. Jun.	16	,,	XVI	Kal. Jul.	16	,,
XVI	Kal. Jun.	17	,,	XV	Kal. Jul.	17	,,
XV	Kal. Jun.	18	,,	XIV	Kal. Jul.	18	,,
XIV	Kal. Jun.	19	,,	XIII	Kal. Jul.	19	,,
XIII	Kal. Jun.	20	,,	XII	Kal. Jul.	20	,,
XII	Kal. Jun.	21	,,	XI	Kal. Jul.	21	,,
XI	Kal. Jun.	22	,,	X	Kal. Jul.	22	,,
X	Kal. Jun.	23	,,	IX	Kal. Jul.	23	,,
IX	Kal. Jun.	24	,,	VIII	Kal. Jul.	24	,,
VIII	Kal. Jun.	25	,,	VII	Kal. Jul.	25	,,
VII	Kal. Jun.	26	,,	VI	Kal. Jul.	26	,,
VI	Kal. Jun.	27	,,	V	Kal. Jul.	27	,,
V	Kal. Jun.	28	,,	IV	Kal. Jul.	28	,,
IV	Kal. Jun.	29	,,	III	Kal. Jul.	29	,,
III	Kal. Jun.	30	,,	Prid.	Kal. Jul.	30	,,
Prid.	Kal. Jun.	31	,,				

JULY				AUGUST			
	Kalendæ	Jul.	1 July		Kalendæ	Aug.	1 August
VI	Non.	Jul.	2 ,,	IV	Non.	Aug.	2 ,,
V	Non.	Jul.	3 ,,	III	Non.	Aug.	3 ,,
IV	Non.	Jul.	4 ,,	Prid.	Non.	Aug.	4 ,,
III	Non.	Jul.	5 ,,		Nonæ	Aug.	5 ,,
Prid.	Non.	Jul.	6 ,,	VIII	Id.	Aug.	6 ,,
	Nonæ	Jul.	7 ,,	VII	Id.	Aug.	7 ,,
VIII	Id.	Jul.	8 ,,	VI	Id.	Aug.	8 ,,
VII	Id.	Jul.	9 ,,	V	Id.	Aug.	9 ,,
VI	Id.	Jul.	10 ,,	IV	Id.	Aug.	10 ,,
V	Id.	Jul.	11 ,,	III	Id.	Aug.	11 ,,
IV	Id.	Jul.	12 ,,	Prid.	Id.	Aug.	12 ,,
III	Id.	Jul.	13 ,,		Idus	Aug.	13 ,,
Prid.	Id.	Jul.	14 ,,	XIX	Kal.	Sep.	14 ,,
	Idus	Jul.	15 ,,	XVIII	Kal.	Sep.	15 ,,
XVII	Kal.	Aug.	16 ,,	XVII	Kal.	Sep.	16 ,,
XVI	Kal.	Aug.	17 ,,	XVI	Kal.	Sep.	17 ,,
XV	Kal.	Aug.	18 ,,	XV	Kal.	Sep.	18 ,,
XIV	Kal.	Aug.	19 ,,	XIV	Kal.	Sep.	19 ,,
XIII	Kal.	Aug.	20 ,,	XIII	Kal.	Sep.	20 ,,
XII	Kal.	Aug.	21 ,,	XII	Kal.	Sep.	21 ,,
XI	Kal.	Aug.	22 ,,	XI	Kal.	Sep.	22 ,,
X	Kal.	Aug.	23 ,,	X	Kal.	Sep.	23 ,,
IX	Kal.	Aug.	24 ,,	IX	Kal.	Sep.	24 ,,
VIII	Kal.	Aug.	25 ,,	VIII	Kal.	Sep.	25 ,,
VII	Kal.	Aug.	26 ,,	VII	Kal.	Sep.	26 ,,
VI	Kal.	Aug.	27 ,,	VI	Kal.	Sep.	27 ,,
V	Kal.	Aug.	28 ,,	V	Kal.	Sep.	28 ,,
IV	Kal.	Aug.	29 ,,	IV	Kal.	Sep.	29 ,,
III	Kal.	Aug.	30 ,,	III	Kal.	Sep.	30 ,,
Prid.	Kal.	Aug.	31 ,,	Prid.	Kal.	Sep.	31 ,,

SEPTEMBER					OCTOBER				
	Kalendæ	Sep.	1	September		Kalendæ	Oct.	1	October
IV	Non.	Sep.	2	,,	VI	Non.	Oct.	2	,,
III	Non.	Sep.	3	,,	V	Non.	Oct.	3	,,
Prid.	Non.	Sep.	4	,,	IV	Non.	Oct.	4	,,
	Nonæ	Sep.	5	,,	III	Non.	Oct.	5	,,
VIII	Id.	Sep.	6	,,	Prid.	Non.	Oct.	6	,,
VII	Id.	Sep.	7	,,		Nonæ	Oct.	7	,,
VI	Id.	Sep.	8	,,	VIII	Id.	Oct.	8	,,
V	Id.	Sep.	9	,,	VII	Id.	Oct.	9	,,
IV	Id.	Sep.	10	,,	VI	Id.	Oct.	10	,,
III	Id.	Sep.	11	,,	V	Id.	Oct.	11	,,
Prid.	Id.	Sep.	12	,,	IV	Id.	Oct.	12	,,
	Idus	Sep.	13	,,	III	Id.	Oct.	13	,,
XVIII	Kal.	Oct.	14	,,	Prid.	Id.	Oct.	14	,,
XVII	Kal.	Oct.	15	,,		Idus	Oct.	15	,,
XVI	Kal.	Oct.	16	,,	XVII	Kal.	Nov.	16	,,
XV	Kal.	Oct.	17	,,	XVI	Kal.	Nov.	17	,,
XIV	Kal.	Oct.	18	,,	XV	Kal.	Nov.	18	,,
XIII	Kal.	Oct.	19	,,	XIV	Kal.	Nov.	19	,,
XII	Kal.	Oct.	20	,,	XIII	Kal.	Nov.	20	,,
XI	Kal.	Oct.	21	,,	XII	Kal.	Nov.	21	,,
X	Kal.	Oct.	22	,,	XI	Kal.	Nov.	22	,,
IX	Kal.	Oct.	23	,,	X	Kal.	Nov.	23	,,
VIII	Kal.	Oct.	24	,,	IX	Kal.	Nov.	24	,,
VII	Kal.	Oct.	25	,,	VIII	Kal.	Nov.	25	,,
VI	Kal.	Oct.	26	,,	VII	Kal.	Nov.	26	,,
V	Kal.	Oct.	27	,,	VI	Kal.	Nov.	27	,,
IV	Kal.	Oct.	28	,,	V	Kal.	Nov.	28	,,
III	Kal.	Oct.	29	,,	IV	Kal.	Nov.	29	,,
Prid.	Kal.	Oct.	30	,,	III	Kal.	Nov.	30	,,
					Prid.	Kal.	Nov.	31	,,

NOVEMBER					DECEMBER				
	Kalendæ	Nov.	1	November		Kalendæ	Dec.	1	December
IV	Non.	Nov.	2	,,	IV	Non.	Dec.	2	,,
III	Non.	Nov.	3	,,	III	Non.	Dec.	3	,,
Prid.	Non.	Nov.	4	,,	Prid.	Non.	Dec.	4	,,
	Nonæ	Nov.	5	,,		Nonæ	Dec.	5	,,
VIII	Id.	Nov.	6	,,	VIII	Id .	Dec.	6	,,
VII	Id.	Nov.	7	,,	VII	Id.	Dec.	7	,,
VI	Id.	Nov.	8	,,	VI	Id.	Dec.	8	,,
V	Id.	Nov.	9	,,	V	Id.	Dec.	9	,,
IV	Id.	Nov.	10	,,	IV	Id.	Dec.	10	,,
III	Id.	Nov.	11	,,	III	Id.	Dec.	11	,,
Prid.	Id.	Nov.	12	,,	Prid.	Id.	Dec.	12	,,
	Idus	Nov.	13	,,		Idus	Dec.	13	,,
XVIII	Kal.	Dec.	14	,,	XIX	Kal.	Jan.	14	,,
XVII	Kal.	Dec.	15	,,	XVIII	Kal.	Jan.	15	,,
XVI	Kal.	Dec.	16	,,	XVII	Kal.	Jan.	16	,,
XV	Kal.	Dec.	17	,,	XVI	Kal.	Jan.	17	,,
XIV	Kal.	Dec.	18	,,	XV	Kal.	Jan.	18	,,
XIII	Kal.	Dec.	19	,,	XIV	Kal.	Jan.	19	,,
XII	Kal.	Dec.	20	,,	XIII	Kal.	Jan.	20	,,
XI	Kal.	Dec.	21	,,	XII	Kal.	Jan.	21	,,
X	Kal.	Dec.	22	,,	XI	Kal.	Jan.	22	,,
IX	Kal.	Dec.	23	,,	X	Kal.	Jan.	23	,,
VIII	Kal.	Dec.	24	,,	IX	Kal.	Jan.	24	,,
VII	Kal.	Dec.	25	,,	VIII	Kal.	Jan.	25	,,
VI	Kal.	Dec.	26	,,	VII	Kal.	Jan.	26	,,
V	Kal.	Dec.	27	,,	VI	Kal.	Jan.	27	,,
IV	Kal.	Dec.	28	,,	V	Kal.	Jan.	28	,,
III	Kal.	Dec.	29	,,	IV	Kal.	Jan.	29	,,
Prid.	Kal.	Dec.	30	,,	III	Kal.	Jan.	30	,,
					Prid.	Kal.	Jan.	31	,,

CALENDARS FOR ALL POSSIBLE DATES
OF EASTER

The following thirty-six tables are based on those of Grotefend and Fry and introduce certain new features. The 'Old Style years' at the head of the left-hand pages include all years of the Julian calendar from A.D. 500 to 1752, when England celebrated Easter according to the Old Style reckoning for the last time. The 'New Style years' on the opposite pages give all years of the Gregorian calendar since its first introduction in Catholic countries abroad in 1582. The example of Fry has been followed in the provision of a special calendar for England in 1752 (table 36). It has not seemed necessary to include in the calendars all the fixed feasts, somewhat capriciously chosen, which Grotefend or Fry included; we have retained only a few which are of special importance in the dating of events (e.g. the quarter days); on the other hand, the Ember days have been added to the series of movable feasts.

The calendars are followed by a chronological table of Easter Days. To find the complete calendar for any year of grace from 500 to 2000, the student has simply to look up the year in the chronological table and then turn to the calendar for the appropriate date of Easter. He must be careful to observe the difference between the dates of Easter as celebrated in Old Style and New Style between 1583 and 1752, and consult the table at p. 161 for New Style calendars in this period.

When the student uses these calendars to check a date, he must first satisfy himself that the year-date is that of the 'historical' year, that is, begins on 1 January; if it is not, he must correct it to the historical year before turning to the table. Thus, an English record dated Wednesday, 29 February 1351 belongs to the historical year A.D. 1352 (a leap year), and table 18 shows that 29 February fell, in that year, on a Wednesday.

Table 1

EASTER DAY

Leap Years		January	February	March	April	May
January	February					
W 1	S 1	T 1	S 1 Quinquag.	S 1 Lent 4	W 1	F 1
T 2	F 2	F 2	M 2 Purific. M.	M 2	T 2	S 2
F 3	S 2 Quinquag.	S 3	T 3 Shrove Tu.	T 3	F 3	
S 4	M 3		W 4 Ash Wed.	W 4	S 4	S 3 Ascens.
	T 4 Shrove Tu.	S 4	T 5	T 5		M 4
S 5	W 5 Ash Wed.	M 5	F 6	F 6	S 5 Easter 2	T 5
M 6 Epiphany	T 6	T 6 Epiphany	S 7	S 7	M 6	W 6
T 7	F 7	W 7			T 7	T 7
W 8	S 8	T 8	S 8 Quadrag.	S 8 Passion	W 8	F 8
T 9		F 9	M 9	M 9	T 9	S 9
F 10	S 9 Quadrag.	S 10	T 10	T 10	F 10	
S 11	M 10		W 11 Ember	W 11	S 11	S 10 Whit Su
	T 11	S 11 Epiph. 1	T 12	T 12		M 11
S 12 Epiph. 1	W 12 Ember	M 12	F 13 Ember	F 13	S 12 Easter 3	T 12
M 13 Hilary	T 13	T 13 Hilary	S 14 Ember	S 14	M 13	W 13 Ember
T 14	F 14 Ember	W 14			T 14	T 14
W 15	S 15 Ember	T 15	S 15 Lent 2	S 15 Palm	W 15	F 15 Ember
T 16		F 16	M 16	M 16	T 16	S 16 Ember
F 17	S 16 Lent 2	S 17	T 17	T 17	F 17	
S 18	M 17		W 18	W 18	S 18	S 17 Trinity
	T 18	S 18 Septuag.	T 19	T 19		M 18
S 19 Septuag.	W 19	M 19	F 20	F 20 Good Fri.	S 19 Easter 4	T 19
M 20	T 20	T 20	S 21	S 21	M 20	W 20
T 21	F 21	W 21			T 21	T 21 Corpus C
W 22	S 22	T 22	S 22 Lent 3	S 22 **Easter Day**	W 22	F 22
T 23		F 23	M 23	M 23	T 23	S 23
F 24	S 23 Lent 3	S 24	T 24 Matthias	T 24	F 24	
S 25	M 24		W 25	W 25 Annunc.	S 25	S 24 Trinity 1
	T 25 Matthias	S 25 Sexages.	T 26	T 26		M 25
S 26 Sexages.	W 26	M 26	F 27	F 27	S 26 Rogation	T 26
M 27	T 27	T 27	S 28	S 28	M 27	W 27
T 28	F 28	W 28			T 28	T 28
W 29	S 29	T 29		S 29 Quasimodo	W 29	F 29
T 30		F 30		M 30	T 30 Ascension	S 30
F 31		S 31		T 31		
						S 31 Trinity 2

OR COMMON YEARS
OR LEAP YEARS (*in bold figures*)
ew Style years 1598, 1693, 1761, 1818

June	July	August	September	October	November	December
1	W 1	S 1 Lammas	T 1	T 1	**S 1 Trinity 24**	T 1
2	T 2		W 2	F 2	M 2	W 2
3	F 3	**S 2 Trinity 11**	T 3	S 3	T 3	T 3
4	S 4	M 3	F 4		W 4	F 4
5		T 4	S 5	**S 4 Trinity 20**	T 5	S 5
6	**S 5 Trinity 7**	W 5		M 5	F 6	
	M 6	T 6	**S 6 Trinity 16**	T 6	S 7	**S 6 Advent 2**
7 Trinity 3	T 7	F 7	M 7	W 7		M 7
8	W 8	S 8	T 8	T 8	**S 8 Trinity 25**	T 8
9	T 9		W 9	F 9	M 9	W 9
10	F 10	**S 9 Trinity 12**	T 10	S 10	T 10	T 10
11	S 11	M 10	F 11		w 11 Martin	F 11
12		T 11	S 12	**S 11 Trinity 21**	T 12	S 12
13	**S 12 Trinity 8**	W 12		M 12	F 13	
	M 13	T 13	**S 13 Trinity 17**	T 13	S 14	**S 13 Advent 3**
14 Trinity 4	T 14	F 14	M 14 Exalt. C.	W 14		M 14
15	W 15	S 15	T 15	T 15	**S 15 Trinity 26**	T 15
16	T 16		w 16 Ember	F 16	M 16	w 16 Ember
17	F 17	**S 16 Trinity 13**	T 17	S 17	T 17	T 17
18	s 18	M 17	F 18 Ember		w 18	F 18 Ember
19		T 18	s 19 Ember	**S 18 Trinity 22**	T 19	s 19 Ember
20	**S 19 Trinity 9**	W 19		M 19	F 20	
	M 20	T 20	**S 20 Trinity 18**	T 20	S 21	**S 20 Advent 4**
21 Trinity 5	T 21	F 21	M 21	W 21		M 21
22	W 22	S 22	T 22	T 22	**S 22 Trinity 27**	T 22
23	T 23		W 23	F 23	M 23	W 23
24 Nat. J. Bap	F 24	**S 23 Trinity 14**	T 24	S 24	T 24	T 24
25	S 25	M 24	F 25		W 25	F 25 Christmas
26		T 25	s 26	**S 25 Trinity 23**	T 26	s 26
27	**S 26 Trinity 10**	W 26		M 26	F 27	
	M 27	T 27	**S 27 Trinity 19**	T 27	S 28	**S 27**
28 Trinity 6	T 28	F 28	M 28	W 28		M 28
29	W 29	S 29	T 29 Michael A.	T 29	**S 29 Advent 1**	T 29
30	T 30		W 30	F 30	M 30	W 30
	F 31	**S 30 Trinity 15**		S 31		T 31
		M 31				

Table 2   EASTER DAY

DOMINICAL LETTER

,,   ,,   F

Old Style years **536,** 699, 783, 794, 878, 889, 973, **984, 1068,** 1231, 1315, 1326, 1410, 1421, 1505, **1516,** 160

Leap Years		January	February	March	April	May
January	February					
T 1	F 1	W 1	S 1	S 1	T 1	T 1 Ascension
W 2	S 2 Purific. M.	T 2			W 2	F 2
T 3		F 3	S 2 Quinquag.	S 2 Lent 4	T 3	S 3
F 4	S 3 Quinquag.	S 4	M 3	M 3	F 4	
S 5	M 4		T 4 Shrove Tu.	T 4	S 5	
	T 5 Shrove Tu.	S 5	W 5 Ash Wed.	W 5		S 4 Ascens. 1
S 6 Epiphany	W 6 Ash Wed.	M 6 Epiphany	T 6	T 6		M 5
M 7	T 7	T 7	F 7	F 7	S 6 Easter 2	T 6
T 8	F 8	W 8	S 8	S 8	M 7	W 7
W 9	S 9	T 9			T 8	T 8
T 10		F 10	S 9 Quadrag.	S 9 Passion	W 9	F 9
F 11	S 10 Quadrag.	S 11	M 10	M 10	T 10	S 10
S 12	M 11		T 11	T 11	F 11	
	T 12	S 12 Epiph. 1	W 12 Ember	W 12	S 12	S 11 Whit Sun.
S 13 Epiph. 1	W 13 Ember	M 13 Hilary	T 13	T 13		M 12
M 14	T 14	T 14	F 14 Ember	F 14	S 13 Easter 3	T 13
T 15	F 15 Ember	W 15	S 15 Ember	S 15	M 14	W 14 Ember
W 16	S 16 Ember	T 16			T 15	T 15
T 17		F 17	S 16 Lent 2	S 16 Palm	W 16	F 16 Ember
F 18	S 17 Lent 2	S 18	M 17	M 17	T 17	S 17 Ember
S 19	M 18		T 18	T 18	F 18	
	T 19	S 19 Septuag.	W 19	W 19	S 19	S 18 Trinity
S 20 Septuag.	W 20	M 20	T 20	T 20		M 19
M 21	T 21	T 21	F 21	F 21 Good Fri.	S 20 Easter 4	T 20
T 22	F 22	W 22	S 22	S 22	M 21	W 21
W 23	S 23	T 23			T 22	T 22 Corpus C.
T 24		F 24	S 23 Lent 3	S 23 **Easter Day**	W 23	F 23
F 25	S 24 Lent 3	S 25	M 24 Matthias	M 24	T 24	S 24
S 26	M 25		T 25	T 25 Annunc.	F 25	
	T 26	S 26 Sexages.	W 26	W 26	S 26	S 25 Trinity 1
S 27 Sexages.	W 27	M 27	T 27	T 27		M 26
M 28	T 28	T 28	F 28	F 28	S 27 Rogation	T 27
T 29	F 29	W 29		S 29	M 28	W 28
W 30		T 30			T 29	T 29
T 31		F 31		S 30 Quasimodo	W 30	F 30
				M 31		S 31

ʀ COMMON YEARS
ʀ LEAP YEARS (*in bold figures*)
ᴡ Style years **1636, 1704,** 1788, 1845, **1856,** 1913

June	July	August	September	October	November	December
ɪ Trinity 2	T ɪ	F ɪ Lammas	M ɪ	W ɪ	S ɪ	M ɪ
2	W 2	S 2	T 2	T 2		T 2
3	T 3		W 3	F 3	**S** 2 Trinity 24	W 3
4	F 4	**S** 3 Trinity 11	T 4	S 4	M 3	T 4
5	S 5	M 4	F 5		T 4	F 5
6		T 5	S 6	**S** 5 Trinity 20	W 5	S 6
7	**S** 6 Trinity 7	W 6		M 6	T 6	
	M 7	T 7	**S** 7 Trinity 16	T 7	F 7	**S** 7 Advent 2
8 Trinity 3	T 8	F 8	M 8	W 8	S 8	M 8
9	W 9	S 9	T 9	T 9		T 9
ɪo	T ɪo		W ɪo	F ɪo	**S** 9 Trinity 25	W ɪo
ɪɪ	F ɪɪ	**S** ɪo Trinity 12	T ɪɪ	S ɪɪ	M ɪo	T ɪɪ
ɪ2	S ɪ2	M ɪɪ	F ɪ2		T ɪɪ Martin	F ɪ2
ɪ3		T ɪ2	S ɪ3	**S** ɪ2 Trinity 21	W ɪ2	S ɪ3
ɪ4	**S** ɪ3 Trinity 8	W ɪ3		M ɪ3	T ɪ3	
	M ɪ4	T ɪ4	**S** ɪ4 Trinity 17	T ɪ4	F ɪ4	**S** ɪ4 Advent 3
ɪ5 Trinity 4	T ɪ5	F ɪ5	M ɪ5	W ɪ5	S ɪ5	M ɪ5
ɪ6	W ɪ6	S ɪ6	T ɪ6	T ɪ6		T ɪ6
ɪ7	T ɪ7		W ɪ7 Ember	F ɪ7	**S** ɪ6 Trinity 26	W ɪ7 Ember
ɪ8	F ɪ8	**S** ɪ7 Trinity 13	T ɪ8	S ɪ8	M ɪ7	T ɪ8
ɪ9	S ɪ9	M ɪ8	F ɪ9 Ember		T ɪ8	F ɪ9 Ember
20		T ɪ9	S 20 Ember	**S** ɪ9 Trinity 22	W ɪ9	S 20 Ember
2ɪ	**S** 20 Trinity 9	W 20		M 20	T 20	
	M 2ɪ	T 2ɪ	**S** 2ɪ Trinity 18	T 2ɪ	F 2ɪ	**S** 2ɪ Advent 4
22 Trinity 5	T 22	F 22	M 22	W 22	S 22	M 22
23	W 23	S 23	T 23	T 23		T 23
24 Nat. J. Bap	T 24		W 24	F 24	**S** 23 Trinity 27	W 24
25	F 25	**S** 24 Trinity 14	T 25	S 25	M 24	T 25 Christmas
26	S 26	M 25	F 26		T 25	F 26
27		T 26	S 27	**S** 26 Trinity 23	W 26	S 27
28	**S** 27 Trinity 10	W 27		M 27	T 27	
	M 28	T 28	**S** 28 Trinity 19	T 28	F 28	**S** 28
29 Trinity 6	T 29	F 29	M 29 Michael A.	W 29	S 29	M 29
30	W 30	S 30	T 30	T 30		T 30
	T 3ɪ			F 3ɪ	**S** 30 Advent ɪ	W 3ɪ
		S 3ɪ Trinity 15				

Table 3

EASTER DAY

Old Style years 547, 631, 642, 726, 737, 821, **832**, **916**, 1079, 1163, 1174, 1258, 1269, 1353, **1364**, **1448**, 1611, 1695, 170

Leap Years		January	February	March	April	May
January	February					
M 1	T 1	T 1	F 1	F 1	M 1	W 1
T 2	F 2 Purific. M.	W 2	S 2 Purific. M.	S 2	T 2	T 2 Ascension
W 3	S 3	T 3			W 3	F 3
T 4		F 4		S 3 Quinquag.	T 4	S 4
F 5	S 4 Quinquag.	S 5	M 4	M 4	F 5	
S 6 Epiphany	M 5		T 5 Shrove Tu.	T 5	S 6	S 5 Ascens. 1
	T 6 Shrove Tu.	S 6 Epiphany	W 6 Ash Wed.	W 6		M 6
S 7 Epiph. 1	W 7 Ash Wed.	M 7	T 7	T 7	S 7 Easter 2	T 7
M 8	T 8	T 8	F 8	F 8	M 8	W 8
T 9	F 9	W 9	S 9	S 9	T 9	T 9
W 10	S 10	T 10			W 10	F 10
T 11		F 11	S 10 Quadrag.	S 10 Passion	T 11	S 11
F 12	S 11 Quadrag.	S 12	M 11	M 11	F 12	
S 13 Hilary	M 12		T 12	T 12	S 13	S 12 Whit Sun.
	T 13	S 13 Epiph. 1	W 13 Ember	W 13		M 13
S 14 Epiph. 2	W 14 Ember	M 14	T 14	T 14	S 14 Easter 3	T 14
M 15	T 15	T 15	F 15 Ember	F 15	M 15	W 15 Ember
T 16	F 16 Ember	W 16	S 16 Ember	S 16	T 16	T 16
W 17	S 17 Ember	T 17			W 17	F 17 Ember
T 18		F 18	S 17 Lent 2	S 17 Palm	T 18	S 18 Ember
F 19	S 18 Lent 2	S 19	M 18	M 18	F 19	
S 20	M 19		T 19	T 19	S 20	S 19 Trinity
	T 20	S 20 Septuag.	W 20	W 20		M 20
S 21 Septuag.	W 21	M 21	T 21	T 21	S 21 Easter 4	T 21
M 22	T 22	T 22	F 22	F 22 Good Fri.	M 22	W 22
T 23	F 23	W 23	S 23	S 23	T 23	T 23 Corpus C.
W 24	S 24	T 24			W 24	F 24
T 25		F 25	S 24 Lent 3	S 24 **Easter Day**	T 25	S 25
F 26	S 25 Lent 3	S 26	M 25	M 25 Annunc.	F 26	
S 27	M 26		T 26	T 26	S 27	S 26 Trinity 1
	T 27	S 27 Sexages.	W 27	W 27		M 27
S 28 Sexages.	W 28	M 28	T 28	T 28	S 28 Rogation	T 28
M 29	T 29	T 29		F 29	M 29	W 29
T 30		W 30		S 30	T 30	T 30
W 31		T 31				F 31
				S 31 Quasimodo		

OR COMMON YEARS
OR LEAP YEARS (*in bold figures*)

ew Style years 1799, **1940**

June	July	August	September	October	November	December
I	M I	T I Lammas	S I Trinity 15	T I	F I	S I Advent I
	T 2	F 2	M 2	W 2	S 2	M 2
2 Trinity 2	W 3	S 3	T 3	T 3		T 3
3	T 4		W 4	F 4	S 3 Trinity 24	W 4
4	F 5	S 4 Trinity 11	T 5	S 5	M 4	T 5
5	S 6	M 5	F 6		T 5	F 6
6		T 6	S 7	S 6 Trinity 20	W 6	S 7
7	S 7 Trinity 7	W 7		M 7	T 7	
8	M 8	T 8	S 8 Trinity 16	T 8	F 8	S 8 Advent 2
	T 9	F 9	M 9	W 9	S 9	M 9
9 Trinity 3	W 10	S 10	T 10	T 10		T 10
10	T 11		W 11	F 11	S 10 Trinity 25	W 11
11	F 12	S 11 Trinity 12	T 12	S 12	M 11 Martin	T 12
12	S 13	M 12	F 13		T 12	F 13
13		T 13	s 14 Exalt. C.	S 13 Trinity 21	W 13	S 14
14	S 14 Trinity 8	W 14		M 14	T 14	
15	M 15	T 15	S 15 Trinity 17	T 15	F 15	S 15 Advent 3
	T 16	F 16	M 16	W 16	S 16	M 16
16 Trinity 4	W 17	S 17	T 17	T 17		T 17
17	T 18		w 18 Ember	F 18	S 17 Trinity 26	w 18 Ember
18	F 19	S 18 Trinity 13	T 19	S 19	M 18	T 19
19	S 20	M 19	F 20 Ember		T 19	F 20 Ember
20		T 20	s 21 Ember	S 20 Trinity 22	W 20	s 21 Ember
21	S 21 Trinity 9	W 21		M 21	T 21	
22	M 22	T 22	S 22 Trinity 18	T 22	F 22	S 22 Advent 4
	T 23	F 23	M 23	W 23	S 23	M 23
23 Trinity 5	W 24	S 24	T 24	T 24		T 24
24 Nat. J. Bap	T 25		W 25	F 25	S 24 Trinity 27	W 25 Christmas
25	F 26	S 25 Trinity 14	T 26	S 26	M 25	T 26
26	S 27	M 26	F 27		T 26	F 27
27		T 27	s 28	S 27 Trinity 23	W 27	S 28
28	S 28 Trinity 10	w 28		M 28	T 28	
29	M 29	T 29	S 29 Trinity 19	T 29	F 29	S 29
	T 30	F 30	M 30	W 30	S 30	M 30
30 Trinity 6	W 31	S 31		T 31		T 31

Table 4

Table 4

Old Style years 563, 574, 585, 658, 669, **680,** 753, **764, 848,** 927, 1011, 1022, 1095, 1106, 1117, 1190, 1201, **1212,** 1285, 129...
1380, 1459, 1543, 1554, 1627, 1638, 1649, 1722, 1733, **1744**

Leap Years		January	February	March	April	May
January	February					
S 1	W 1	M 1	T 1	T 1	S 1 Quasimodo	T 1
M 2	T 2 Purific. M.	T 2	F 2 Purific. M.	F 2	M 2	W 2
T 3	F 3	W 3	S 3	S 3	T 3	T 3 Ascension
W 4	S 4	T 4			W 4	F 4
T 5		F 5	S 4 Quinquag.	S 4 Lent 4	T 5	S 5
F 6 Epiphany	S 5 Quinquag.	s 6 Epiphany	M 5	M 5	F 6	
S 7	M 6		T 6 Shrove Tu.	T 6	S 7	S 6 Ascens. 1
	T 7 Shrove Tu.	S 7 Epiph. 1	w 7 Ash Wed.	w 7		M 7
S 8 Epiph. 1	w 8 Ash Wed.	M 8	T 8	T 8	S 8 Easter 2	T 8
M 9	T 9	T 9	F 9	F 9	M 9	W 9
T 10	F 10	W 10	S 10	S 10	T 10	T 10
W 11	S 11	T 11			W 11	F 11
T 12		F 12	S 11 Quadrag.	S 11 Passion	T 12	S 12
F 13 Hilary	S 12 Quadrag.	s 13 Hilary	M 12	M 12	F 13	
S 14	M 13		T 13	T 13	S 14	S 13 Whit Sun.
	T 14	S 14 Epiph. 2	w 14 Ember	w 14		M 14
S 15 Epiph. 2	w 15 Ember	M 15	T 15	T 15	S 15 Easter 3	T 15
M 16	T 16	T 16	F 16 Ember	F 16	M 16	w 16 Ember
T 17	F 17 Ember	W 17	s 17 Ember	s 17	T 17	T 17
w 18	s 18 Ember	T 18			w 18	F 18 Ember
T 19		F 19	S 18 Lent 2	S 18 Palm	T 19	s 19 Ember
F 20	S 19 Lent 2	S 20	M 19	M 19	F 20	
S 21	M 20		T 20	T 20	S 21	S 20 Trinity
	T 21	S 21 Septuag.	w 21	w 21		M 21
S 22 Septuag.	w 22	M 22	T 22	T 22	S 22 Easter 4	T 22
M 23	T 23	T 23	F 23	F 23 Good Fri.	M 23	W 23
T 24	F 24	W 24	s 24 Matthias	s 24	T 24	T 24 Corpus C.
W 25	s 25 Matthias	T 25			w 25	F 25
T 26		F 26	S 25 Lent 3	S 25 **Easter Day**	T 26	s 26
F 27	S 26 Lent 3	S 27	M 26	M 26	F 27	
s 28	M 27		T 27	T 27	s 28	S 27 Trinity 1
	T 28	S 28 Sexages.	w 28	w 28		M 28
S 29 Sexages.	W 29	M 29		T 29	S 29 Rogation	T 29
M 30		T 30		F 30	M 30	W 30
T 31		W 31		S 31		T 31

OR COMMON YEARS
OR LEAP YEARS (*in bold figures*)
w Style years 1663, 1674, 1731, 1742, 1883, 1894, 1951

June	July	August	September	October	November	December
1	S 1 Trinity 6	W 1 Lammas	S 1	M 1	T 1	S 1
2	M 2	T 2		T 2	F 2	
	T 3	F 3	S 2 Trinity 15	W 3	S 3	S 2 Advent 1
3 Trinity 2	W 4	S 4	M 3	T 4		M 3
4	T 5		T 4	F 5	S 4 Trinity 24	T 4
5	F 6	S 5 Trinity 11	W 5	S 6	M 5	W 5
6	S 7	M 6	T 6		T 6	T 6
7		T 7	F 7	S 7 Trinity 20	W 7	F 7
8	S 8 Trinity 7	W 8	S 8	M 8	T 8	S 8
9	M 9	T 9		T 9	F 9	
	T 10	F 10	S 9 Trinity 16	W 10	S 10	S 9 Advent 2
10 Trinity 3	W 11	S 11	M 10	T 11		M 10
11	T 12		T 11	F 12	S 11 Trinity 25	T 11
12	F 13	S 12 Trinity 12	W 12	S 13	M 12	W 12
13	S 14	M 13	T 13		T 13	T 13
14		T 14	F 14 Exalt. C.	S 14 Trinity 21	W 14	F 14
15	S 15 Trinity 8	W 15	S 15	M 15	T 15	S 15
16	M 16	T 16		T 16	F 16	
	T 17	F 17	S 16 Trinity 17	W 17	S 17	S 16 Advent 3
17 Trinity 4	W 18	S 18	M 17	T 18		M 17
18	T 19		T 18	F 19	S 18 Trinity 26	T 18
19	F 20	S 19 Trinity 13	W 19 Ember	S 20	M 19	W 19 Ember
20	S 21	M 20	T 20		T 20	T 20
21		T 21	F 21 Ember	S 21 Trinity 22	W 21	F 21 Ember
22	S 22 Trinity 9	W 22	S 22 Ember	M 22	T 22	S 22 Ember
23	M 23	T 23		T 23	F 23	
	T 24	F 24	S 23 Trinity 18	W 24	S 24	S 23 Advent 4
24 Trinity 5	W 25	S 25	M 24	T 25		M 24
25	T 26		T 25	F 26	S 25 Trinity 27	T 25 Christmas
26	F 27	S 26 Trinity 14	W 26	S 27	M 26	W 26
27	S 28	M 27	T 27		T 27	T 27
28		T 28	F 28	S 28 Trinity 23	W 28	F 28
29	S 29 Trinity 10	W 29	S 29 Michael A.	M 29	T 29	S 29
30	M 30	T 30		T 30	F 30	
	T 31	F 31	S 30 Trinity 19	W 31		S 30 Advent 4
						M 31

Table 5

EASTER DA

DOMINICAL LETTER
,,   ,,

Old Style years 506, 517, **528**, 590, 601, **612**, 685, **696**, 775, **780**, 859, 870, 943, 954, 965, 1027, 1038, 1049, **1060**, 1122, 11
1144, 1217, **1228**, 1307, **1312**, 1391, 1402, 1475, 1486, 1497, 1559, 1570, 1581, **1592**, 1654, 1665, **1676**, 1749

Leap Years		January	February	March	April	May
January	February					
S 1	T 1	S 1	W 1	W 1	S 1	M 1
	W 2 Purific. M.	M 2	T 2 Purific. M.	T 2		T 2
S 2	T 3	T 3	F 3	F 3	S 2 Quasimodo	W 3
M 3	F 4	W 4	S 4	S 4	M 3	T 4 Ascension
T 4	S 5	T 5			T 4	F 5
W 5		F 6 Epiphany	S 5 Quinquag.	S 5 Lent 4	W 5	S 6
T 6 Epiphany	S 6 Quinquag.	S 7	M 6	M 6	T 6	
F 7	M 7		T 7 Shrove Tu.	T 7	F 7	S 7 Ascens. 1
S 8	T 8 Shrove Tu.	S 8 Epiph. 1	W 8 Ash Wed.	W 8	S 8	M 8
	W 9 Ash Wed.	M 9	T 9	T 9		T 9
S 9 Epiph. 1	T 10	T 10	F 10	F 10	S 9 Easter 2	W 10
M 10	F 11	W 11	S 11	S 11	M 10	T 11
T 11	S 12	T 12			T 11	F 12
W 12		F 13 Hilary	S 12 Quadrag.	S 12 Passion	W 12	S 13
T 13 Hilary	S 13 Quadrag.	S 14	M 13	M 13	T 13	
F 14	M 14		T 14	T 14	F 14	S 14 Whit Sun.
S 15	T 15	S 15 Epiph. 2	W 15 Ember	W 15	S 15	M 15
	W 16 Ember	M 16	T 16	T 16		T 16
S 16 Epiph. 2	T 17	T 17	F 17 Ember	F 17	S 16 Easter 3	W 17 Ember
M 17	F 18 Ember	W 18	S 18 Ember	S 18	M 17	T 18
T 18	S 19 Ember	T 19			T 18	F 19 Ember
W 19		F 20	S 19 Lent 2	S 19 Palm	W 19	S 20 Ember
T 20	S 20 Lent 2	S 21	M 20	M 20	T 20	
F 21	M 21		T 21	T 21	F 21	S 21 Trinity
S 22	T 22	S 22 Septuag.	W 22	W 22	S 22	M 22
	W 23	M 23	T 23	T 23		T 23
S 23 Septuag.	T 24	T 24	F 24 Matthias	F 24 Good Fri.	S 23 Easter 4	W 24
M 24	F 25 Matthias	W 25	S 25	S 25 Annunc.	M 24	T 25 Corpus C.
T 25	S 26	T 26			T 25	F 26
W 26		F 27	S 26 Lent 3	S 26 **Easter Day**	W 26	S 27
T 27	S 27 Lent 3	S 28	M 27	M 27	T 27	
F 28	M 28		T 28	T 28	F 28	S 28 Trinity 1
S 29	T 29	S 29 Sexages.		W 29	S 29	M 29
		M 30		T 30		T 30
S 30 Sexages.		T 31		F 31	S 30 Rogation	W 31
M 31						

R COMMON YEARS
R LEAP YEARS (*in bold figures*)
w Style years 1595, 1606, 1617, 1690, 1758, 1769, **1780,** 1815, 1826, 1837, 1967, 1978, 1989

June	July	August	September	October	November	December
1	S 1	T 1 Lammas	F 1	S 1 Trinity 19	W 1	F 1
2	W 2		S 2	M 2	T 2	S 2
3	S 2 Trinity 6	T 3		T 3	F 3	
	M 3	F 4	S 3 Trinity 15	W 4	S 4	S 3　Advent 1
4 Trinity 2	T 4	S 5	M 4	T 5		M 4
5	W 5		T 5	F 6	S 5 Trinity 24	T 5
6	T 6	S 6 Trinity 11	W 6	S 7	M 6	W 6
7	F 7	M 7	T 7		T 7	T 7
8	S 8	T 8	F 8	S 8 Trinity 20	W 8	F 8
9		W 9	S 9	M 9	T 9	S 9
10	S 9 Trinity 7	T 10		T 10	F 10	
	M 10	F 11	S 10 Trinity 16	W 11	s 11 Martin	S 10 Advent 2
11 Trinity 3	T 11	s 12	M 11	T 12		M 11
12	W 12		T 12	F 13	S 12 Trinity 25	T 12
13	T 13	S 13 Trinity 12	W 13	s 14	M 13	W 13
14	F 14	M 14	T 14 Exalt. C.		T 14	T 14
15	S 15	T 15	F 15	S 15 Trinity 21	W 15	F 15
16		W 16	s 16	M 16	T 16	s 16
17	S 16 Trinity 8	T 17		T 17	F 17	
	M 17	F 18	S 17 Trinity 17	W 18	s 18	S 17 Advent 3
18 Trinity 4	T 18	S 19	M 18	T 19		M 18
19	W 19		T 19	F 20	S 19 Trinity 26	T 19
20	T 20	S 20 Trinity 13	w 20 Ember	s 21	M 20	w 20 Ember
21	F 21	M 21	T 21		T 21	T 21
22	S 22	T 22	F 22 Ember	S 22 Trinity 22	W 22	F 22 Ember
23		W 23	s 23 Ember	M 23	T 23	s 23 Ember
24 Nat. J. Bap	S 23 Trinity 9	T 24		T 24	F 24	
	M 24	F 25	S 24 Trinity 18	W 25	S 25	S 24 Advent 4
25 Trinity 5	T 25	s 26	M 25	T 26		M 25 Christmas
26	W 26		T 26	F 27	S 26 Trinity 27	T 26
27	T 27	S 27 Trinity 14	W 27	s 28	M 27	W 27
28	F 28	M 28	T 28		T 28	T 28
29	S 29	T 29	F 29 Michael A.	S 29 Trinity 23	W 29	F 29
30		W 30	s 30	M 30	T 30	s 30
	S 30 Trinity 10	T 31		T 31		
	M 31					S 31

Table 6

EASTER DA

DOMINICAL LETTER
„   „

Old Style years 533, **544**, 623, **628**, 707, 718, 791, 802, 813, 875, 886, 897, **908**, 970, 981, **992**, 1065, **1076**, 1155, **1160**, 1... 1250, 1323, 1334, 1345, 1407, 1418, 1429, **1440**, 1502, 1513, **1524**, 1597, **1608**, 1687, **1692**

Leap Years		January	February	March	April	May
January	**February**					
F 1	M 1	S 1	T 1	T 1	F 1	S 1 Rogation
S 2	T 2 Purific. M.		W 2 Purific. M.	W 2	S 2	M 2
	W 3	S 2	T 3	T 3		T 3
S 3	T 4	M 3	F 4	F 4	S 3 Quasimodo	W 4
M 4	F 5	T 4	S 5	S 5	M 4	T 5 Ascensio
T 5	S 6	W 5			T 5	F 6
W 6 Epiphany		T 6 Epiphany	S 6 Quinquag.	S 6 Lent 4	W 6	S 7
T 7	S 7 Quinquag.	F 7	M 7	M 7	T 7	
F 8	M 8	S 8	T 8 Shrove Tu.	T 8	F 8	S 8 Ascens.
S 9	T 9 Shrove Tu.		W 9 Ash Wed.	W 9	S 9	M 9
	W 10 Ash Wed.	S 9 Epiph. 1	T 10	T 10		T 10
S 10 Epiph. 1	T 11	M 10	F 11	F 11	S 10 Easter 2	W 11
M 11	F 12	T 11	S 12	S 12	M 11	T 12
T 12	S 13	W 12			T 12	F 13
W 13 Hilary		T 13 Hilary	S 13 Quadrag.	S 13 Passion	W 13	S 14
T 14	S 14 Quadrag.	F 14	M 14	M 14	T 14	
F 15	M 15	S 15	T 15	T 15	F 15	S 15 Whit Sun
S 16	T 16		W 16 Ember	W 16	S 16	M 16
	W 17 Ember	S 16 Epiph. 2	T 17	T 17		T 17
S 17 Epiph. 2	T 18	M 17	F 18 Ember	F 18	S 17 Easter 3	W 18 Ember
M 18	F 19 Ember	T 18	S 19 Ember	S 19	M 18	T 19
T 19	S 20 Ember	W 19			T 19	F 20 Ember
W 20		T 20	S 20 Lent 2	S 20 Palm	W 20	S 21 Ember
T 21	S 21 Lent 2	F 21	M 21	M 21	T 21	
F 22	M 22	S 22	T 22	T 22	F 22	S 22 Trinity
S 23	T 23		W 23	W 23	S 23	M 23
	W 24	S 23 Septuag.	T 24 Matthias	T 24		T 24
S 24 Septuag.	T 25 Matthias	M 24	F 25	F 25 Good Fri.	S 24 Easter 4	W 25
M 25	F 26	T 25	S 26	S 26	M 25	T 26 Corpus C.
T 26	S 27	W 26			T 26	F 27
W 27		T 27	S 27 Lent 3	S 27 **Easter Day**	W 27	S 28
T 28	S 28 Lent 3	F 28	M 28	M 28	T 28	
F 29	M 29	S 29		T 29	F 29	S 29 Trinity 1
S 30				W 30	S 30	M 30
		S 30 Sexages.		T 31		T 31
S 31 Sexages.		M 31				

94

R COMMON YEARS
R LEAP YEARS (*in bold figures*)
w Style years 1622, 1633, **1644**, 1701, **1712**, 1785, **1796**, 1842, 1853, **1864**, 1910, 1921, **1932**

June	July	August	September	October	November	December
1	F 1	M 1 Lammas	T 1	S 1	T 1	T 1
2	S 2	T 2	F 2		W 2	F 2
3		W 3	S 3	S 2 Trinity 19	T 3	S 3
4	S 3 Trinity 6	T 4		M 3	F 4	
	M 4	F 5	S 4 Trinity 15	T 4	S 5	S 4 Advent 2
5 Trinity 2	T 5	S 6	M 5	W 5		M 5
6	W 6		T 6	T 6	S 6 Trinity 24	T 6
7	T 7	S 7 Trinity 11	W 7	F 7	M 7	W 7
8	F 8	M 8	T 8	S 8	T 8	T 8
9	S 9	T 9	F 9		W 9	F 9
10	W 10	W 10	S 10	S 9 Trinity 20	T 10	S 10
1	S 10 Trinity 7	T 11		M 10	F 11 Martin	
	M 11	F 12	S 11 Trinity 16	T 11	S 12	S 11 Advent 3
12 Trinity 3	T 12	S 13	M 12	W 12		M 12
13	W 13		T 13	T 13	S 13 Trinity 25	T 13
14	T 14	S 14 Trinity 12	W 14 Exalt. C.	F 14	M 14	W 14 Ember
15	F 15	M 15	T 15	S 15	T 15	T 15
16	S 16	T 16	F 16		W 16	F 16 Ember
17		W 17	S 17	S 16 Trinity 21	T 17	S 17 Ember
18	S 17 Trinity 8	T 18		M 17	F 18	
	M 18	F 19	S 18 Trinity 17	T 18	S 19	S 18 Advent 4
19 Trinity 4	T 19	S 20	M 19	W 19		M 19
20	W 20		T 20	T 20	S 20 Trinity 26	T 20
21	T 21	S 21 Trinity 13	W 21 Ember	F 21	M 21	W 21
22	F 22	M 22	T 22	S 22	T 22	T 22
23	S 23	T 23	F 23 Ember		W 23	F 23
24 Nat. J. Bap		W 24	S 24 Ember	S 23 Trinity 22	T 24	S 24
25	S 24 Trinity 9	T 25		M 24	F 25	
	M 25	F 26	S 25 Trinity 18	T 25	S 26	S 25 Christmas
26 Trinity 5	T 26	S 27	M 26	W 26		M 26
27	W 27		T 27	T 27	S 27 Advent 1	T 27
28	T 28	S 28 Trinity 14	W 28	F 28	M 28	W 28
29	F 29	M 29	T 29 Michael A.	S 29	T 29	T 29
30	S 30	T 30	F 30		W 30	F 30
		W 31		S 30 Trinity 23		S 31
	S 31 Trinity 10			M 31		

Table 7

EASTER DAY
DOMINICAL LETTER

Old Style years 555, **560,** 566, 639, 650, 661, 723, 734, 745, **756,** 807, 818, 829, **840,** 902, 913, **924,** 997, 1003, **1008,** 1087, 1⬛
1098, 1171, 1182, 1193, 1255, 1266, 1277, **1288,** 1339, 1350, 1361, **1372,** 1434, 1445, **1456,** 1529, 1535, **1540,** 1619, 1⬛
1630, 1703, 1714, 1725

Leap Years		January	February	March	April	May
January	February					
T 1	S 1 Sexages.	F 1	M 1	M 1	T 1	S 1
F 2	M 2 Purific. M.	S 2	T 2 Purific. M.	T 2	F 2	
S 3	T 3		W 3	W 3	S 3	S 2 Rogation
	W 4		T 4	T 4		M 3
S 4	T 5	S 3	F 5	F 5	S 4 Quasimodo	T 4
M 5	F 6	M 4	s 6	s 6	M 5	W 5
T 6 Epiphany	S 7	T 5			T 6	T 6 Ascension
W 7		W 6 Epiphany	S 7 Quinquag.	S 7 Lent 4	W 7	F 7
T 8	S 8 Quinquag.	T 7	M 8	M 8	T 8	S 8
F 9	M 9	F 8	T 9 Shrove Tu.	T 9	F 9	
S 10	T 10 Shrove Tu.	S 9	W 10 Ash Wed.	W 10	S 10	S 9 Ascens.
	W 11 Ash Wed.		T 11	T 11		M 10
S 11 Epiph. 1	T 12	S 10 Epiph. 1	F 12	F 12	S 11 Easter 2	T 11
M 12	F 13	M 11	s 13	s 13	M 12	W 12
T 13 Hilary	S 14	T 12			T 13	T 13
W 14		W 13 Hilary	S 14 Quadrag.	S 14 Passion	W 14	F 14
T 15	S 15 Quadrag.	T 14	M 15	M 15	T 15	S 15
F 16	M 16	F 15	T 16	T 16	F 16	
S 17	T 17	s 16	w 17 Ember	W 17	S 17	S 16 Whit Sun
	w 18 Ember		T 18	T 18		M 17
S 18 Epiph. 2	T 19	S 17 Epiph. 2	F 19 Ember	F 19	S 18 Easter 3	T 18
M 19	F 20 Ember	M 18	s 20 Ember	s 20	M 19	w 19 Ember
T 20	s 21 Ember	T 19			T 20	T 20
W 21		W 20	S 21 Lent 2	S 21 Palm	W 21	F 21 Ember
T 22	S 22 Lent 2	T 21	M 22	M 22	T 22	s 22 Ember
F 23	M 23	F 22	T 23	T 23	F 23	
S 24	T 24	S 23	w 24 Matthias	W 24	S 24	S 23 Trinity
	w 25 Matthias		T 25	T 25 Annunc.		M 24
S 25 Septuag.	T 26	S 24 Septuag.	F 26	F 26 Good Fri.	S 25 Easter 4	T 25
M 26	F 27	M 25	s 27	s 27	M 26	w 26
T 27	s 28	T 26			T 27	T 27 Corpus C
W 28		W 27	S 28 Lent 3	S 28 **Easter Day**	W 28	F 28
T 29	S 29 Lent 3	T 28		M 29	T 29	S 29
F 30		F 29		T 30	F 30	
S 31		S 30		W 31		S 30 Trinity 1
		S 31 Sexages.				M 31

96

R COMMON YEARS
R LEAP YEARS (*in bold figures*)
Style years 1655, **1660**, 1717, 1723, **1728**, 1869, 1875, **1880**, 1937, **1948**

June	July	August	September	October	November	December
1	T 1	S 1 Trinity 10	W 1	F 1	M 1	W 1
2	F 2	M 2	T 2	S 2	T 2	T 2
3	S 3	T 3	F 3		W 3	F 3
4		W 4	S 4		T 4	S 4
5	S 4 Trinity 6	T 5		S 3 Trinity 19	F 5	
	M 5	F 6	S 5 Trinity 15	M 4	S 6	S 5 Advent 2
6 Trinity 2	T 6	S 7	M 6	T 5		M 6
7	W 7		T 7	W 6		T 7
8	T 8	S 8 Trinity 11	W 8	T 7	S 7 Trinity 24	W 8
9	F 9	M 9	T 9	F 8	M 8	T 9
10	S 10	T 10	F 10	S 9	T 9	F 10
11		W 11	S 11		W 10	S 11
12	S 11 Trinity 7	T 12		S 10 Trinity 20	T 11 Martin	
	M 12	F 13	S 12 Trinity 16	M 11	F 12	S 12 Advent 3
13 Trinity 3	T 13	S 14	M 13	T 12	S 13	M 13
14	W 14		T 14 Exalt. C.	W 13		T 14
15	T 15	S 15 Trinity 12	W 15 Ember	T 14	S 14 Trinity 25	W 15 Ember
16	F 16	M 16	T 16	F 15	M 15	T 16
17	S 17	T 17	F 17 Ember	S 16	T 16	F 17 Ember
18		W 18	S 18 Ember		W 17	S 18 Ember
19	S 18 Trinity 8	T 19		S 17 Trinity 21	T 18	
	M 19	F 20	S 19 Trinity 17	M 18	F 19	S 19 Advent 4
20 Trinity 4	T 20	S 21	M 20	T 19	S 20	M 20
21	W 21		T 21	W 20		T 21
22	T 22	S 22 Trinity 13	W 22	T 21	S 21 Trinity 26	W 22
23	F 23	M 23	T 23	F 22	M 22	T 23
24 Nat. J. Bap	S 24	T 24	F 24	S 23	T 23	F 24
25		W 25	S 25		W 24	s 25 Christmas
26	S 25 Trinity 9	T 26		S 24 Trinity 22	T 25	
	M 26	F 27	S 26 Trinity 18	M 25	F 26	S 26
27 Trinity 5	T 27	S 28	M 27	T 26	S 27	M 27
28	W 28		T 28	W 27		T 28
29	T 29	S 29 Trinity 14	W 29 Michael A.	T 28	S 28 Advent 1	W 29
30	F 30	M 30	T 30	F 29	M 29	T 30
	S 31	T 31		S 30	T 30	F 31
				S 31 Trinity 23		

Table 8

DOMINICAL LETTER

Old Style years 571, 582, 593, 655, 666, 677, **688,** 750, 761, **772,** 845, **856,** 935, **940,** 1019, 1030, 1103, 1114, 1125, 1187, 1... 1209, **1220,** 1282, 1293, **1304,** 1377, **1388,** 1467, **1472,** 1551, 1562, 1635, 1646, 1657, 1719, 1730, 1741 [for **1752** see spe... table]

Leap Years — January

W 1
T 2
F 3
S 4

S 5
M 6 Epiphany
T 7
W 8
T 9
F 10
S 11

S 12 Epiph. 1
M 13 Hilary
T 14
W 15
T 16
F 17
s 18

S 19 Epiph. 2
M 20
T 21
W 22
T 23
F 24
s 25

S 26 Septuag.
M 27
T 28
W 29
T 30
F 31

Leap Years — February

S 1
F 2
S 2 Sexages.
M 3
T 4
W 5
T 6
F 7
s 8
S 9 Quinquag.
M 10
T 11 Shrove Tu.
W 12 Ash Wed.
T 13
F 14
S 15
S 16 Quadrag.
M 17
T 18
W 19 Ember
T 20
F 21 Ember
s 22 Ember
S 23 Lent 2
M 24
T 25 Matthias
W 26
T 27
F 28
S 29

January

T 1
F 2
S 3

S 4
M 5
T 6 Epiphany
W 7
T 8
F 9
S 10

S 11 Epiph. 1
M 12
T 13 Hilary
W 14
T 15
F 16
s 17

S 18 Epiph. 2
M 19
T 20
W 21
T 22
F 23
S 24

S 25 Septuag.
M 26
T 27
w 28
T 29
F 30
S 31

February

S 1 Sexages.
M 2 Purific. M.
T 3
W 4
T 5
F 6
S 7

S 8 Quinquag.
M 9
T 10 Shrove Tu.
W 11 Ash Wed.
T 12
F 13
S 14

S 15 Quadrag.
M 16
T 17
w 18 Ember
T 19
F 20 Ember
s 21 Ember

S 22 Lent 2
M 23
T 24 Matthias
W 25
T 26
F 27
s 28

March

S 1 Lent 3
M 2
T 3
W 4
T 5
F 6
S 7

S 8 Lent 4
M 9
T 10
W 11
T 12
F 13
S 14

S 15 Passion
M 16
T 17
w 18
T 19
F 20
s 21

S 22 Palm
M 23
T 24
w 25 Annunc.
T 26
F 27 Good Fri.
s 28

S 29 **Easter Day**
M 30
T 31

April

W 1
T 2
F 3
S 4

S 5 Quasimodo
M 6
T 7
W 8
T 9
F 10
S 11

S 12 Easter 2
M 13
T 14
W 15
T 16
F 17
s 18

S 19 Easter 3
M 20
T 21
W 22
T 23
F 24
s 25

S 26 Easter 4
M 27
T 28
W 29
T 30

May

F 1
S 2

S 3 Rogatio...
M 4
T 5
w 6
T 7 Ascensi...
F 8
S 9

S 10 Ascens.
M 11
T 12
W 13
T 14
F 15
s 16

S 17 Whit Su...
M 18
T 19
w 20 Ember
T 21
F 22 Ember
s 23 Ember

S 24 Trinity
M 25
T 26
W 27
T 28 Corpus
F 29
s 30

S 31 Trinity

R COMMON YEARS
R LEAP YEARS (*in bold figures*)
w Style years 1587, **1592**, 1671, 1682, 1739, **1744** (German Protestant Style), 1750, 1807, **1812**, 1891, 1959, **1964**, 1970

June	July	August	September	October	November	December
1	W 1	S 1 Lammas	T 1	**T 1**	**S** 1 Trinity 23	T 1
2	T 2		W 2	F 2	M 2	W 2
3	F 3	**S** 2 Trinity 10	T 3	S 3	T 3	T 3
4	S 4	M 3	F 4		W 4	F 4
5		T 4	S 5	**S** 4 Trinity 19	T 5	S 5
6	**S** 5 Trinity 6	W 5		M 5	F 6	
	M 6	T 6	**S** 6 Trinity 15	T 6	S 7	**S** 6 Advent 2
7 Trinity 2	T 7	F 7	M 7	W 7		M 7
8	W 8	S 8	T 8	T 8	**S** 8 Trinity 24	T 8
9	T 9		W 9	F 9	M 9	W 9
10	**F** 10	**S** 9 Trinity 11	T 10	S 10	T 10	T 10
11	S 11	M 10	F 11		W 11 Martin	F 11
12		T 11	S 12	**S** 11 Trinity 20	T 12	S 12
13	**S** 12 Trinity 7	W 12		M 12	F 13	
	M 13	T 13	**S** 13 Trinity 16	T 13	S 14	**S** 13 Advent 3
14 Trinity 3	T 14	F 14	M 14 Exalt. C.	W 14		M 14
15	W 15	S 15	T 15	T 15	**S** 15 Trinity 25	T 15
16	T 16		w 16 Ember	F 16	M 16	w 16 Ember
17	F 17	**S** 16 Trinity 12	T 17	S 17	T 17	T 17
18	S 18	M 17	F 18 Ember		W 18	F 18 Ember
19		T 18	s 19 Ember	**S** 18 Trinity 21	T 19	s 19 Ember
20	**S** 19 Trinity 8	W 19		M 19	F 20	
	M 20	T 20	**S** 20 Trinity 17	T 20	S 21	**S** 20 Advent 4
21 Trinity 4	T 21	F 21	M 21	W 21		M 21
22	W 22	S 22	T 22	T 22	**S** 22 Trinity 26	T 22
23	T 23		W 23	F 23	M 23	W 23
24 Nat. J. Bap	F 24	**S** 23 Trinity 13	T 24	S 24	T 24	T 24
25	S 25	M 24	F 25		W 25	F 25 Christmas
26		**T** 25	s 26	**S** 25 Trinity 22	T 26	s 26
27	**S** 26 Trinity 9	w 26		M 26	F 27	
	M 27	T 27	**S** 27 Trinity 18	T 27	S 28	**S** 27
28 Trinity 5	T 28	F 28	M 28	W 28		M 28
29	W 29	S 29	T 29 Michael A.	T 29	**S** 29 Advent 1	T 29
30	T 30		W 30	F 30	M 30	W 30
	F 31	**S** 30 Trinity 14		S 31		T 31
		M 31				

Table 9 **EASTER DAY**

DOMINICAL LETTER
,,   ,,   F

Old Style years 503, 514, 525, 587, 598, 609, **620**, 682, 693, **704**, 777, **788**, 867, **872**, 951, 962, 1035, 1046, 1057, 1119, 11
1141, **1152**, 1214, 1225, **1236**, 1309, **1320**, 1399, **1404**, 1483, 1494, 1567, 1578, 1589, 1651, 1662, 1673, **1684**, 1746

Leap Years		January	February	March	April	May
January	February					
T 1	F 1	W 1	S 1	S 1	T 1	T 1
W 2	s 2 Purific. M.	T 2			W 2	F 2
T 3		F 3	S 2 Sexages.	S 2 Lent 3	T 3	s 3
F 4	S 3 Sexages.	s 4	M 3	M 3	F 4	
s 5	M 4		T 4	T 4	s 5	S 4 Rogation
	T 5	S 5	W 5	W 5		M 5
S 6 Epiphany	w 6	M 6 Epiphany	T 6	T 6	S 6 Quasimodo	T 6
M 7	T 7	T 7	F 7	F 7	M 7	W 7
T 8	F 8	W 8	s 8	s 8	T 8	T 8 Ascension
W 9	s 9	T 9			W 9	F 9
T 10		F 10	S 9 Quinquag.	S 9 Lent 4	T 10	S 10
F 11	S 10 Quinquag.	s 11	M 10	M 10	F 11	
s 12	M 11		T 11 Shrove Tu.	T 11	s 12	S 11 Ascens. 1
	T 12 Shrove Tu.	S 12 Epiph. 1	w 12 Ash Wed.	w 12		M 12
S 13 Epiph. 1	w 13 Ash Wed.	M 13 Hilary	T 13	T 13	S 13 Easter 2	T 13
M 14	T 14	T 14	F 14	F 14	M 14	W 14
T 15	F 15	W 15	s 15	s 15	T 15	T 15
W 16	s 16	T 16			w 16	F 16
T 17		F 17	S 16 Quadrag.	S 16 Passion	T 17	s 17
F 18	S 17 Quadrag.	s 18	M 17	M 17	F 18	
s 19	M 18		T 18	T 18	s 19	S 18 Whit Sun
	T 19	S 19 Epiph. 2	w 19 Ember	w 19		M 19
S 20 Epiph. 2	w 20 Ember	M 20	T 20	T 20	S 20 Easter 3	T 20
M 21	T 21	T 21	F 21 Ember	F 21	M 21	w 21 Ember
T 22	F 22 Ember	W 22	s 22 Ember	s 22	T 22	T 22
W 23	s 23 Ember	T 23			w 23	F 23 Ember
T 24		F 24	S 23 Lent 2	S 23 Palm	T 24	s 24 Ember
F 25	S 24 Lent 2	s 25	M 24 Matthias	M 24	F 25	
s 26	M 25 Matthias		T 25	T 25 Annunc.	s 26	S 25 Trinity
	T 26	S 26 Septuag.	w 26	w 26		M 26
S 27 Septuag.	w 27	M 27	T 27	T 27	S 27 Easter 4	T 27
M 28	T 28	T 28	F 28	F 28 Good Fri.	M 28	w 28
T 29	F 29	W 29		s 29	T 29	T 29 Corpus C
W 30		T 30			w 30	F 30
T 31		F 31		S 30 **Easter Day**		s 31
				M 31		

COMMON YEARS
LEAP YEARS (*in bold figures*)
Style years 1603, 1614, 1625, 1687, 1698, 1755, 1766, 1777, 1823, 1834, 1902, 1975, 1986, 1997

June	July	August	September	October	November	December
1 Trinity 1	T 1	F 1 Lammas	M 1	W 1	S 1	M 1
2	W 2	S 2	T 2	T 2	⊣	T 2
3	T 3		W 3	F 3	S 2 Trinity 23	W 3
4	F 4	S 3 Trinity 10	T 4	S 4	M 3	T 4
5	S 5	M 4	F 5		T 4	F 5
6		T 5	S 6	S 5 Trinity 19	W 5	S 6
7	S 6 Trinity 6	W 6		M 6	T 6	
	M 7	T 7	S 7 Trinity 15	T 7	F 7	S 7 Advent 2
8 Trinity 2	T 8	F 8	M 8	W 8	S 8	M 8
9	W 9	S 9	T 9	T 9		T 9
10	T 10		W 10	F 10	S 9 Trinity 24	W 10
11	F 11	S 10 Trinity 11	T 11	S 11	M 10	T 11
12	S 12	M 11	F 12		T 11 Martin	F 12
13		T 12	S 13	S 12 Trinity 20	W 12	S 13
14	S 13 Trinity 7	W 13		M 13	T 13	
	M 14	T 14	S 14 Trinity 16	T 14	F 14	S 14 Advent 3
15 Trinity 3	T 15	F 15	M 15	W 15	S 15	M 15
16	W 16	S 16	T 16	T 16		T 16
17	T 17		W 17 Ember	F 17	S 16 Trinity 25	W 17 Ember
18	F 18	S 17 Trinity 12	T 18	S 18	M 17	T 18
19	S 19	M 18	F 19 Ember		T 18	F 19 Ember
20		T 19	S 20 Ember	S 19 Trinity 21	W 19	S 20 Ember
21	S 20 Trinity 8	W 20		M 20	T 20	
	M 21	T 21	S 21 Trinity 17	T 21	F 21	S 21 Advent 4
22 Trinity 4	T 22	F 22	M 22	W 22	S 22	M 22
23	W 23	S 23	T 23	T 23		T 23
24 Nat. J. Bap	T 24		W 24	F 24	S 23 Trinity 26	W 24
25	F 25	S 24 Trinity 13	T 25	S 25	M 24	T 25 Christmas
26	S 26	M 25	F 26		T 25	F 26
27		T 26	S 27	S 26 Trinity 22	W 26	S 27
28	S 27 Trinity 9	W 27		M 27	T 27	
	M 28	T 28	S 28 Trinity 18	T 28	F 28	S 28
29 Trinity 5	T 29	F 29	M 29 Michael A.	W 29	S 29	M 29
30	W 30	S 30	T 30	T 30		T 30
	T 31			F 31	S 30 Advent 1	W 31
		S 31 Trinity 14				

Table 10

Old Style years 519, 530, 541, **552**, 614, 625, **636**, 709, 715, **720**, 799, **804**, 810, 883, 894, 905, 967, 978, 989, **1000**, 1051, 106
1073, **1084**, 1146, 1157, **1168**, 1241, 1247, **1252**, 1331, **1336**, 1342, 1415, 1426, 1437, 1499, 1510, 1521, **1532**, 1583, 159
1605, **1616**, 1678, 1689, **1700**

| Leap Years | | January | February | March | April | May |
January	February					
M 1	T 1	T 1	F 1	F 1	M 1	W 1
T 2	F 2 Purific. M.	W 2	S 2 Purific. M.	S 2	T 2	T 2
W 3	S 3	T 3			W 3	F 3
T 4		F 4	S 3 Sexages.	S 3 Lent 3	T 4	S 4
F 5	S 4 Sexages.	S 5	M 4	M 4	F 5	
s 6 Epiphany	M 5		T 5	T 5	s 6	S 5 Rogation
	T 6	S 6 Epiphany	w 6	w 6		M 6
S 7 Epiph. 1	W 7	M 7	T 7	T 7	S 7 Quasimodo	T 7
M 8	T 8	T 8	F 8	F 8	M 8	w 8
T 9	F 9	W 9	S 9	S 9	T 9	T 9 Ascension
W 10	S 10	T 10			W 10	F 10
T 11		F 11	S 10 Quinquag.	S 10 Lent 4	T 11	S 11
F 12	S 11 Quinquag.	S 12	M 11	M 11	F 12	
s 13 Hilary	M 12		T 12 Shrove Tu.	T 12	s 13	S 12 Ascens. 1
	T 13 Shrove Tu.	S 13 Epiph. 1	w 13 Ash Wed.	w 13		M 13
S 14 Epiph. 2	w 14 Ash Wed.	M 14	T 14	T 14	S 14 Easter 2	T 14
M 15	T 15	T 15	F 15	F 15	M 15	W 15
T 16	F 16	w 16	s 16	s 16	T 16	T 16
W 17	S 17	T 17			W 17	F 17
T 18		F 18	S 17 Quadrag.	S 17 Passion	T 18	s 18
F 19	S 18 Quadrag.	S 19	M 18	M 18	F 19	
S 20	M 19		T 19	T 19	S 20	S 19 Whit Sun
	T 20	S 20 Epiph. 2	w 20 Ember	w 20		M 20
S 21 Epiph. 3	w 21 Ember	M 21	T 21	T 21	S 21 Easter 3	T 21
M 22	T 22	T 22	F 22 Ember	F 22	M 22	w 22 Ember
T 23	F 23 Ember	W 23	s 23 Ember	s 23	T 23	T 23
W 24	s 24 Ember	T 24			W 24	F 24 Ember
T 25		F 25	S 24 Lent 2	S 24 Palm	T 25	s 25 Ember
F 26	S 25 Lent 2	s 26	M 25	M 25 Annunc.	F 26	
s 27	M 26		T 26	T 26	s 27	S 26 Trinity
	T 27	S 27 Septuag.	w 27	w 27		M 27
S 28 Septuag.	w 28	M 28	T 28	T 28	S 28 Easter 4	T 28
M 29	T 29	T 29		F 29 Good Fri.	M 29	w 29
T 30		W 30		S 30	T 30	T 30 Corpus C.
W 31		T 31				F 31
				S 31 **Easter Day**		

ᴏʀ Cᴏᴍᴍᴏɴ Yᴇᴀʀs
ᴏʀ Lᴇᴀᴘ Yᴇᴀʀs (*in bold figures*)
w Style years 1619, 1630, 1641, **1652,** 1709, **1720,** 1771, 1782, 1793, 1839, 1850, 1861, **1872,** 1907, 1918, 1929, 1991

June	July	August	September	October	November	December
ɪ	M ɪ	T ɪ Lammas	S ɪ Trinity 14	T ɪ	F ɪ	S ɪ Advent ɪ
	T 2	F 2	M 2	W 2	S 2	M 2
2 Trinity ɪ	W 3	S 3	T 3	T 3		T 3
3	T 4		W 4	F 4	S 3 Trinity 23	W 4
4	F 5	S 4 Trinity 10	T 5	S 5	M 4	T 5
5	S 6	M 5	F 6		T 5	F 6
6		T 6	S 7	S 6 Trinity 19	W 6	S 7
7	S 7 Trinity 6	W 7		M 7	T 7	
8	M 8	T 8	S 8 Trinity 15	T 8	F 8	S 8 Advent 2
	T 9	F 9	M 9	W 9	S 9	M 9
9 Trinity 2	W 10	S 10	T 10	T 10		T 10
10	T 11		W 11	F 11	S 10 Trinity 24	W 11
11	F 12	S 11 Trinity 11	T 12	S 12	M 11 Martin	T 12
12	S 13	M 12	F 13		T 12	F 13
13		T 13	S 14 Exalt. C.	S 13 Trinity 20	W 13	S 14
14	S 14 Trinity 7	W 14		M 14	T 14	
15	M 15	T 15	S 15 Trinity 16	T 15	F 15	S 15 Advent 3
	T 16	F 16	M 16	W 16	S 16	M 16
16 Trinity 3	W 17	S 17	T 17	T 17		T 17
17	T 18		W 18 Ember	F 18	S 17 Trinity 25	W 18 Ember
18	F 19	S 18 Trinity 12	T 19	S 19	M 18	T 19
19	S 20	M 19	F 20 Ember		T 19	F 20 Ember
20		T 20	S 21 Ember	S 20 Trinity 21	W 20	S 21 Ember
21	S 21 Trinity 8	W 21		M 21	T 21	
22	M 22	T 22	S 22 Trinity 17	T 22	F 22	S 22 Advent 4
	T 23	F 23	M 23	W 23	S 23	M 23
23 Trinity 4	W 24	S 24	T 24	T 24		T 24
24 Nat. J. Bap	T 25		W 25	F 25	S 24 Trinity 26	W 25 Christmas
25	F 26	S 25 Trinity 13	T 26	S 26	M 25	T 26
26	S 27	M 26	F 27		T 26	F 27
27		T 27	S 28	S 27 Trinity 22	W 27	S 28
28	S 28 Trinity 9	W 28		M 28	T 28	
29	M 29	T 29	S 29 Trinity 18	T 29	F 29	S 29
	T 30	F 30	M 30	W 30	S 30	M 30
30 Trinity 5	W 31	S 31		T 31		T 31

Table 11   EASTER DAY

DOMINICAL LETTER ●
      ,,   ,, A●

Old Style years 557, **568**, 647, **652**, 731, 742, 815, 826, 837, 899, 910, 921, **932**, 994, 1005, **1016**, 1089, **1100**, 1179, **1184**, 126
1274, 1347, 1358, 1369, 1431, 1442, 1453, **1464**, 1526, 1537, **1548**, 1621, **1632**, 1711, **1716**

Leap Years		January	February	March	April	May
January	February					
S 1	W 1	M 1	T 1	T 1	S 1 Easter Day	T 1
M 2	T 2 Purific. M.	T 2	F 2 Purific. M.	F 2	M 2	W 2
T 3	F 3	W 3	S 3	S 3	T 3	T 3
W 4	S 4	T 4			W 4	F 4
T 5		F 5			T 5	S 5
F 6 Epiphany	S 5 Sexages.	S 6 Epiphany	S 4 Sexages.	S 4 Lent 3	F 6	
S 7	M 6		M 5	M 5	S 7	S 6 Rogation
	T 7	S 7 Epiph. 1	T 6	T 6		M 7
S 8 Epiph. 1	W 8	M 8	W 7	W 7	S 8 Quasimodo	T 8
M 9	T 9	T 9	T 8	T 8	M 9	W 9
T 10	F 10	W 10	F 9	F 9	T 10	T 10 Ascension
W 11	S 11	T 11	S 10	S 10	W 11	F 11
T 12		F 12			T 12	S 12
F 13 Hilary	S 12 Quinquag.	S 13 Hilary	S 11 Quinquag.	S 11 Lent 4	F 13	
S 14	M 13		M 12	M 12	S 14	S 13 Ascens. 1
	T 14 Shrove Tu.	S 14 Epiph. 2	T 13 Shrove Tu.	T 13		M 14
S 15 Epiph. 2	W 15 Ash Wed.	M 15	W 14 Ash Wed.	W 14	S 15 Easter 2	T 15
M 16	T 16	T 16	T 15	T 15	M 16	W 16
T 17	F 17	W 17	F 16	F 16	T 17	T 17
W 18	S 18	T 18	S 17	S 17	W 18	F 18
T 19		F 19			T 19	S 19
F 20	S 19 Quadrag.	S 20	S 18 Quadrag.	S 18 Passion	F 20	
S 21	M 20		M 19	M 19	S 21	S 20 Whit Sun.
	T 21	S 21 Epiph. 3	T 20	T 20		M 21
S 22 Epiph. 3	W 22 Ember	M 22	W 21 Ember	W 21	S 22 Easter 3	T 22
M 23	T 23	T 23	T 22	T 22	M 23	W 23 Ember
T 24	F 24 Ember	W 24	F 23 Ember	F 23	T 24	T 24
W 25	S 25 Ember	T 25	S 24 Ember	S 24	W 25	F 25 Ember
T 26		F 26			T 26	S 26 Ember
F 27	S 26 Lent 2	S 27	S 25 Lent 2	S 25 Palm	F 27	
S 28	M 27		M 26	M 26	S 28	S 27 Trinity
	T 28	S 28 Septuag.	T 27	T 27		M 28
S 29 Septuag.	W 29	M 29	W 28	W 28	S 29 Easter 4	T 29
M 30		T 30		T 29	M 30	W 30
T 31		W 31		F 30 Good Fri.		T 31 Corpus C.
				S 31		

R COMMON YEARS
R LEAP YEARS (*in bold figures*)
w Style years **1584**, 1646, 1657, **1668**, 1714, 1725, **1736**, **1804**, 1866, 1877, **1888**, 1923, 1934, 1945, **1956**

June	July	August	September	October	November	December
1	S 1 Trinity 5	w 1 Lammas	s 1	M 1	T 1	s 1
2	M 2	T 2		T 2	F 2	
	T 3	F 3	S 2 Trinity 14	w 3	s 3	S 2 Advent 1
3 Trinity 1	w 4	s 4	M 3	T 4		M 3
4	T 5		T 4	F 5	S 4 Trinity 23	T 4
5	F 6	S 5 Trinity 10	w 5	s 6	M 5	w 5
6	s 7	M 6	T 6		T 6	T 6
7		T 7	F 7	S 7 Trinity 19	w 7	F 7
8	S 8 Trinity 6	w 8	s 8	M 8	T 8	s 8
9	M 9	T 9		T 9	F 9	
	T 10	F 10	S 9 Trinity 15	w 10	s 10	S 9 Advent 2
10 Trinity 2	w 11	s 11	M 10	T 11		M 10
11	T 12		T 11	F 12	S 11 Trinity 24	T 11
12	F 13	S 12 Trinity 11	w 12	s 13	M 12	w 12
13	s 14	M 13	T 13		T 13	T 13
14		T 14	F 14 Exalt. C.	S 14 Trinity 20	w 14	F 14
15	S 15 Trinity 7	w 15	s 15	M 15	T 15	s 15
16	M 16	T 16		T 16	F 16	
	T 17	F 17	S 16 Trinity 16	w 17	s 17	S 16 Advent 3
17 Trinity 3	w 18	s 18	M 17	T 18		M 17
18	T 19		T 18	F 19	S 18 Trinity 25	T 18
19	F 20	S 19 Trinity 12	w 19 Ember	s 20	M 19	w 19 Ember
20	s 21	M 20	T 20		T 20	T 20
21		T 21	F 21 Ember	S 21 Trinity 21	w 21	F 21 Ember
22	S 22 Trinity 8	w 22	s 22 Ember	M 22	T 22	s 22 Ember
23	M 23	T 23		T 23	F 23	
	T 24	F 24	S 23 Trinity 17	w 24	s 24	S 23 Advent 4
24 Trinity 4	w 25	s 25	M 24	T 25		M 24
25	T 26		T 25	F 26	S 25 Trinity 26	T 25 Christmas
26	F 27	S 26 Trinity 13	w 26	s 27	M 26	w 26
27	s 28	M 27	T 27		T 27	T 27
28		T 28	F 28	S 28 Trinity 22	w 28	F 28
29	S 29 Trinity 9	w 29	s 29 Michael A.	M 29	T 29	s 29
30	M 30	T 30		T 30	F 30	
	T 31	F 31	S 30 Trinity 18	w 31		S 30
						M 31

Table 12

EASTER DAY

DOMINICAL LETTER
„
„ B

Old Style years **500**, 579, **584**, 663, 674, 747, 758, 769, 831, 842, 853, **864**, 926, 937, **948**, 1021, **1032**, 1111, **1116**, 1195, 12○ 1279, 1290, 1301, 1363, 1374, 1385, **1396**, 1458, 1469, **1480**, 1553, **1564**, 1643, **1648**, 1727, 1738

| Leap Years | | | | | | |
January	February	January	February	March	April	May
S 1	T 1	S 1	W 1	W 1	S 1	M 1
	w 2 Purific. M.	M 2	T 2 Purific. M.	T 2		T 2
S 2	T 3	T 3	F 3	F 3	S 2 Easter Day	W 3
M 3	F 4	W 4	S 4	S 4	M 3	T 4
T 4	S 5	T 5			T 4	F 5
W 5		F 6 Epiphany	S 5 Sexages.	S 5 Lent 3	W 5	s 6
T 6 Epiphany	S 6 Sexages.	S 7	M 6	M 6	T 6	
F 7	M 7		T 7	T 7	F 7	S 7 Rogation
s 8	T 8	S 8 Epiph. 1	w 8	w 8	s 8	M 8
	W 9	M 9	T 9	T 9		T 9
S 9 Epiph. 1	T 10	T 10	F 10	F 10	S 9 Quasimodo	W 10
M 10	F 11	W 11	S 11	S 11	M 10	T 11 Ascension
T 11	S 12	T 12			T 11	F 12
W 12		F 13 Hilary	S 12 Quinquag.	S 12 Lent 4	W 12	s 13
T 13 Hilary	S 13 Quinquag.	S 14	M 13	M 13	T 13	
F 14	M 14		T 14 Shrove Tu.	T 14	F 14	S 14 Ascens. 1
S 15	T 15 Shrove Tu.	S 15 Epiph. 2	w 15 Ash Wed.	w 15	S 15	M 15
	w 16 Ash Wed.	M 16	T 16	T 16		T 16
S 16 Epiph. 2	T 17	T 17	F 17	F 17	S 16 Easter 2	W 17
M 17	F 18	w 18	s 18	s 18	M 17	T 18
T 18	S 19	T 19			T 18	F 19
W 19		F 20	S 19 Quadrag.	S 19 Passion	W 19	S 20
T 20	S 20 Quadrag.	S 21	M 20	M 20	T 20	
F 21	M 21		T 21	T 21	F 21	S 21 Whit Sun.
S 22	T 22	S 22 Epiph. 3	w 22 Ember	w 22	S 22	M 22
	w 23 Ember	M 23	T 23	T 23		T 23
S 23 Epiph. 3	T 24	T 24	F 24 Ember	F 24	S 23 Easter 3	w 24 Ember
M 24	F 25 Ember	w 25	s 25 Ember	s 25 Annunc.	M 24	T 25
T 25	s 26 Ember	T 26			T 25	F 26 Ember
w 26		F 27	S 26 Lent 2	S 26 Palm	w 26	s 27 Ember
T 27	S 27 Lent 2	s 28	M 27	M 27	T 27	
F 28	M 28		T 28	T 28	F 28	S 28 Trinity
S 29	T 29	S 29 Septuag.		w 29	S 29	M 29
		M 30		T 30		T 30
S 30 Septuag.		T 31		F 31 Good Fri.	S 30 Easter 4	W 31
M 31						

or Common Years
or Leap Years (*in bold figures*)
ew Style years 1589, **1600**, 1673, 1679, **1684**, 1741, 1747, **1752**, 1809, **1820**, 1893, 1899, 1961, **1972**

June	July	August	September	October	November	December
T 1 Corpus C.	S 1	T 1 Lammas	F 1	**S** 1 Trinity 18	W 1	F 1
F 2		W 2	S 2	M 2	T 2	S 2
S 3	**S** 2 Trinity 5	T 3		T 3	F 3	
	M 3	F 4	**S** 3 Trinity 14	W 4	S 4	**S** 3 Advent 1
S 4 Trinity 1	T 4	S 5	M 4	T 5		M 4
M 5	W 5		T 5	F 6	**S** 5 Trinity 23	T 5
T 6	T 6	**S** 6 Trinity 10	W 6	S 7	M 6	W 6
W 7	F 7	M 7	T 7		T 7	T 7
T 8	S 8	T 8	F 8	**S** 8 Trinity 19	W 8	F 8
F 9		W 9	S 9	M 9	T 9	S 9
S 10	**S** 9 Trinity 6	T 10		T 10	F 10	
	M 10	F 11	**S** 10 Trinity 15	W 11	S 11 Martin	**S** 10 Advent 2
S 11 Trinity 2	T 11	S 12	M 11	T 12		M 11
M 12	W 12		T 12	F 13	**S** 12 Trinity 24	T 12
T 13	T 13	**S** 13 Trinity 11	W 13	S 14	M 13	W 13
W 14	F 14	M 14	T 14 Exalt. C.		T 14	T 14
T 15	S 15	T 15	F 15	**S** 15 Trinity 20	W 15	F 15
F 16		W 16	S 16	M 16	T 16	S 16
S 17	**S** 16 Trinity 7	T 17		T 17	F 17	
	M 17	F 18	**S** 17 Trinity 16	W 18	S 18	**S** 17 Advent 3
S 18 Trinity 3	T 18	S 19	M 18	T 19		M 18
M 19	W 19		T 19	F 20	**S** 19 Trinity 25	T 19
T 20	T 20	**S** 20 Trinity 12	W 20 Ember	S 21	M 20	W 20 Ember
W 21	F 21	M 21	T 21		T 21	T 21
T 22	S 22	T 22	F 22 Ember	**S** 22 Trinity 21	W 22	F 22 Ember
F 23		W 23	S 23 Ember	M 23	T 23	S 23 Ember
S 24 Nat. J. Bap	**S** 23 Trinity 8	T 24		T 24	F 24	
	M 24	F 25	**S** 24 Trinity 17	W 25	S 25	**S** 24 Advent 4
S 25 Trinity 4	T 25	S 26	M 25	T 26		M 25 Christmas
M 26	W 26		T 26	F 27	**S** 26 Trinity 26	T 26
T 27	T 27	**S** 27 Trinity 13	W 27	S 28	M 27	W 27
W 28	F 28	M 28	T 28		T 28	T 28
T 29	S 29	T 29	F 29 Michael A.	**S** 29 Trinity 22	W 29	F 29
F 30		W 30	S 30	M 30	T 30	S 30
	S 30 Trinity 9	T 31		T 31		
	M 31					**S** 31

Table 13

Old Style years 511, **516,** 522, 595, 606, 617, 679, 690, 701, **712,** 763, 774, 785, **796,** 858, 869, **880,** 953, 959, **964,** 1043, **1048,** 1054, 1127, 1138, 1149, 1211, 1222, 1233, **1244,** 1295, 1306, 1317, **1328,** 1390, 1401, **1412,** 1485, 1491, **1496,** 1575, **1580,** 1586, 1659, 1670, 1681, 1743

Leap Years		January	February	March	April	May
January	February					
F 1	M 1	S 1	T 1	T 1	F 1 Good Fri.	S 1 Easter 4
S 2	T 2 Purific. M.		W 2 Purific. M.	W 2	S 2	M 2
	W 3	S 2	T 3	T 3		T 3
S 3	T 4	M 3	F 4	F 4	S 3 Easter Day	W 4
M 4	F 5	T 4	S 5	S 5	M 4	T 5
T 5	S 6	W 5			T 5	F 6
W 6 Epiphany		T 6 Epiphany	S 6 Sexages.	S 6 Lent 3	W 6	S 7
T 7	S 7 Sexages.	F 7	M 7	M 7	T 7	
F 8	M 8	S 8	T 8	T 8	F 8	S 8 Rogation
S 9	T 9		W 9	W 9	S 9	M 9
	W 10	S 9 Epiph. 1	T 10	T 10		T 10
S 10 Epiph. 1	T 11	M 10	F 11	F 11	S 10 Quasimodo	W 11
M 11	F 12	T 11	S 12	S 12	M 11	T 12 Ascension
T 12	S 13	W 12			T 12	F 13
W 13 Hilary		T 13 Hilary	S 13 Quinquag.	S 13 Lent 4	W 13	S 14
T 14	S 14 Quinquag.	F 14	M 14	M 14	T 14	
F 15	M 15	S 15	T 15 Shrove Tu.	T 15	F 15	S 15 Ascens. 1
S 16	T 16 Shrove Tu.		W 16 Ash Wed.	W 16	S 16	M 16
	W 17 Ash Wed.	S 16 Epiph. 2	T 17	T 17		T 17
S 17 Epiph. 2	T 18	M 17	F 18	F 18	S 17 Easter 2	W 18
M 18	F 19	T 18	S 19	S 19	M 18	T 19
T 19	S 20	W 19			T 19	F 20
W 20		T 20	S 20 Quadrag.	S 20 Passion	W 20	S 21
T 21	S 21 Quadrag.	F 21	M 21	M 21	T 21	
F 22	M 22	S 22	T 22	T 22	F 22	S 22 Whit Sun.
S 23	T 23		W 23 Ember	W 23	S 23	M 23
	W 24 Ember	S 23 Epiph. 3	T 24 Matthias	T 24		T 24
S 24 Epiph. 3	T 25 Matthias	M 24	F 25 Ember	F 25 Annunc.	S 24 Easter 3	W 25 Ember
M 25	F 26 Ember	T 25	S 26 Ember	S 26	M 25	T 26
T 26	S 27 Ember	W 26			T 26	F 27 Ember
W 27		T 27	S 27 Lent 2	S 27 Palm	W 27	S 28 Ember
T 28	S 28 Lent 2	F 28	M 28	M 28	T 28	
F 29	M 29	S 29		T 29	F 29	S 29 Trinity
S 30				W 30	S 30	M 30
		S 30 Septuag.		T 31		T 31
S 31 Septuag.		M 31				

OR COMMON YEARS
OR LEAP YEARS (*in bold figures*)
ew Style years 1611, **1616**, 1695, 1763, **1768**, 1774, 1825, 1831, **1836**, **1904**, 1983, **1988**, 1994

June	July	August	September	October	November	December
1	F 1	M 1 Lammas	T 1	S 1	T 1	T 1
2 Corpus C.	S 2	T 2	F 2		W 2	F 2
3		W 3	S 3		T 3	S 3
4		T 4		S 2 Trinity 18	F 4	
	S 3 Trinity 5	F 5		M 3	S 5	
	M 4	s 6	S 4 Trinity 14	T 4		S 4 Advent 2
5 Trinity 1	T 5		M 5	W 5		M 5
6	W 6		T 6	T 6	S 6 Trinity 23	T 6
7	T 7	S 7 Trinity 10	W 7	F 7	M 7	W 7
8	F 8	M 8	T 8	s 8	T 8	T 8
9	S 9	T 9	F 9		W 9	F 9
10		W 10	S 10		T 10	S 10
11		T 11		S 9 Trinity 19	F 11 Martin	
	S 10 Trinity 6	F 12	S 11 Trinity 15	M 10	s 12	S 11 Advent 3
	M 11	s 13	M 12	T 11		M 12
12 Trinity 2	T 12		T 13	W 12		T 13
13	W 13		w 14 Exalt. C.	T 13	S 13 Trinity 24	w 14 Ember
14	T 14	S 14 Trinity 11	T 15	F 14	M 14	T 15
15	F 15	M 15	F 16	s 15	T 15	F 16 Ember
16	s 16	T 16	s 17		W 16	s 17 Ember
17		W 17		S 16 Trinity 20	T 17	
18	S 17 Trinity 7	T 18	S 18 Trinity 16	M 17	F 18	S 18 Advent 4
	M 18	F 19	M 19	T 18	s 19	M 19
19 Trinity 3	T 19	S 20	T 20	W 19		T 20
20	W 20		w 21 Ember	T 20	S 20 Trinity 25	W 21
21	T 21	S 21 Trinity 12	T 22	F 21	M 21	T 22
22	F 22	M 22	F 23 Ember	s 22	T 22	F 23
23	S 23	T 23	s 24 Ember		W 23	S 24
24 Nat. J. Bap		W 24		S 23 Trinity 21	T 24	
25	S 24 Trinity 8	T 25	S 25 Trinity 17	M 24	F 25	S 25 Christmas
	M 25	F 26	M 26	T 25	s 26	M 26
26 Trinity 4	T 26	s 27	T 27	W 26		T 27
27	W 27		w 28	T 27	S 27 Advent 1	W 28
28	T 28	S 28 Trinity 13	T 29 Michael A.	F 28	M 28	T 29
29	F 29	M 29	F 30	s 29	T 29	F 30
30	S 30	T 30			W 30	S 31
		W 31		S 30 Trinity 22		
	S 31 Trinity 9			M 31		

Table 14

EASTER DAY

Old Style years 527, 538, 549, 611, 622, 633, **644**, 706, 717, **728**, 801, **812**, 891, **896**, 975, 986, 1059, 1070, 1081, 1143, 11
1165, **1176**, 1238, 1249, **1260**, 1333, **1344**, 1423, **1428**, 1507, 1518, 1591, 1602, 1613, 1675, 1686, 1697, **1708**

Leap Years		January	February	March	April	May
January	February					
T 1	S 1 Septuag.	F 1	M 1	M 1	T 1	S 1
F 2	M 2 Purific. M.	S 2	T 2 Purific. M.	T 2	F 2 Good Fri.	
S 3	T 3		W 3	W 3	S 3	S 2 Easter 4
	W 4	S 3	T 4	T 4		M 3
S 4	T 5	M 4	F 5	F 5	S 4 **Easter Day**	T 4
M 5	F 6	T 5	S 6	S 6	M 5	W 5
T 6 Epiphany	S 7	W 6 Epiphany			T 6	T 6
W 7		T 7	S 7 Sexages.	S 7 Lent 3	W 7	F 7
T 8	S 8 Sexages.	F 8	M 8	M 8	T 8	S 8
F 9	M 9	S 9	T 9	T 9	F 9	
S 10	T 10		W 10	W 10	S 10	S 9 Rogation
	W 11	S 10 Epiph. 1	T 11	T 11		M 10
S 11 Epiph. 1	T 12	M 11	F 12	F 12	S 11 Quasimodo	T 11
M 12	F 13	T 12	S 13	S 13	M 12	W 12
T 13 Hilary	S 14	W 13 Hilary			T 13	T 13 Ascension
W 14		T 14	S 14 Quinquag.	S 14 Lent 4	W 14	F 14
T 15	S 15 Quinquag.	F 15	M 15	M 15	T 15	S 15
F 16	M 16	S 16	T 16 Shrove Tu.	T 16	F 16	
S 17	T 17 Shrove Tu.		w 17 Ash Wed.	W 17	S 17	S 16 Ascens. 1
	w 18 Ash Wed.	S 17 Epiph. 2	T 18	T 18		M 17
S 18 Epiph. 2	T 19	M 18	F 19	F 19	S 18 Easter 2	T 18
M 19	F 20	T 19	S 20	S 20	M 19	W 19
T 20	S 21	W 20			T 20	T 20
W 21		T 21	S 21 Quadrag.	S 21 Passion	W 21	F 21
T 22	S 22 Quadrag.	F 22	M 22	M 22	T 22	S 22
F 23	M 23	S 23	T 23	T 23	F 23	
S 24	T 24		w 24 Ember	W 24	S 24	S 23 Whit Sun.
	w 25 Ember	S 24 Epiph. 3	T 25	T 25 Annunc.		M 24
S 25 Epiph. 3	T 26	M 25	F 26 Ember	F 26	S 25 Easter 3	T 25
M 26	F 27 Ember	T 26	s 27 Ember	S 27	M 26	w 26 Ember
T 27	s 28 Ember	W 27			T 27	T 27
W 28		T 28	S 28 Lent 2	S 28 Palm	W 28	F 28 Ember
T 29	S 29 Lent 2	F 29		M 29	T 29	s 29 Ember
F 30		S 30		T 30	F 30	
S 31				W 31		S 30 Trinity
		S 31 Septuag.				M 31

ꞁʀ COMMON YEARS
ꞁʀ LEAP YEARS (*in bold figures*)
ꞁ·w Style years 1627, 1638, 1649, 1706, 1779, 1790, 1847, 1858, 1915, **1920**, 1926, 1999

June	July	August	September	October	November	December
1	T 1	S 1 Trinity 9	W 1	F 1	M 1	W 1
2	F 2	M 2	T 2	S 2	T 2	T 2
3 Corpus C.	S 3	T 3	F 3		W 3	F 3
4		W 4	S 4		T 4	S 4
5	S 4 Trinity 5	T 5		S 3 Trinity 18	F 5	
	M 5	F 6	S 5 Trinity 14	M 4	S 6	S 5 Advent 2
6 Trinity 1	T 6	S 7	M 6	T 5		M 6
7	W 7		T 7	W 6	S 7 Trinity 23	T 7
8	T 8	S 8 Trinity 10	W 8	T 7	M 8	W 8
9	F 9	M 9	T 9	F 8	T 9	T 9
10	S 10	T 10	F 10	S 9	W 10	F 10
11		W 11	S 11		T 11 Martin	S 11
12	S 11 Trinity 6	T 12		S 10 Trinity 19	F 12	
	M 12	F 13	S 12 Trinity 15	M 11	S 13	S 12 Advent 3
13 Trinity 2	T 13	S 14	M 13	T 12		M 13
14	W 14		T 14 Exalt. C.	W 13	S 14 Trinity 24	T 14
15	T 15	S 15 Trinity 11	W 15 Ember	T 14	M 15	W 15 Ember
16	F 16	M 16	T 16	F 15	T 16	T 16
17	S 17	T 17	F 17 Ember	S 16	W 17	F 17 Ember
18		W 18	S 18 Ember		T 18	S 18 Ember
19	S 18 Trinity 7	T 19		S 17 Trinity 20	F 19	
	M 19	F 20	S 19 Trinity 16	M 18	S 20	S 19 Advent 4
20 Trinity 3	T 20	S 21	M 20	T 19		M 20
21	W 21		T 21	W 20	S 21 Trinity 25	T 21
22	T 22	S 22 Trinity 12	W 22	T 21	M 22	W 22
23	F 23	M 23	T 23	F 22	T 23	T 23
24 Nat. J. Bap	S 24	T 24	F 24	S 23	W 24	F 24
25		W 25	S 25		T 25	S 25 Christmas
26	S 25 Trinity 8	T 26		S 24 Trinity 21	F 26	
	M 26	F 27	S 26 Trinity 17	M 25	S 27	S 26
27 Trinity 4	T 27	S 28	M 27	T 26		M 27
28	W 28		T 28	W 27	S 28 Advent 1	T 28
29	T 29	S 29 Trinity 13	W 29 Michael A.	T 28	M 29	W 29
30	F 30	M 30	T 30	F 29	T 30	T 30
	S 31	T 31		S 30		F 31
				S 31 Trinity 22		

Table 15

Old Style years 543, 554, 565, **576**, 638, 649, **660**, 733, 739, **744**, 823, **828**, 834, 907, 918, 929, 991, 1002, 1013, **1024**, 10
1086, 1097, **1108**, 1170, 1181, **1192**, 1265, 1271, **1276**, 1355, **1360**, 1366, 1439, 1450, 1461, 1523, 1534, 1545, **1556**, 16
1618, 1629, **1640**, 1702, 1713, **1724**

Leap Years		January	February	March	April	May
January	**February**					
W 1	S 1	T 1	S 1 Septuag.	S 1 Lent 2	W 1	F 1
T 2	F 2	M 2 Purific. M.	M 2	M 2	T 2	S 2
F 3	S 2 Septuag.	S 3	T 3	T 3	F 3 Good Fri.	
S 4	M 3		W 4	W 4	S 4	S 3 Easter 4
	T 4	S 4	T 5	T 5		M 4
S 5	W 5	M 5	F 6	F 6	S 5 **Easter Day**	T 5
M 6 Epiphany	T 6	T 6 Epiphany	S 7	S 7	M 6	W 6
T 7	F 7	W 7			T 7	T 7
W 8	S 8	T 8	S 8 Sexages.	S 8 Lent 3	W 8	F 8
T 9		F 9	M 9	M 9	T 9	S 9
F 10	S 9 Sexages.	S 10	T 10	T 10	F 10	
S 11	M 10		W 11	W 11	S 11	S 10 Rogation
	T 11	S 11 Epiph. 1	T 12	T 12		M 11
S 12 Epiph. 1	W 12	M 12	F 13	F 13	S 12 Quasimodo	T 12
M 13 Hilary	T 13	T 13 Hilary	S 14	S 14	M 13	W 13
T 14	F 14	W 14			T 14	T 14 Ascension
W 15	S 15	T 15	S 15 Quinquag.	S 15 Lent 4	W 15	F 15
T 16		F 16	M 16	M 16	T 16	S 16
F 17	S 16 Quinquag.	S 17	T 17 Shrove Tu.	T 17	F 17	
S 18	M 17		W 18 Ash Wed.	W 18	S 18	S 17 Ascens. 1
	T 18 Shrove Tu.	S 18 Epiph. 2	T 19	T 19		M 18
S 19 Epiph. 2	W 19 Ash Wed.	M 19	F 20	F 20	S 19 Easter 2	T 19
M 20	T 20	T 20	S 21	S 21	M 20	W 20
T 21	F 21	W 21			T 21	T 21
W 22	S 22	T 22	S 22 Quadrag.	S 22 Passion	W 22	F 22
T 23		F 23	M 23	M 23	T 23	S 23
F 24	S 23 Quadrag.	S 24	T 24 Matthias	T 24	F 24	
S 25	M 24		W 25 Ember	W 25 Annunc.	S 25	S 24 Whit Sun
	T 25 Matthias	S 25 Epiph. 3	T 26	T 26		M 25
S 26 Epiph. 3	W 26 Ember	M 26	F 27 Ember	F 27	S 26 Easter 3	T 26
M 27	T 27	T 27	S 28 Ember	S 28	M 27	W 27 Ember
T 28	F 28 Ember	W 28			T 28	T 28
W 29	S 29 Ember	T 29		S 29 Palm	W 29	F 29 Ember
T 30		F 30		M 30	T 30	S 30 Ember
F 31		S 31		T 31		
						S 31 Trinity

OR COMMON YEARS
OR LEAP YEARS (*in bold figures*)

ew Style years 1643, 1654, 1665, 1676, 1711, 1722, 1733, **1744**, 1795, 1801, 1863, 1874, 1885, **1896**, 1931, 1942, 1953

June	July	August	September	October	November	December
1	W 1	S 1 Lammas	T 1	T 1	S 1 Trinity 22	T 1
2	T 2		W 2	F 2	M 2	W 2
3	F 3	S 2 Trinity 9	T 3	S 3	T 3	T 3
4 Corpus C.	S 4	M 3	F 4		W 4	F 4
5		T 4	S 5	S 4 Trinity 18	T 5	S 5
6	S 5 Trinity 5	W 5		M 5	F 6	
	M 6	T 6	S 6 Trinity 14	T 6	S 7	S 6 Advent 2
7 Trinity 1	T 7	F 7	M 7	W 7		M 7
8	W 8	S 8	T 8	T 8	S 8 Trinity 23	T 8
9	T 9		W 9	F 9	M 9	W 9
10	F 10	S 9 Trinity 10	T 10	S 10	T 10	T 10
11	S 11	M 10	F 11		W 11 Martin	F 11
12		T 11	S 12	S 11 Trinity 19	T 12	S 12
13	S 12 Trinity 6	W 12		M 12	F 13	
	M 13	T 13	S 13 Trinity 15	T 13	S 14	S 13 Advent 3
14 Trinity 2	T 14	F 14	M 14 Exalt. C.	W 14		M 14
15	W 15	S 15	T 15	T 15	S 15 Trinity 24	T 15
16	T 16		W 16 Ember	F 16	M 16	W 16 Ember
17	F 17	S 16 Trinity 11	T 17	S 17	T 17	T 17
18	S 18	M 17	F 18 Ember		W 18	F 18 Ember
19		T 18	S 19 Ember	S 18 Trinity 20	T 19	S 19 Ember
20	S 19 Trinity 7	W 19		M 19	F 20	
	M 20	T 20	S 20 Trinity 16	T 20	S 21	S 20 Advent 4
21 Trinity 3	T 21	F 21	M 21	W 21		M 21
22	W 22	S 22	T 22	T 22	S 22 Trinity 25	T 22
23	T 23		W 23	F 23	M 23	W 23
24 Nat. J. Bap	F 24	S 23 Trinity 12	T 24	S 24	T 24	T 24
25	S 25	M 24	F 25		W 25	F 25 Christmas
26		T 25	S 26	S 25 Trinity 21	T 26	S 26
27	S 26 Trinity 8	W 26		M 26	F 27	
	M 27	T 27	S 27 Trinity 17	T 27	S 28	S 27
28 Trinity 4	T 28	F 28	M 28	W 28		M 28
29	W 29	S 29	T 29 Michael A.	T 29	S 29 Advent 1	T 29
30	T 30		W 30	F 30	M 30	W 30
	F 31	S 30 Trinity 13		S 31		T 31
		M 31				

Table 16

EASTER DAY

DOMINICAL LETTER
,,   ,,   F

Old Style years **508**, 570, 581, **592**, 665, 671, **676**, 755, **760**, 766, 839, 850, 861, 923, 934, 945, **956**, 1007, 1018, 1029, 10
1102, 1113, **1124**, 1197, 1203, **1208**, 1287, **1292**, 1298, 1371, 1382, 1393, 1455, 1466, 1477, **1488**, 1539, 1550, 1561, 15
1634, 1645, **1656**, 1729, 1735, **1740**

Leap Years		January	February	March	April	May
January	February					
T 1	F 1	W 1	S 1	s 1 Ember	T 1	T 1
W 2	s 2 Purific. M.	T 2			W 2	F 2
T 3		F 3	**S** 2 Septuag.	**S** 2 Lent 2	T 3	s 3
F 4	**S** 3 Septuag.	s 4	M 3	M 3	F 4 Good Fri.	
s 5	M 4		T 4	T 4	s 5	**S** 4 Easter 4
	T 5	**S** 5	W 5	W 5		M 5
S 6 Epiphany	W 6	M 6 Epiphany	T 6	T 6	**S** 6 **Easter Day**	T 6
M 7	T 7	T 7	F 7	F 7	M 7	W 7
T 8	F 8	W 8	s 8	s 8	T 8	T 8
W 9	s 9	T 9			W 9	F 9
T 10		F 10	**S** 9 Sexages.	**S** 9 Lent 3	T 10	s 10
F 11	**S** 10 Sexages.	s 11	M 10	M 10	F 11	
s 12	M 11		T 11	T 11	s 12	**S** 11 Rogation
	T 12	**S** 12 Epiph. 1	W 12	W 12		M 12
S 13 Epiph. 1	W 13	M 13 Hilary	T 13	T 13	**S** 13 Quasimodo	T 13
M 14	T 14	T 14	F 14	F 14	M 14	W 14
T 15	F 15	W 15	s 15	s 15	T 15	T 15 Ascension
W 16	s 16	T 16			W 16	F 16
T 17		F 17	**S** 16 Quinquag.	**S** 16 Lent 4	T 17	s 17
F 18	**S** 17 Quinquag.	s 18	M 17	M 17	F 18	
s 19	M 18		T 18 Shrove Tu.	T 18	s 19	**S** 18 Ascens. 1
	T 19 Shrove Tu.	**S** 19 Epiph. 2	w 19 Ash Wed.	W 19		M 19
S 20 Epiph. 2	w 20 Ash Wed.	M 20	T 20	T 20	**S** 20 Easter 2	T 20
M 21	T 21	T 21	F 21	F 21	M 21	W 21
T 22	F 22	W 22	S 22	S 22	T 22	T 22
W 23	s 23	T 23			w 23	F 23
T 24		F 24	**S** 23 Quadrag.	**S** 23 Passion	T 24	s 24
F 25	**S** 24 Quadrag.	s 25	M 24 Matthias	M 24	F 25	
s 26	M 25 Matthias		T 25	T 25 Annunc.	s 26	**S** 25 Whit Sun
	T 26	**S** 26 Epiph. 3	w 26 Ember	w 26		M 26
S 27 Epiph. 3	w 27 Ember	M 27	T 27	T 27	**S** 27 Easter 3	T 27
M 28	T 28	T 28	F 28 Ember	F 28	M 28	w 28 Ember
T 29	F 29 Ember	W 29		s 29	T 29	T 29
W 30		T 30			w 30	F 30 Ember
T 31		F 31		**S** 30 Palm		s 31 Ember
				M 31		

114

FOR COMMON YEARS

FOR LEAP YEARS (*in bold figures*)

New Style years 1586, 1597, **1608,** 1670, 1681, **1692,** 1738, 1749, **1760,** 1806, 1817, **1828,** 1890, 1947, 1958, 1969, **1980**

June	July	August	September	October	November	December
S 1 Trinity	T 1	F 1 Lammas	M 1	W 1	S 1	M 1
M 2	W 2	S 2	T 2	T 2		T 2
T 3	T 3		W 3	F 3	S 2 Trinity 22	W 3
W 4	F 4	S 3 Trinity 9	T 4	S 4	M 3	T 4
T 5 Corpus C.	S 5	M 4	F 5		T 4	F 5
F 6		T 5	S 6	S 5 Trinity 18	W 5	S 6
S 7	S 6 Trinity 5	W 6		M 6	T 6	
	M 7	T 7	S 7 Trinity 14	T 7	F 7	S 7 Advent 2
S 8 Trinity 1	T 8	F 8	M 8	W 8	S 8	M 8
M 9	W 9	S 9	T 9	T 9		T 9
T 10	T 10		W 10	F 10	S 9 Trinity 23	W 10
W 11	F 11	S 10 Trinity 10	T 11	S 11	M 10	T 11
T 12	S 12	M 11	F 12		T 11 Martin	F 12
F 13		T 12	S 13	S 12 Trinity 19	W 12	S 13
S 14	S 13 Trinity 6	W 13		M 13	T 13	
	M 14	T 14	S 14 Trinity 15	T 14	F 14	S 14 Advent 3
S 15 Trinity 2	T 15	F 15	M 15	W 15	S 15	M 15
M 16	W 16	S 16	T 16	T 16		T 16
T 17	T 17		W 17 Ember	F 17	S 16 Trinity 24	W 17 Ember
W 18	F 18	S 17 Trinity 11	T 18	S 18	M 17	T 18
T 19	S 19	M 18	F 19 Ember		T 18	F 19 Ember
F 20		T 19	S 20 Ember	S 19 Trinity 20	W 19	S 20 Ember
S 21	S 20 Trinity 7	W 20		M 20	T 20	
	M 21	T 21	S 21 Trinity 16	T 21	F 21	S 21 Advent 4
S 22 Trinity 3	T 22	F 22	M 22	W 22	S 22	M 22
M 23	W 23	S 23	T 23	T 23		T 23
T 24 Nat. J. Bap	T 24		W 24	F 24	S 23 Trinity 25	W 24
W 25	F 25	S 24 Trinity 12	T 25	S 25	M 24	T 25 Christmas
T 26	S 26	M 25	F 26		T 25	F 26
F 27		T 26	S 27	S 26 Trinity 21	W 26	S 27
S 28	S 27 Trinity 8	W 27		M 27	T 27	
	M 28	T 28	S 28 Trinity 17	T 28	F 28	S 28
S 29 Trinity 4	T 29	F 29	M 29 Michael A.	W 29	S 29	M 29
M 30	W 30	S 30	T 30	T 30		T 30
	T 31			F 31	S 30 Advent 1	W 31
		S 31 Trinity 13				

Table 17

EASTER DAY

DOMINICAL LETTER
,,   ,, G

Old Style years 513, **524**, 603, **608**, 687, 698, 771, 782, 793, 855, 866, 877, **888**, 950, 961, **972**, 1045, **1056**, 1135, **1140**, 12
1230, 1303, 1314, 1325, 1387, 1398, 1409, **1420**, 1482, 1493, **1504**, 1577, **1588**, 1667, **1672**, 1751

Leap Years		January	February	March	April	May
January	February					
M 1	T 1	T 1	F 1	F 1 Ember	M 1	W 1
T 2	F 2 Purific. M.	W 2	S 2 Purific. M.	S 2 Ember	T 2	T 2
W 3	S 3	T 3			W 3	F 3
T 4		F 4	S 3 Septuag.	S 3 Lent 2	T 4	S 4
F 5	S 4 Septuag.	S 5	M 4	M 4	F 5 Good Fri.	
s 6 Epiphany	M 5		T 5	T 5	s 6	S 5 Easter 4
	T 6	S 6 Epiphany	W 6	W 6		M 6
S 7 Epiph. 1	W 7	M 7	T 7	T 7	S 7 **Easter Day**	T 7
M 8	T 8	T 8	F 8	F 8	M 8	W 8
T 9	F 9	W 9	S 9	S 9	T 9	T 9
W 10	S 10	T 10			W 10	F 10
T 11		F 11	S 10 Sexages.	S 10 Lent 3	T 11	S 11
F 12	S 11 Sexages.	S 12	M 11	M 11	F 12	
s 13 Hilary	M 12		T 12	T 12	S 13	S 12 Rogation
	T 13	S 13 Epiph. 1	W 13	W 13		M 13
S 14 Epiph. 2	W 14	M 14	T 14	T 14	S 14 Quasimodo	T 14
M 15	T 15	T 15	F 15	F 15	M 15	W 15
T 16	F 16	W 16	s 16	s 16	T 16	T 16 Ascension
W 17	S 17	T 17			W 17	F 17
T 18		F 18	S 17 Quinquag.	S 17 Lent 4	T 18	s 18
F 19	S 18 Quinquag.	S 19	M 18	M 18	F 19	
S 20	M 19		T 19 Shrove Tu.	T 19	S 20	S 19 Ascens. 1
	T 20 Shrove Tu.	S 20 Epiph. 2	W 20 Ash Wed.	W 20		M 20
S 21 Epiph. 3	W 21 Ash Wed.	M 21	T 21	T 21	S 21 Easter 2	T 21
M 22	T 22	T 22	F 22	F 22	M 22	W 22
T 23	F 23	W 23	S 23	S 23	T 23	T 23
W 24	S 24	T 24			W 24	F 24
T 25		F 25	S 24 Quadrag.	S 24 Passion	T 25	S 25
F 26	S 25 Quadrag.	S 26	M 25	M 25 Annunc.	F 26	
S 27	M 26		T 26	T 26	S 27	S 26 Whit Sun.
	T 27	S 27 Epiph. 3	W 27 Ember	W 27		M 27
S 28 Epiph. 4	W 28 Ember	M 28	T 28	T 28	S 28 Easter 3	T 28
M 29	T 29	T 29		F 29	M 29	W 29 Ember
T 30		W 30		S 30	T 30	T 30
W 31		T 31				F 31 Ember
				S 31 Palm		

or Common Years
or Leap Years (*in bold figures*)
ew Style years 1602, 1613, **1624**, 1697, 1765, **1776**, 1822, 1833, **1844**, 1901, **1912**, 1985, **1996**

June	July	August	September	October	November	December
1 Ember	M 1	T 1 Lammas	S 1 Trinity 13	T 1	F 1	S 1 Advent 1
2 Trinity	T 2	F 2	M 2	W 2	S 2	M 2
3	W 3	S 3	T 3	T 3	S 3 Trinity 22	T 3
4	T 4	S 4 Trinity 9	W 4	F 4	M 4	W 4
5	F 5	M 5	T 5	S 5	T 5	T 5
6 Corpus C.	S 6	T 6	F 6	S 6 Trinity 18	w 6	F 6
7	S 7 Trinity 5	W 7	s 7	M 7	T 7	S 7
8	M 8	T 8	S 8 Trinity 14	T 8	F 8	S 8 Advent 2
9 Trinity 1	T 9	F 9	M 9	W 9	S 9	M 9
10	W 10	S 10	T 10	T 10	S 10 Trinity 23	T 10
11	T 11	S 11 Trinity 10	W 11	F 11	M 11 Martin	W 11
12	F 12	M 12	T 12	S 12	T 12	T 12
13	S 13	T 13	F 13	S 13 Trinity 19	W 13	F 13
14	S 14 Trinity 6	W 14	s 14 Exalt. C.	M 14	T 14	s 14
15	M 15	T 15	S 15 Trinity 15	T 15	F 15	S 15 Advent 3
16 Trinity 2	T 16	F 16	M 16	w 16	s 16	M 16
17	W 17	S 17	T 17	T 17	S 17 Trinity 24	T 17
18	T 18	S 18 Trinity 11	w 18 Ember	F 18	M 18	w 18 Ember
19	F 19	M 19	T 19	S 19	T 19	T 19
20	S 20	T 20	F 20 Ember	S 20 Trinity 20	W 20	F 20 Ember
21	S 21 Trinity 7	W 21	s 21 Ember	M 21	T 21	s 21 Ember
22	M 22	T 22	S 22 Trinity 16	T 22	F 22	S 22 Advent 4
23 Trinity 3	T 23	F 23	M 23	W 23	S 23	M 23
24 Nat. J. Bap	W 24	S 24	T 24	T 24	S 24 Trinity 25	T 24
25	T 25	S 25 Trinity 12	w 25	F 25	M 25	w 25 Christmas
26	F 26	M 26	T 26	s 26	T 26	T 26
27	S 27	T 27	F 27	S 27 Trinity 21	W 27	F 27
28	S 28 Trinity 8	W 28	s 28	M 28	T 28	s 28
29	M 29	T 29	S 29 Trinity 17	T 29	F 29	S 29
30 Trinity 4	T 30	F 30	M 30	W 30	S 30	M 30
	W 31	S 31		T 31		T 31

Table 18   EASTER DAY

DOMINICAL LETTER
,,
,, A

Old Style years 535, **540,** 546, 619, 630, 641, 703, 714, 725, **736,** 787, 798, 809, **820,** 882, 893, **904,** 977, 983, **988,** 1067, 107
1078, 1151, 1162, 1173, 1235, 1246, 1257, **1268,** 1319, 1330, 1341, **1352,** 1414, 1425, **1436,** 1509, 1515, **1520,** 1599, 160
1610, 1683, 1694, 1705

Leap Years		January	February	March	April	May
January	February					
S 1	W 1	M 1	T 1	T 1	S 1 Palm	T 1
M 2	T 2 Purific. M.	T 2	F 2 Purific. M.	F 2 Ember	M 2	W 2
T 3	F 3	W 3	S 3	s 3 Ember	T 3	T 3
W 4	S 4	T 4			W 4	F 4
T 5		F 5	S 4 Septuag.	S 4 Lent 2	T 5	s 5
F 6 Epiphany	S 5 Septuag.	s 6 Epiphany	M 5	M 5	F 6 Good Fri.	
s 7	M 6		T 6	T 6	s 7	S 6 Easter 4
	T 7	S 7 Epiph. 1	w 7	w 7		M 7
S 8 Epiph. 1	w 8	M 8	T 8	T 8	S 8 **Easter Day**	T 8
M 9	T 9	T 9	F 9	F 9	M 9	W 9
T 10	F 10	W 10	s 10	s 10	T 10	T 10
W 11	s 11	T 11			W 11	F 11
T 12		F 12	S 11 Sexages.	S 11 Lent 3	T 12	s 12
F 13 Hilary	S 12 Sexages.	s 13 Hilary	M 12	M 12	F 13	
s 14	M 13		T 13	T 13	s 14	S 13 Rogation
	T 14	S 14 Epiph. 2	w 14	w 14		M 14
S 15 Epiph. 2	w 15	M 15	T 15	T 15	S 15 Quasimodo	T 15
M 16	T 16	T 16	F 16	F 16	M 16	w 16
T 17	F 17	W 17	s 17	s 17	T 17	T 17 Ascension
w 18	s 18	T 18			w 18	F 18
T 19		F 19	S 18 Quinquag.	S 18 Lent 4	T 19	s 19
F 20	S 19 Quinquag.	s 20	M 19	M 19	F 20	
S 21	M 20		T 20 Shrove Tu.	T 20	s 21	S 20 Ascens. 1
	T 21 Shrove Tu.	S 21 Epiph. 3	w 21 Ash Wed.	w 21		M 21
S 22 Epiph. 3	w 22 Ash Wed.	M 22	T 22	T 22	S 22 Easter 2	T 22
M 23	T 23	T 23	F 23	F 23	M 23	w 23
T 24	F 24	W 24	s 24 Matthias	s 24	T 24	T 24
W 25	s 25 Matthias	T 25			W 25	F 25
T 26		F 26	S 25 Quadrag.	S 25 Passion	T 26	s 26
F 27	S 26 Quadrag.	s 27	M 26	M 26	F 27	
s 28	M 27		T 27	T 27	s 28	S 27 Whit Sun
	T 28	S 28 Epiph. 4	w 28 Ember	w 28		M 28
S 29 Epiph. 4	w 29 Ember	M 29		T 29	S 29 Easter 3	T 29
M 30		T 30		F 30	M 30	w 30 Ember
T 31		W 31		s 31		T 31

ᴏʀ Cᴏᴍᴍᴏɴ Yᴇᴀʀs
ᴏʀ Lᴇᴀᴘ Yᴇᴀʀs (*in bold figures*)
ᴇw Style years 1635, **1640**, 1703, **1708**, 1787, **1792**, 1798, 1849, 1855, **1860**, 1917, **1928**

June	July	August	September	October	November	December
1 Ember	S 1 Trinity 4	w 1 Lammas	s 1	M 1	T 1	s 1
2 Ember	M 2	T 2		T 2	F 2	
	T 3	F 3	S 2 Trinity 13	w 3	s 3	S 2 Advent 1
3 Trinity	w 4	s 4	M 3	T 4		M 3
4	T 5		T 4	F 5	S 4 Trinity 22	T 4
5	F 6	S 5 Trinity 9	w 5	s 6	M 5	w 5
6	s 7	M 6	T 6		T 6	T 6
7 Corpus C.		T 7	F 7	S 7 Trinity 18	w 7	F 7
8	S 8 Trinity 5	w 8	s 8	M 8	T 8	s 8
9	M 9	T 9		T 9	F 9	
	T 10	F 10	S 9 Trinity 14	w 10	s 10	S 9 Advent 2
10 Trinity 1	w 11	s 11	M 10	T 11		M 10
11	T 12		T 11	F 12	S 11 Trinity 23	T 11
12	F 13	S 12 Trinity 10	w 12	s 13	M 12	w 12
13	s 14	M 13	T 13		T 13	T 13
14		T 14	F 14 Exalt. C.	S 14 Trinity 19	w 14	F 14
15	S 15 Trinity 6	w 15	s 15	M 15	T 15	s 15
16	M 16	T 16		T 16	F 16	
	T 17	F 17	S 16 Trinity 15	w 17	s 17	S 16 Advent 3
17 Trinity 2	w 18	s 18	M 17	T 18		M 17
18	T 19		T 18	F 19	S 18 Trinity 24	T 18
19	F 20	S 19 Trinity 11	w 19 Ember	s 20	M 19	w 19 Ember
20	s 21	M 20	T 20		T 20	T 20
21		T 21	F 21 Ember	S 21 Trinity 20	w 21	F 21 Ember
22	S 22 Trinity 7	w 22	s 22 Ember	M 22	T 22	s 22 Ember
23	M 23	T 23		T 23	F 23	
	T 24	F 24	S 23 Trinity 16	w 24	s 24	S 23 Advent 4
24 Trinity 3	w 25	s 25	M 24	T 25		M 24
25	T 26		T 25	F 26	S 25 Trinity 25	T 25 Christmas
26	F 27	S 26 Trinity 12	w 26	s 27	M 26	w 26
27	s 28	M 27	T 27		T 27	T 27
28		T 28	F 28	S 28 Trinity 21	w 28	F 28
29	S 29 Trinity 8	w 29	s 29 Michael A.	M 29	T 29	s 29
30	M 30	T 30		T 30	F 30	
	T 31	F 31	S 30 Trinity 17	w 31		S 30 Advent 5
						M 31

Table 19

EASTER DAY

DOMINICAL LETTER

„　　　„　I

Old Style years 551, 562, 573, 635, 646, 657, **668**, 730, 741, 752, 825, **836**, 915, **920**, 999, 1010, 1083, 1094, 1105, 1167, 11
1189, **1200**, 1262, 1273, **1284**, 1357, **1368**, 1447, **1452**, 1531, 1542, 1615, 1626, 1637, 1699, 1710, 1721, **1732**

Leap Years		January	February	March	April	May
January	February					
S 1	T 1	S 1	W 1	W 1 Ember	S 1	M 1
	W 2 Purific. M.	M 2	T 2 Purific. M.	T 2		T 2
S 2	T 3	T 3	F 3	F 3 Ember	S 2 Palm	W 3
M 3	F 4	W 4	S 4	S 4 Ember	M 3	T 4
T 4	S 5	T 5			T 4	F 5
W 5		F 6 Epiphany	S 5 Septuag.	S 5 Lent 2	W 5	S 6
T 6 Epiphany	S 6 Septuag.	S 7	M 6	M 6	T 6	
F 7	M 7		T 7	T 7	F 7 Good Fri.	S 7 Easter 4
S 8	T 8	S 8 Epiph. 1	W 8	W 8	S 8	M 8
	W 9	M 9	T 9	T 9		T 9
S 9 Epiph. 1	T 10	T 10	F 10	F 10	S 9 Easter Day	W 10
M 10	F 11	W 11	S 11	S 11	M 10	T 11
T 11	S 12	T 12			T 11	F 12
W 12		F 13 Hilary	S 12 Sexages.	S 12 Lent 3	W 12	S 13
T 13 Hilary	S 13 Sexages.	S 14	M 13	M 13	T 13	
F 14	M 14		T 14	T 14	F 14	S 14 Rogation
S 15	T 15	S 15 Epiph. 2	W 15	W 15	S 15	M 15
	W 16	M 16	T 16	T 16		T 16
S 16 Epiph. 2	T 17	T 17	F 17	F 17	S 16 Quasimodo	W 17
M 17	F 18	W 18	S 18	S 18	M 17	T 18 Ascension
T 18	S 19	T 19			T 18	F 19
W 19		F 20	S 19 Quinquag.	S 19 Lent 4	W 19	S 20
T 20	S 20 Quinquag.	S 21	M 20	M 20	T 20	
F 21	M 21		T 21 Shrove Tu.	T 21	F 21	S 21 Ascens. 1
S 22	T 22 Shrove Tu.	S 22 Epiph. 3	W 22 Ash Wed.	W 22	S 22	M 22
	W 23 Ash Wed.	M 23	T 23	T 23		T 23
S 23 Epiph. 3	T 24	T 24	F 24 Matthias	F 24	S 23 Easter 2	W 24
M 24	F 25 Matthias	W 25	S 25	S 25 Annunc.	M 24	T 25
T 25	S 26	T 26			T 25	F 26
W 26		F 27	S 26 Quadrag.	S 26 Passion	W 26	S 27
T 27	S 27 Quadrag.	S 28	M 27	M 27	T 27	
F 28	M 28		T 28	T 28	F 28	S 28 Whit Sun.
S 29	T 29	S 29 Epiph. 4		W 29	S 29	M 29
		M 30		T 30		T 30
S 30 Epiph. 4		T 31		F 31	S 30 Easter 3	W 31 Ember
M 31						

r COMMON YEARS

r LEAP YEARS (*in bold figures*)

w Style years 1651, 1662, 1719, **1724** (German Protestant Style), 1730, 1871, 1882, 1939, **1944,** 1950

June	July	August	September	October	November	December
1	S 1	T 1 Lammas	F 1	§ 1 Trinity 17	W 1	F 1
2 Ember	W 2	W 2	S 2	M 2	T 2	S 2
3 Ember	T 3	T 3		T 3	F 3	
	§ 2 Trinity 4	F 4	§ 3 Trinity 13	W 4	S 4	§ 3 Advent 1
4 Trinity	M 3	S 5	M 4	T 5		M 4
5	T 4		T 5	F 6	§ 5 Trinity 22	T 5
6	W 5	§ 6 Trinity 9	W 6	S 7	M 6	W 6
7	T 6	M 7	T 7		T 7	T 7
8 Corpus C.	F 7	T 8	F 8	§ 8 Trinity 18	W 8	F 8
9	S 8	W 9	S 9	M 9	T 9	S 9
10		T 10		T 10	F 10	
	§ 9 Trinity 5	F 11	§ 10 Trinity 14	W 11	S 11 Martin	§ 10 Advent 2
11 Trinity 1	M 10	S 12	M 11	T 12		M 11
12	T 11		T 12	F 13	§ 12 Trinity 23	T 12
13	W 12	§ 13 Trinity 10	W 13	S 14	M 13	W 13
14	T 13	M 14	T 14 Exalt. C.		T 14	T 14
15	F 14	T 15	F 15	§ 15 Trinity 19	W 15	F 15
16	S 15	W 16	S 16	M 16	T 16	S 16
17		T 17		T 17	F 17	
	§ 16 Trinity 6	F 18	§ 17 Trinity 15	W 18	S 18	§ 17 Advent 3
18 Trinity 2	M 17	S 19	M 18	T 19		M 18
19	T 18		T 19	F 20	§ 19 Trinity 24	T 19
20	W 19	§ 20 Trinity 11	W 20 Ember	S 21	M 20	W 20 Ember
21	T 20	M 21	T 21		T 21	T 21
22	F 21	T 22	F 22 Ember	§ 22 Trinity 20	W 22	F 22 Ember
23	S 22	W 23	S 23 Ember	M 23	T 23	S 23 Ember
24 Nat. J. Bap		T 24		T 24	F 24	
	§ 23 Trinity 7	F 25	§ 24 Trinity 16	W 25	S 25	§ 24 Advent 4
25 Trinity 3	M 24	S 26	M 25	T 26		M 25 Christmas
26	T 25		T 26	F 27	§ 26 Trinity 25	T 26
27	W 26	§ 27 Trinity 12	W 27	S 28	M 27	W 27
28	T 27	M 28	T 28		T 28	T 28
29	F 28	T 29	F 29 Michael A.	§ 29 Trinity 21	W 29	F 29
30	S 29	W 30	S 30	M 30	T 30	S 30
		T 31		T 31		
	§ 30 Trinity 8					§ 31
	M 31					

Table 20   EASTER DAY

Old Style years 505, 567, 578, 589, **600**, 662, 673, **684**, 757, **768**, 847, **852**, 931, 942, 1015, 1026, 1037, 1099, 1110, 1121, 11... 1194, 1205, **1216**, 1289, **1300**, 1379, **1384**, 1463, 1474, 1547, 1558, 1569, 1631, 1642, 1653, **1664**, 1726, 1737, **1748**

	Leap Years January	Leap Years February	January	February	March	April	May
1	F 1	M 1	S 1	T 1	T 1	F 1	S 1 Easter 3
2	S 2	T 2 Purific. M.	S 2	W 2 Purific. M.	W 2 Ember	S 2	M 2
3	S 3	W 3	M 3	T 3	T 3	S 3 Palm	T 3
4	M 4	T 4	T 4	F 4	F 4 Ember	M 4	W 4
5	T 5	F 5	W 5	S 5	S 5 Ember	T 5	T 5
6	W 6 Epiphany	S 6	T 6 Epiphany	S 6 Septuag.	S 6 Lent 2	W 6	F 6
7	T 7	S 7 Septuag.	F 7	M 7	M 7	T 7	S 7
8	F 8	M 8	S 8	T 8	T 8	F 8 Good Fri.	S 8 Easter 4
9	S 9	T 9	S 9 Epiph. 1	W 9	W 9	S 9	M 9
10	S 10 Epiph. 1	W 10	M 10	T 10	T 10	S 10 **Easter Day**	T 10
11	M 11	T 11	T 11	F 11	F 11	M 11	W 11
12	T 12	F 12	W 12	S 12	S 12	T 12	T 12
13	W 13 Hilary	S 13	T 13 Hilary	S 13 Sexages.	S 13 Lent 3	W 13	F 13
14	T 14	S 14 Sexages.	F 14	M 14	M 14	T 14	S 14
15	F 15	M 15	S 15	T 15	T 15	F 15	S 15 Rogation
16	S 16	T 16	S 16 Epiph. 2	W 16	W 16	S 16	M 16
17	S 17 Epiph. 2	W 17	M 17	T 17	T 17	S 17 Quasimodo	T 17
18	M 18	T 18	T 18	F 18	F 18	M 18	W 18
19	T 19	F 19	W 19	S 19	S 19	T 19	T 19 Ascension
20	W 20	S 20	T 20	S 20 Quinquag.	S 20 Lent 4	W 20	F 20
21	T 21	S 21 Quinquag.	F 21	M 21	M 21	T 21	S 21
22	F 22	M 22	S 22	T 22 Shrove Tu.	T 22	F 22	S 22 Ascens.
23	S 23	T 23 Shrove Tu.	S 23 Epiph. 3	W 23 Ash Wed.	W 23	S 23	M 23
24	S 24 Epiph. 3	W 24 Ash Wed.	M 24	T 24 Matthias	T 24	S 24 Easter 2	T 24
25	M 25	T 25 Matthias	T 25	F 25	F 25 Annunc.	M 25	W 25
26	T 26	F 26	W 26	S 26	S 26	T 26	T 26
27	W 27	S 27	T 27	S 27 Quadrag.	S 27 Passion	W 27	F 27
28	T 28	S 28 Quadrag.	F 28	M 28	M 28	T 28	S 28
29	F 29	M 29	S 29		T 29	F 29	S 29 Whit Su
30	S 30		S 30 Epiph. 4		W 30	S 30	M 30
31	S 31 Epiph. 4		M 31		T 31		T 31

R COMMON YEARS

R LEAP YEARS (*in bold figures*)

w Style years 1583, 1594, 1605, 1667, 1678, 1689, 1735 1746, 1757, 1803, 1814, 1887, 1898, 1955, 1966, 1977

June	July	August	September	October	November	December
1 Ember	F 1	M 1 Lammas	T 1	S 1	T 1	T 1
2	S 2	T 2	F 2		W 2	F 2
3 Ember		W 3	S 3	**S** 2 Trinity 17	T 3	S 3
4 Ember	**S** 3 Trinity 4	T 4		M 3	F 4	
	M 4	F 5	**S** 4 Trinity 13	T 4	S 5	**S** 4 Advent 2
5 Trinity	T 5	S 6	M 5	W 5		M 5
6	W 6		T 6	T 6	**S** 6 Trinity 22	T 6
7	T 7	**S** 7 Trinity 9	W 7	F 7	M 7	W 7
8	F 8	M 8	T 8	S 8	T 8	T 8
9 Corpus C.	S 9	T 9	F 9		W 9	F 9
10		W 10	S 10		T 10	S 10
11	**S** 10 Trinity 5	T 11		**S** 9 Trinity 18	F 11 Martin	
	M 11	F 12	**S** 11 Trinity 14	M 10	S 12	**S** 11 Advent 3
12 Trinity 1	T 12	S 13	M 12	T 11		M 12
13	W 13		T 13	W 12	**S** 13 Trinity 23	T 13
14	T 14	**S** 14 Trinity 10	W 14 Exalt. C.	T 13	M 14	W 14 Ember
15	F 15	M 15	T 15	F 14	T 15	T 15
16	S 16	T 16	F 16	S 15	W 16	F 16 Ember
17		W 17	S 17		T 17	S 17 Ember
18	**S** 17 Trinity 6	T 18		**S** 16 Trinity 19	F 18	
	M 18	F 19	**S** 18 Trinity 15	M 17	S 19	**S** 18 Advent 4
19 Trinity 2	T 19	S 20	M 19	T 18		M 19
20	W 20		T 20	W 19	**S** 20 Trinity 24	T 20
21	T 21	**S** 21 Trinity 11	W 21 Ember	T 20	M 21	W 21
22	F 22	M 22	T 22	F 21	T 22	T 22
23	S 23	T 23	F 23 Ember	S 22	W 23	F 23
24 Nat. J. Bap		W 24	S 24 Ember		T 24	S 24
25	**S** 24 Trinity 7	T 25		**S** 23 Trinity 20	F 25	
	M 25	F 26	**S** 25 Trinity 16	M 24	S 26	**S** 25 Christmas
26 Trinity 3	T 26	S 27	M 26	T 25		M 26
27	W 27		T 27	W 26	**S** 27 Advent 1	T 27
28	T 28	**S** 28 Trinity 12	W 28	T 27	M 28	W 28
29	F 29	M 29	T 29 Michael A.	F 28	T 29	T 29
30	S 30	T 30	F 30	S 29	W 30	F 30
		W 31				S 31
	S 31 Trinity 8			**S** 30 Trinity 21		
				M 31		

Table 21

EASTER DAY

DOMINICAL LETTER
,,   ,,

Old Style years 510, 521, **532**, 594, 605, **616**, 689, 695, **700**, 779, **784**, 790, 863, 874, 885, 947, 958, 969, **980**, 1031, 1042, 1c
1064, 1126, 1137, **1148**, 1221, 1227, **1232**, 1311, **1316**, 1322, 1395, 1406, 1417, 1479, 1490, 1501, **1512**, 1563, 1574, 15
1596, 1658, 1669, **1680**

Leap Years		January	February	March	April	May
January	**February**					
T 1	§ 1 Epiph. 4	F 1	M 1	M 1	T 1	S 1
F 2	M 2 Purific. M.	S 2	T 2 Purific. M.	T 2	F 2	
S 3	T 3		W 3	W 3 Ember	S 3	
	W 4		T 4	T 4		§ 2 Easter 3
§ 4	T 5	§ 3	F 5	F 5 Ember		M 3
M 5	F 6	M 4	s 6	s 6 Ember	§ 4 Palm	T 4
T 6 Epiphany	S 7	T 5			M 5	W 5
W 7		W 6 Epiphany			T 6	T 6
T 8	§ 8 Septuag.	T 7	§ 7 Septuag.	§ 7 Lent 2	W 7	F 7
F 9	M 9	F 8	M 8	M 8	T 8	s 8
S 10	T 10	S 9	T 9	T 9	F 9 Good Fri.	
	W 11		W 10	W 10	S 10	
§ 11 Epiph. 1	T 12	§ 10 Epiph. 1	T 11	T 11		§ 9 Easter 4
M 12	F 13	M 11	F 12	F 12		M 10
T 13 Hilary	S 14	T 12	S 13	S 13	§ 11 **Easter Day**	T 11
W 14		W 13 Hilary			M 12	W 12
T 15	§ 15 Sexages.	T 14	§ 14 Sexages.	§ 14 Lent 3	T 13	T 13
F 16	M 16	F 15	M 15	M 15	W 14	F 14
S 17	T 17	s 16	T 16	T 16	T 15	S 15
	W 18		W 17	W 17	T 16	
§ 18 Epiph. 2	T 19	§ 17 Epiph. 2	T 18	T 18	S 17	§ 16 Rogation
M 19	F 20	M 18	F 19	F 19		M 17
T 20	S 21	T 19	S 20	S 20	§ 18 Quasimodo	T 18
W 21		W 20			M 19	W 19
T 22	§ 22 Quinquag.	T 21	§ 21 Quinquag.	§ 21 Lent 4	T 20	T 20 Ascension
F 23	M 23	F 22	M 22	M 22	W 21	F 21
S 24	T 24 Shrove Tu.	S 23	T 23 Shrove Tu.	T 23	T 22	S 22
	W 25 Ash Wed.		W 24 Ash Wed.	W 24	F 23	
§ 25 Epiph. 3	T 26	§ 24 Epiph. 3	T 25	T 25 Annunc.	S 24	§ 23 Ascens. 1
M 26	F 27	M 25	F 26	F 26		M 24
T 27	s 28	T 26	S 27	S 27	§ 25 Easter 2	T 25
W 28		W 27			M 26	W 26
T 29	§ 29 Quadrag.	T 28	§ 28 Quadrag.	§ 28 Passion	T 27	T 27
F 30		F 29		M 29	W 28	F 28
s 31		S 30		T 30	T 29	S 29
				W 31	F 30	
		§ 31 Epiph. 4				§ 30 Whit Sun.
						M 31

OR COMMON YEARS
OR LEAP YEARS (*in bold figures*)
w Style years 1599, 1610, 1621, **1632**, 1694, 1700 (*not* a leap year), 1751, 1762, 1773, **1784**, 1819, 1830, 1841, **1852**, 1909, 1971, 1982, 1993

June	July	August	September	October	November	December
1	T 1	§ 1 Trinity 8	W 1	F 1	M 1	W 1
2 Ember	F 2	M 2	T 2	S 2	T 2	T 2
3	S 3	T 3	F 3		W 3	F 3
4 Ember		W 4	S 4		T 4	S 4
5 Ember	§ 4 Trinity 4	T 5		§ 3 Trinity 17	F 5	
	M 5	F 6	§ 5 Trinity 13	M 4	s 6	§ 5 Advent 2
6 Trinity	T 6	S 7	M 6	T 5		M 6
7	W 7		T 7	w 6	§ 7 Trinity 22	T 7
8	T 8	§ 8 Trinity 9	W 8	T 7	M 8	W 8
9	F 9	M 9	T 9	F 8	T 9	T 9
10 Corpus C.	S 10	T 10	F 10	S 9	W 10	F 10
11		W 11	S 11		T 11 Martin	S 11
12	§ 11 Trinity 5	T 12		§ 10 Trinity 18·	F 12	
	M 12	F 13	§ 12 Trinity 14	M 11	S 13	§ 12 Advent 3
13 Trinity 1	T 13	S 14	M 13	T 12		M 13
14	W 14		T 14 Exalt. C.	W 13	§ 14 Trinity 23	T 14
15	T 15	§ 15 Trinity 10	W 15 Ember	T 14	M 15	w 15 Ember
16	F 16	M 16	T 16	F 15	T 16	T 16
17	S 17	T 17	F 17 Ember	S 16	W 17	F 17 Ember
18		W 18	s 18 Ember		T 18	s 18 Ember
19	§ 18 Trinity 6	T 19		§ 17 Trinity 19	F 19	
	M 19	F 20	§ 19 Trinity 15	M 18	S 20	§ 19 Advent 4
20 Trinity 2	T 20	S 21	M 20	T 19		M 20
21	W 21		T 21	W 20	§ 21 Trinity 24	T 21
22	T 22	§ 22 Trinity 11	W 22	T 21	M 22	W 22
23	F 23	M 23	T 23	F 22	T 23	T 23
24 Nat. J. Bap	s 24	T 24	F 24	S 23	W 24	F 24
25		W 25	s 25		T 25	s 25 Christmas
26	§ 25 Trinity 7	T 26		§ 24 Trinity 20	F 26	
	M 26	F 27	§ 26 Trinity 16	M 25	S 27	§ 26
27 Trinity 3	T 27	s 28	M 27	T 26		M 27
28	W 28		T 28	W 27	§ 28 Advent 1	T 28
29	T 29	§ 29 Trinity 12	W 29 Michael A.	T 28	M 29	W 29
30	F 30	M 30	T 30	F 29	T 30	T 30
	S 31	T 31		S 30		F 31
				§ 31 Trinity 21		

Table 22

EASTER DAY
DOMINICAL LETTER I
,,   ,, EI

Old Style years 537, **548**, 627, **632**, 711, 722, 795, 806, 817, 879, 890, 901, **912**, 974, 985, **996**, 1069, **1080**, 1159, **1164**, 124
1254, 1327, 1338, 1349, 1411, 1422, 1433, **1444**, 1506, 1517, **1528**, 1601, **1612**, 1691, **1696**

Leap Years		January	February	March	April	May
January	February					
W 1	S 1	T 1	S 1 Epiph. 4	S 1 Quadrag.	W 1	F 1
T 2	F 2	M 2 Purific. M.	M 2	T 2	S 2
F 3	S 2 Epiph. 4	S 3	T 3	T 3	F 3	
S 4	M 3	W 4	W 4 Ember	S 4	S 3 Easter 3
	T 4	S 4	T 5	T 5		M 4
S 5	W 5	M 5	F 6	F 6 Ember	S 5 Palm	T 5
M 6 Epiphany	T 6	T 6 Epiphany	S 7	S 7 Ember	M 6	W 6
T 7	F 7	W 7			T 7	T 7
W 8	S 8	T 8	S 8 Septuag.	S 8 Lent 2	W 8	F 8
T 9		F 9	M 9	M 9	T 9	S 9
F 10	S 9 Septuag.	S 10	T 10	T 10	F 10 Good Fri.	
S 11	M 10		W 11	W 11	S 11	S 10 Easter 4
	T 11	S 11 Epiph. 1	T 12	T 12		M 11
S 12 Epiph. 1	W 12	M 12	F 13	F 13	S 12 **Easter Day**	T 12
M 13 Hilary	T 13	T 13 Hilary	S 14	S 14	M 13	W 13
T 14	F 14	W 14			T 14	T 14
W 15	S 15	T 15	S 15 Sexages.	S 15 Lent 3	W 15	F 15
T 16		F 16	M 16	M 16	T 16	S 16
F 17	S 16 Sexages.	S 17	T 17	T 17	F 17	
S 18	M 17		W 18	W 18	S 18	S 17 Rogation
	T 18	S 18 Epiph. 2	T 19	T 19		M 18
S 19 Epiph. 2	W 19	M 19	F 20	F 20	S 19 Quasimodo	T 19
M 20	T 20	T 20	S 21	S 21	M 20	W 20
T 21	F 21	W 21			T 21	T 21 Ascension
W 22	S 22	T 22	S 22 Quinquag.	S 22 Lent 4	W 22	F 22
T 23		F 23	M 23	M 23	T 23	S 23
F 24	S 23 Quinquag.	S 24	T 24 Shrove Tu.	T 24	F 24	
S 25	M 24		W 25 Ash Wed.	W 25 Annunc.	S 25	S 24 Ascens. 1
	T 25 Shrove Tu.	S 25 Epiph. 3	T 26	T 26		M 25
S 26 Epiph. 3	W 26 Ash Wed.	M 26	F 27	F 27	S 26 Easter 2	T 26
M 27	T 27	T 27	S 28	S 28	M 27	W 27
T 28	F 28	W 28			T 28	T 28
W 29	S 29	T 29		S 29 Passion	W 29	F 29
T 30		F 30		M 30	T 30	S 30
F 31		S 31		T 31		
						S 31 Whit Sun.

or Common Years
or Leap Years (*in bold figures*)
ew Style years 1626, 1637, **1648**, 1705, **1716**, 1789, 1846, 1857, **1868**, 1903, 1914, 1925, 1936, 1998

June	July	August	September	October	November	December
1	W 1	S 1 Lammas	T 1	T 1	S 1 Trinity 21	T 1
2	T 2		W 2	F 2	M 2	W 2
3 Ember	F 3	S 2 Trinity 8	T 3	S 3	T 3	T 3
4	S 4	M 3	F 4		W 4	F 4
5 Ember		T 4	S 5		T 5	S 5
6 Ember	S 5 Trinity 4	W 5		S 4 Trinity 17	F 6	
	M 6	T 6	S 6 Trinity 13	M 5	S 7	S 6 Advent 2
7 Trinity	T 7	F 7	M 7	T 6		M 7
8	W 8	S 8	T 8	W 7	S 8 Trinity 22	T 8
9	T 9		W 9	T 8	M 9	W 9
10	F 10	S 9 Trinity 9	T 10	F 9	T 10	T 10
11 Corpus C.	S 11	M 10	F 11	S 10	W 11 Martin	F 11
12		T 11	S 12		T 12	S 12
13	S 12 Trinity 5	W 12		S 11 Trinity 18	F 13	
	M 13	T 13	S 13 Trinity 14	M 12	S 14	S 13 Advent 3
14 Trinity 1	T 14	F 14	M 14 Exalt. C.	T 13		M 14
15	W 15	S 15	T 15	W 14	S 15 Trinity 23	T 15
16	T 16		W 16 Ember	T 15	M 16	W 16 Ember
17	F 17	S 16 Trinity 10	T 17	F 16	T 17	T 17
18	S 18	M 17	F 18 Ember	S 17	W 18	F 18 Ember
19		T 18	S 19 Ember		T 19	S 19 Ember
20	S 19 Trinity 6	W 19		S 18 Trinity 19	F 20	
	M 20	T 20	S 20 Trinity 15	M 19	S 21	S 20 Advent 4
21 Trinity 2	T 21	F 21	M 21	T 20		M 21
22	W 22	S 22	T 22	W 21	S 22 Trinity 24	T 22
23	T 23		W 23	T 22	M 23	W 23
24 Nat. J. Bap	F 24	S 23 Trinity 11	T 24	F 23	T 24	T 24
25	S 25	M 24	F 25	S 24	W 25	F 25 Christmas
26		T 25	S 26		T 26	S 26
27	S 26 Trinity 7	W 26		S 25 Trinity 20	F 27	
	M 27	T 27	S 27 Trinity 16	M 26	S 28	S 27
28 Trinity 3	T 28	F 28	M 28	T 27		M 28
29	W 29	S 29	T 29 Michael A.	W 28	S 29 Advent 1	T 29
30	T 30		W 30	T 29	M 30	W 30
	F 31	S 30 Trinity 12		F 30		T 31
		M 31		S 31		

DOMINICAL LETTER
   ,,   ,,   F

Old Style years 559, **564,** 643, 654, 727, 738, 749, 811, 822, 833, **844,** 906, 917, **928,** 1001, **1012,** 1091, **1096,** 1175, 1186, 125
1270, 1281, 1343, 1354, 1365, **1376,** 1438, 1449, **1460,** 1533, **1544,** 1623, **1628,** 1707, 1718

Leap Years		January	February	March	April	May
January	February					
T 1	F 1	W 1	S 1	S 1	T 1	T 1
W 2	S 2 Purific. M.	T 2			W 2	F 2
T 3		F 3	S 2 Epiph. 4	S 2 Quadrag.	T 3	S 3
F 4	S 3 Epiph. 4	S 4	M 3	M 3	F 4	
S 5	M 4		T 4	T 4	S 5	S 4 Easter 3
	T 5	S 5	W 5	W 5 Ember		M 5
S 6 Epiphany	W 6	M 6 Epiphany	T 6	T 6	S 6 Palm	T 6
M 7	T 7	T 7	F 7	F 7 Ember	M 7	W 7
T 8	F 8	W 8	S 8	S 8 Ember	T 8	T 8
W 9	S 9	T 9			W 9	F 9
T 10		F 10	S 9 Septuag.	S 9 Lent 2	T 10	S 10
F 11	S 10 Septuag.	S 11	M 10	M 10	F 11 Good Fri.	
S 12	M 11		T 11	T 11	S 12	S 11 Easter 4
	T 12	S 12 Epiph. 1	W 12	W 12		M 12
S 13 Epiph. 1	W 13	M 13 Hilary	T 13	T 13	S 13 **Easter Day**	T 13
M 14	T 14	T 14	F 14	F 14	M 14	W 14
T 15	F 15	W 15	S 15	S 15	T 15	T 15
W 16	S 16	T 16			W 16	F 16
T 17		F 17	S 16 Sexages.	S 16 Lent 3	T 17	S 17
F 18	S 17 Sexages.	S 18	M 17	M 17	F 18	
S 19	M 18		T 18	T 18	S 19	S 18 Rogation
	T 19	S 19 Epiph. 2	W 19	W 19		M 19
S 20 Epiph. 2	W 20	M 20	T 20	T 20	S 20 Quasimodo	T 20
M 21	T 21	T 21	F 21	F 21	M 21	W 21
T 22	F 22	W 22	S 22	S 22	T 22	T 22 Ascension
W 23	S 23	T 23			W 23	F 23
T 24		F 24	S 23 Quinquag.	S 23 Lent 4	T 24	S 24
F 25	S 24 Quinquag.	S 25	M 24 Matthias	M 24	F 25	
S 26	M 25 Matthias		T 25 Shrove Tu.	T 25 Annunc.	S 26	S 25 Ascens. 1
	T 26 Shrove Tu.	S 26 Epiph. 3	W 26 Ash Wed.	W 26		M 26
S 27 Epiph. 3	W 27 Ash Wed.	M 27	T 27	T 27	S 27 Easter 2	T 27
M 28	T 28	T 28	F 28	F 28	M 28	W 28
T 29	F 29	W 29		S 29	T 29	T 29
W 30		T 30		W 26	W 30	F 30
T 31		F 31		S 30 Passion		S 31
				M 31		

128

OR COMMON YEARS
OR LEAP YEARS (*in bold figures*)
w Style years 1653, 1659, **1664**, 1721, 1727, **1732**, 1800 (*not* a leap year), 1873, 1879, **1884**, 1941, **1952**

June
1 Whit Sun.
2
3
4 Ember
5
6 Ember
7 Ember
8 Trinity
9
10
11
12 Corpus C.
13
14
15 Trinity 1
16
17
18
19
20
21
22 Trinity 2
23
24 Nat. J. Bap
25
26
27
28
29 Trinity 3
30

July
T 1
W 2
T 3
F 4
S 5
S 6 Trinity 4
M 7
T 8
W 9
T 10
F 11
S 12
S 13 Trinity 5
M 14
T 15
W 16
T 17
F 18
S 19
S 20 Trinity 6
M 21
T 22
W 23
T 24
F 25
S 26
S 27 Trinity 7
M 28
T 29
W 30
T 31

August
F 1 Lammas
S 2
S 3 Trinity 8
M 4
T 5
W 6
T 7
F 8
S 9
S 10 Trinity 9
M 11
T 12
W 13
T 14
F 15
S 16
S 17 Trinity 10
M 18
T 19
W 20
T 21
F 22
S 23
S 24 Trinity 11
M 25
T 26
W 27
T 28
F 29
S 30
S 31 Trinity 12

September
M 1
T 2
W 3
T 4
F 5
S 6
S 7 Trinity 13
M 8
T 9
W 10
T 11
F 12
S 13
S 14 Trinity 14
M 15
T 16
W 17 Ember
T 18
F 19 Ember
S 20 Ember
S 21 Trinity 15
M 22
T 23
W 24
T 25
F 26
S 27
S 28 Trinity 16
M 29 Michael A.
T 30

October
W 1
T 2
F 3
S 4
S 5 Trinity 17
M 6
T 7
W 8
T 9
F 10
S 11
S 12 Trinity 18
M 13
T 14
W 15
T 16
F 17
S 18
S 19 Trinity 19
M 20
T 21
W 22
T 23
F 24
S 25
S 26 Trinity 20
M 27
T 28
W 29
T 30
F 31

November
S 1
S 2 Trinity 21
M 3
T 4
W 5
T 6
F 7
S 8
S 9 Trinity 22
M 10
T 11 Martin
W 12
T 13
F 14
S 15
S 16 Trinity 23
M 17
T 18
W 19
T 20
F 21
S 22
S 23 Trinity 24
M 24
T 25
W 26
T 27
F 28
S 29
S 30 Advent 1

December
M 1
T 2
W 3
T 4
F 5
S 6
S 7 Advent 2
M 8
T 9
W 10
T 11
F 12
S 13
S 14 Advent 3
M 15
T 16
W 17 Ember
T 18
F 19 Ember
S 20 Ember
S 21 Advent 4
M 22
T 23
W 24
T 25 Christmas
F 26
S 27
S 28
M 29
T 30
W 31

Table 24

EASTER DAY

DOMINICAL LETTER
„   „   C

Old Style years 502, 575, 586, 597, 659, 670, 681, **692**, 743, 754, 765, **776**, 838, 849, **860**, 933, 939, **944**, 1023, **1028**, 10
1107, 1118, 1129, 1191, 1202, 1213, **1224**, 1275, 1286, 1297, **1308**, 1370, 1381, **1392**, 1465, 1471, **1476**, 1555, **1560**, 15
1639, 1650, 1661, 1723, 1734, 1745

Leap Years		January	February	March	April	May
January	February					
M 1	T 1	T 1	F 1	F 1	M 1	W 1
T 2	F 2 Purific. M.	W 2	S 2 Purific M.	S 2	T 2	T 2
W 3	S 3	T 3			W 3	F 3
T 4		F 4	S 3 Epiph. 4	S 3 Quadrag.	T 4	S 4
F 5	S 4 Epiph. 5	S 5	M 4	M 4	F 5	
S 6 Epiphany	M 5		T 5	T 5	S 6	S 5 Easter 3
	T 6	S 6 Epiphany	W 6	W 6 Ember		M 6
S 7 Epiph. 1	W 7	M 7	T 7	T 7	S 7 Palm	T 7
M 8	T 8	T 8	F 8	F 8 Ember	M 8	W 8
T 9	F 9	W 9	S 9	S 9 Ember	T 9	T 9
W 10	S 10	T 10			W 10	F 10
T 11		F 11	S 10 Septuag.	S 10 Lent 2	T 11	S 11
F 12	S 11 Septuag.	S 12	M 11	M 11	F 12 Good Fri.	
S 13 Hilary	M 12		T 12	T 12	S 13	S 12 Easter 4
	T 13	S 13 Epiph. 1	W 13	W 13		M 13
S 14 Epiph. 2	W 14	M 14	T 14	T 14	S 14 **Easter Day**	T 14
M 15	T 15	T 15	F 15	F 15	M 15	W 15
T 16	F 16	W 16	S 16	S 16	T 16	T 16
W 17	S 17	T 17			W 17	F 17
T 18		F 18	S 17 Sexages.	S 17 Lent 3	T 18	S 18
F 19	S 18 Sexages.	S 19	M 18	M 18	F 19	
S 20	M 19		T 19	T 19	S 20	S 19 Rogation
	T 20	S 20 Epiph. 2	W 20	W 20		M 20
S 21 Epiph. 3	W 21	M 21	T 21	T 21	S 21 Quasimodo	T 21
M 22	T 22	T 22	F 22	F 22	M 22	W 22
T 23	F 23	W 23	S 23	S 23	T 23	T 23 Ascensio
W 24	S 24	T 24			W 24	F 24
T 25		F 25			T 25	S 25
F 26	S 25 Quinquag.	S 26	S 24 Quinquag.	S 24 Lent 4	F 26	
S 27	M 26		M 25	M 25 Annunc.	S 27	S 26 Ascens.
	T 27 Shrove Tu.	S 27 Epiph. 3	T 26 Shrove Tu.	T 26		M 27
S 28 Epiph. 4	W 28 Ash Wed.	M 28	W 27 Ash Wed.	W 27	S 28 Easter 2	T 28
M 29	T 29	T 29	T 28	T 28	M 29	W 29
T 30		W 30		F 29	T 30	T 30
W 31		T 31		S 30		F 31
				S 31 Passion		

r Common Years
r Leap Years (*in bold figures*)
w Style years 1591, **1596,** 1675, 1686, 1743, **1748,** 1754, 1805, 1811, **1816,** 1895, 1963, **1968,** 1974

June	July	August	September	October	November	December
1	M 1	T 1 Lammas	**S** 1 Trinity 12	T 1	F 1	**S** 1 Advent 1
	T 2	F 2	M 2	W 2	S 2	M 2
2 Whit Sun.	W 3	S 3	T 3	T 3		T 3
3	T 4		W 4	F 4	**S** 3 Trinity 21	W 4
4	F 5	**S** 4 Trinity 8	T 5	S 5	M 4	T 5
5 Ember	S 6	M 5	F 6		T 5	F 6
6		T 6	S 7	**S** 6 Trinity 17	W 6	S 7
7 Ember	**S** 7 Trinity 4	W 7		M 7	T 7	
8 Ember	M 8	T 8	**S** 8 Trinity 13	T 8	F 8	**S** 8 Advent 2
	T 9	F 9	M 9	W 9	S 9	M 9
9 Trinity	W 10	S 10	T 10	T 10		T 10
10	T 11		W 11	F 11	**S** 10 Trinity 22	W 11
11	F 12	**S** 11 Trinity 9	T 12	S 12	M 11 Martin	T 12
12	S 13	M 12	F 13		T 12	F 13
13 Corpus C.		T 13	s 14 Exalt. C.	**S** 13 Trinity 18	W 13	S 14
14	**S** 14 Trinity 5	W 14		M 14	T 14	
15	M 15	T 15	**S** 15 Trinity 14	T 15	F 15	**S** 15 Advent 3
	T 16	F 16	M 16	W 16	S 16	M 16
16 Trinity 1	W 17	S 17	T 17	T 17		T 17
17	T 18		W 18 Ember	F 18	**S** 17 Trinity 23	W 18 Ember
18	F 19	**S** 18 Trinity 10	T 19	S 19	M 18	T 19
19	S 20	M 19	F 20 Ember		T 19	F 20 Ember
20		T 20	s 21 Ember	**S** 20 Trinity 19	W 20	s 21 Ember
21	**S** 21 Trinity 6	W 21		M 21	T 21	
22	M 22	T 22	**S** 22 Trinity 15	T 22	F 22	**S** 22 Advent 4
	T 23	F 23	M 23	W 23	S 23	M 23
23 Trinity 2	W 24	S 24	T 24	T 24		T 24
24 Nat. J. Bap	T 25		W 25	F 25	**S** 24 Trinity 24	W 25 Christmas
25	F 26	**S** 25 Trinity 11	T 26	S 26	M 25	T 26
26	S 27	M 26	F 27		T 26	F 27
27		T 27	s 28	**S** 27 Trinity 20	W 27	s 28
28	**S** 28 Trinity 7	W 28		M 28	T 28	
29	M 29	T 29	**S** 29 Trinity 16	T 29	F 29	**S** 29
	T 30	F 30	M 30	W 30	S 30	M 30
30 Trinity 3	W 31	S 31		T 31		T 31

Table 25 EASTER DAY

DOMINICAL LETTER

,,   ,, A

Old Style years 507, 518, 529, 591, 602, 613, **624**, 686, 697, **703**, 781, **792**, 871, 876, 955, 966, 1039, 1050, 1061, 1123, 11 1145, **1156**, 1218, 1229, **1240**, 1313, **1324**, 1403, **1408**, 1487, 1498, 1571, 1582, 1593, 1655, 1666, 1677, **1688**, 1750

Leap Years		January	February	March	April	May
January	February					
S 1	W 1	M 1	T 1	T 1	S 1 Passion	T 1
M 2	T 2 Purific. M.	T 2	F 2 Purific. M.	F 2	M 2	W 2
T 3	F 3	W 3	s 3	s 3	T 3	T 3
W 4	s 4	T 4			W 4	F 4
T 5		F 5	S 4 Epiph. 5	S 4 Quadrag.	T 5	S 5
F 6 Epiphany	S 5 Epiph. 5	s 6 Epiphany	M 5	M 5	F 6	
s 7	M 6		T 6	T 6	S 7	S 6 Easter 3
	T 7	S 7 Epiph. 1	W 7	w 7 Ember		M 7
S 8 Epiph. 1	w 8	M 8	T 8	T 8	S 8 Palm	T 8
M 9	T 9	T 9	F 9	F 9 Ember	M 9	W 9
T 10	F 10	W 10	s 10	s 10 Ember	T 10	T 10
W 11	s 11	T 11			W 11	F 11
T 12		F 12	S 11 Septuag.	S 11 Lent 2	T 12	S 12
F 13 Hilary	S 12 Septuag.	s 13 Hilary	M 12	M 12	F 13 Good Fri.	
s 14	M 13		T 13	T 13	s 14	S 13 Easter 4
	T 14	S 14 Epiph. 2	W 14	W 14		M 14
S 15 Epiph. 2	w 15	M 15	T 15	T 15	S 15 **Easter Day**	T 15
M 16	T 16	T 16	F 16	F 16	M 16	w 16
T 17	F 17	W 17	s 17	s 17	T 17	T 17
w 18	s 18	T 18			W 18	F 18
T 19		F 19	S 18 Sexages.	S 18 Lent 3	T 19	s 19
F 20	S 19 Sexages.	s 20	M 19	M 19	F 20	
s 21	M 20		T 20	T 20	s 21	S 20 Rogation
	T 21	S 21 Epiph. 3	w 21	W 21		M 21
S 22 Epiph. 3	w 22	M 22	T 22	T 22	S 22 Quasimodo	T 22
M 23	T 23	T 23	F 23	F 23	M 23	w 23
T 24	F 24	W 24	s 24 Matthias	s 24	T 24	T 24 Ascension
W 25	s 25 Matthias	T 25			W 25	F 25
T 26		F 26	S 25 Quinquag.	S 25 Lent 4	T 26	s 26
F 27	S 26 Quinquag.	s 27	M 26	M 26	F 27	
s 28	M 27		T 27 Shrove Tu.	T 27	s 28	S 27 Ascens. 1
	T 28 Shrove Tu.	S 28 Epiph. 4	w 28 Ash Wed.	w 28		M 28
S 29 Epiph. 4	w 29 Ash Wed.	M 29		T 29	S 29 Easter 2	T 29
M 30		T 30		F 30	M 30	W 30
T 31		W 31		s 31		T 31

FOR COMMON YEARS
FOR LEAP YEARS (*in bold figures*)
New Style years 1607, 1618, 1629, 1691, 1759, 1770, 1781, 1827, 1838, 1900 *not* a leap year), 1906, 1979, 1990

June	July	August	September	October	November	December
F 1	S 1 Trinity 3	W 1 Lammas	S 1	M 1	T 1	S 1
S 2	M 2	T 2		T 2	F 2	
	T 3	F 3		W 3	S 3	S 2 Advent 1
S 3 Whit Sun.	W 4	S 4	S 2 Trinity 12	T 4		M 3
M 4	T 5		M 3	F 5	S 4 Trinity 21	T 4
T 5	F 6		T 4	S 6	M 5	W 5
W 6 Ember	S 7	S 5 Trinity 8	W 5		T 6	T 6
T 7		M 6	T 6		W 7	F 7
F 8 Ember	S 8 Trinity 4	T 7	F 7	S 7 Trinity 17	T 8	S 8
S 9 Ember	M 9	W 8	S 8	M 8	F 9	
	T 10	T 9		T 9	S 10	S 9 Advent 2
S 10 Trinity	W 11	F 10	S 9 Trinity 13	W 10		M 10
M 11	T 12	S 11	M 10	T 11	S 11 Trinity 22	T 11
T 12	F 13		T 11	F 12	M 12	W 12
W 13	S 14	S 12 Trinity 9	W 12	S 13	T 13	T 13
T 14 Corpus C.		M 13	T 13		W 14	F 14
F 15	S 15 Trinity 5	T 14	F 14 Exalt. C.	S 14 Trinity 18	T 15	S 15
S 16	M 16	W 15	S 15	M 15	F 16	
	T 17	T 16		T 16	S 17	S 16 Advent 3
S 17 Trinity 1	W 18	F 17	S 16 Trinity 14	W 17		M 17
M 18	T 19	S 18	M 17	T 18	S 18 Trinity 23	T 18
T 19	F 20		T 18	F 19	M 19	W 19 Ember
W 20	S 21	S 19 Trinity 10	W 19 Ember	S 20	T 20	T 20
T 21		M 20	T 20		W 21	F 21 Ember
F 22	S 22 Trinity 6	T 21	F 21 Ember	S 21 Trinity 19	T 22	S 22 Ember
S 23	M 23	W 22	S 22 Ember	M 22	F 23	
	T 24	T 23		T 23	S 24	S 23 Advent 4
S 24 Trinity 2	W 25	F 24	S 23 Trinity 15	W 24		M 24
M 25	T 26	S 25	M 24	T 25	S 25 Trinity 24	T 25 Christmas
T 26	F 27		T 25	F 26	M 26	W 26
W 27	S 28	S 26 Trinity 11	W 26	S 27	T 27	T 27
T 28		M 27	T 27		W 28	F 28
F 29	S 29 Trinity 7	T 28	F 28	S 28 Trinity 20	T 29	S 29
S 30	M 30	W 29	S 29 Michael A.	M 29	F 30	
	T 31	T 30		T 30		S 30 Advent 4
		F 31	S 30 Trinity 16	W 31		M 31

Table 26 — EASTER DAY,

„ „ BA...

Old Style years 523, 534, 545, **556**, 618, 629, **640**, 713, 719, **724**, 803, **808**, 814, 887, 898, 909, 971, 982, 993, **1004**, 1055, 1066, 1077, **1088**, 1150, 1161, **1172**, 1245, 1251, **1256**, 1335, **1340**, 1346, 1419, 1430, 1441, 1503, 1514, 1525, **1536**, 1587, 1598, 1609, **1620**, 1682, 1693, **1704**

Leap Years		January	February	March	April	May
January	February					
S 1	T 1	S 1	W 1	W 1 Ash Wed.	S 1	M 1
	W 2 Purific. M.	M 2	T 2 Purific. M.	T 2		T 2
S 2	T 3	T 3	F 3	F 3	S 2 Passion	W 3
M 3	F 4	W 4	S 4	S 4	M 3	T 4
T 4	S 5	T 5			T 4	F 5
W 5		F 6 Epiphany	S 5 Epiph. 5	S 5 Quadrag.	W 5	S 6
T 6 Epiphany	S 6 Epiph. 5	S 7	M 6	M 6	T 6	
F 7	M 7		T 7	T 7	F 7	S 7 Easter 3
S 8	T 8	S 8 Epiph. 1	W 8	W 8 Ember	S 8	M 8
	W 9	M 9	T 9	T 9		T 9
S 9 Epiph. 1	T 10	T 10	F 10	F 10 Ember	S 9 Palm	W 10
M 10	F 11	W 11	S 11	S 11 Ember	M 10	T 11
T 11	S 12	T 12			T 11	F 12
W 12		F 13 Hilary	S 12 Septuag.	S 12 Lent 2	W 12	S 13
T 13 Hilary	S 13 Septuag.	S 14	M 13	M 13	T 13	
F 14	M 14		T 14	T 14	F 14 Good Fri.	S 14 Easter 4
S 15	T 15	S 15 Epiph. 2	W 15	W 15	S 15	M 15
	W 16	M 16	T 16	T 16		T 16
S 16 Epiph. 2	T 17	T 17	F 17	F 17	S 16 **Easter Day**	W 17
M 17	F 18	W 18	S 18	S 18	M 17	T 18
T 18	S 19	T 19			T 18	F 19
W 19		F 20	S 19 Sexages.	S 19 Lent 3	W 19	S 20
T 20	S 20 Sexages.	S 21	M 20	M 20	T 20	
F 21	M 21		T 21	T 21	F 21	S 21 Rogation
S 22	T 22	S 22 Epiph. 3	W 22	W 22	S 22	M 22
	W 23	M 23	T 23	T 23		T 23
S 23 Epiph. 3	T 24	T 24	F 24 Matthias	F 24	S 23 Quasimodo	W 24
M 24	F 25 Matthias	W 25	S 25	S 25 Annunc.	M 24	T 25 Ascension
T 25	S 26	T 26			T 25	F 26
W 26		F 27	S 26 Quinquag.	S 26 Lent 4	W 26	S 27
T 27	S 27 Quinquag.	S 28	M 27	M 27	T 27	
F 28	M 28		T 28 Shrove Tu.	T 28	F 28	S 28 Ascens. 1
S 29	T 29 Shrove Tu.	S 29 Epiph. 4		W 29	S 29	M 29
		M 30		T 30		T 30
S 30 Epiph. 4		T 31		F 31	S 30 Easter 2	W 31
M 31						

FOR COMMON YEARS
FOR LEAP YEARS (*in bold figures*)
New Style years 1623, 1634, 1645, **1656**, 1702, 1713, **1724**, 1775, 1786, 1797, 1843, 1854, 1865, **1876**, 1911, 1922, 1933, 1995

June

- T 1
- F 2
- S 3
- S 4 Whit Sun.
- M 5
- T 6
- W 7 Ember
- T 8
- F 9 Ember
- S 10 Ember
- S 11 Trinity
- M 12
- T 13
- W 14
- T 15 Corpus C.
- F 16
- S 17
- S 18 Trinity 1
- M 19
- T 20
- W 21
- T 22
- F 23
- S 24 Nat. J. Bap
- S 25 Trinity 2
- M 26
- T 27
- W 28
- T 29
- F 30

July

- S 1
- S 2 Trinity 3
- M 3
- T 4
- W 5
- T 6
- F 7
- S 8
- S 9 Trinity 4
- M 10
- T 11
- W 12
- T 13
- F 14
- S 15
- S 16 Trinity 5
- M 17
- T 18
- W 19
- T 20
- F 21
- S 22
- S 23 Trinity 6
- M 24
- T 25
- W 26
- T 27
- F 28
- S 29
- S 30 Trinity 7
- M 31

August

- T 1 Lammas
- W 2
- T 3
- F 4
- S 5
- S 6 Trinity 8
- M 7
- T 8
- W 9
- T 10
- F 11
- S 12
- S 13 Trinity 9
- M 14
- T 15
- W 16
- T 17
- F 18
- S 19
- S 20 Trinity 10
- M 21
- T 22
- W 23
- T 24
- F 25
- S 26
- S 27 Trinity 11
- M 28
- T 29
- W 30
- T 31

September

- F 1
- S 2
- S 3 Trinity 12
- M 4
- T 5
- W 6
- T 7
- F 8
- S 9
- S 10 Trinity 13
- M 11
- T 12
- W 13
- T 14 Exalt. C.
- F 15
- S 16
- S 17 Trinity 14
- M 18
- T 19
- W 20 Ember
- T 21
- F 22 Ember
- S 23 Ember
- S 24 Trinity 15
- M 25
- T 26
- W 27
- T 28
- F 29 Michael A.
- S 30

October

- S 1 Trinity 16
- M 2
- T 3
- W 4
- T 5
- F 6
- S 7
- S 8 Trinity 17
- M 9
- T 10
- W 11
- T 12
- F 13
- S 14
- S 15 Trinity 18
- M 16
- T 17
- W 18
- T 19
- F 20
- S 21
- S 22 Trinity 19
- M 23
- T 24
- W 25
- T 26
- F 27
- S 28
- S 29 Trinity 20
- M 30
- T 31

November

- W 1
- T 2
- F 3
- S 4
- S 5 Trinity 21
- M 6
- T 7
- W 8
- T 9
- F 10
- S 11 Martin
- S 12 Trinity 22
- M 13
- T 14
- W 15
- T 16
- F 17
- S 18
- S 19 Trinity 23
- M 20
- T 21
- W 22
- T 23
- F 24
- S 25
- S 26 Trinity 24
- M 27
- T 28
- W 29
- T 30

December

- F 1
- S 2
- S 3 Advent 1
- M 4
- T 5
- W 6
- T 7
- F 8
- S 9
- S 10 Advent 2
- M 11
- T 12
- W 13
- T 14
- F 15
- S 16
- S 17 Advent 3
- M 18
- T 19
- W 20 Ember
- T 21
- F 22 Ember
- S 23 Ember
- S 24 Advent 4
- M 25 Christmas
- T 26
- W 27
- T 28
- F 29
- S 30
- S 31

Table 27

Old Style years 561, **572**, 651, 656, 735, 746, 819, 830, 841, 903, 914, 925, **936**, 998, 1009, **1020**, 1093, **1104**, 1183, **1188**, 1267
1278, 1351, 1362, 1373, 1435, 1446, 1457, **1468**, 1530, 1541, **1552**, 1625, **1636**, 1715, **1720**

Leap Years		January	February	March	April	May
January	February					
F 1	M 1	S 1	T 1	T 1 Shrove Tu.	F 1	S 1 Easter 2
S 2	T 2 Purific. M.		W 2 Purific. M.	W 2 Ash Wed.	S 2	M 2
	W 3	S 2	T 3	T 3		T 3
S 3	T 4	M 3	F 4	F 4	S 3 Passion	W 4
M 4	F 5	T 4	S 5	S 5	M 4	T 5
T 5	S 6	W 5			T 5	F 6
W 6 Epiphany		T 6 Epiphany	S 6 Epiph. 5	S 6 Quadrag.	W 6	S 7
T 7	S 7 Epiph. 5	F 7	M 7	M 7	T 7	
F 8	M 8	S 8	T 8	T 8	F 8	S 8 Easter 3
S 9	T 9		W 9	W 9 Ember	S 9	M 9
	W 10	S 9 Epiph. 1	T 10	T 10		T 10
S 10 Epiph. 1	T 11	M 10	F 11	F 11 Ember	S 10 Palm	W 11
M 11	F 12	T 11	S 12	S 12 Ember	M 11	T 12
T 12	S 13	W 12			T 12	F 13
W 13 Hilary		T 13 Hilary	S 13 Septuag.	S 13 Lent 2	W 13	S 14
T 14	S 14 Septuag.	F 14	M 14	M 14	T 14	
F 15	M 15	S 15	T 15	T 15	F 15 Good Fri.	S 15 Easter 4
S 16	T 16		W 16	W 16	S 16	M 16
	W 17	S 16 Epiph. 2	T 17	T 17		T 17
S 17 Epiph. 2	T 18	M 17	F 18	F 18	S 17 **Easter Day**	W 18
M 18	F 19	T 18	S 19	S 19	M 18	T 19
T 19	S 20	W 19			T 19	F 20
W 20		T 20	S 20 Sexages.	S 20 Lent 3	W 20	S 21
T 21	S 21 Sexages.	F 21	M 21	M 21	T 21	
F 22	M 22	S 22	T 22	T 22	F 22	S 22 Rogation
S 23	T 23		W 23	W 23	S 23	M 23
	W 24	S 23 Epiph. 3	T 24 Matthias	T 24		T 24
S 24 Epiph. 3	T 25 Matthias	M 24	F 25	F 25 Annunc.	S 24 Quasimodo	W 25
M 25	F 26	T 25	S 26	S 26	M 25	T 26 Ascension
T 26	S 27	W 26			T 26	F 27
W 27		T 27	S 27 Quinquag.	S 27 Lent 4	W 27	S 28
T 28	S 28 Quinquag.	F 28	M 28	M 28	T 28	
F 29	M 29	S 29		T 29	F 29	S 29 Ascens. 1
S 30				W 30	S 30	M 30
		S 30 Epiph. 4		T 31		T 31
S 31 Epiph. 4		M 31				

FOR COMMON YEARS
FOR LEAP YEARS (*in bold figure*
New Style years **1588**, 1650, 1661, **1672**, 1718, 1729, **1740**, **1808**, 1870, 1881, **1892**, 1927, 1938, 1949, **1960**

June	July	August	September	October	November	December
T 1	F 1	M 1 Lammas	T 1	S 1	T 1	T 1
2	S 2	T 2	F 2	―――	W 2	F 2
3		W 3	S 3	S 2 Trinity 16	T 3	S 3
4	S 3 Trinity 3	T 4	―――	M 3	F 4	―――
	M 4	F 5	S 4 Trinity 12	T 4	S 5	S 4 Advent 2
5 Whit Sun.	T 5	S 6	M 5	W 5		M 5
6	W 6		T 6	T 6	S 6 Trinity 21	T 6
7	T 7	S 7 Trinity 8	W 7	F 7	M 7	W 7
8 Ember	F 8	M 8	T 8	S 8	T 8	T 8
9	S 9	T 9	F 9		W 9	F 9
10 Ember		W 10	S 10	S 9 Trinity 17	T 10	S 10
11 Ember	S 10 Trinity 4	T 11		M 10	F 11 Martin	
	M 11	F 12	S 11 Trinity 13	T 11	S 12	S 11 Advent 3
12 Trinity	T 12	S 13	M 12	W 12		M 12
13	W 13		T 13	T 13	S 13 Trinity 22	T 13
14	T 14	S 14 Trinity 9	W 14 Exalt. C.	F 14	M 14	W 14 Ember
15	F 15	M 15	T 15	S 15	T 15	T 15
16 Corpus C.	S 16	T 16	F 16		W 16	F 16 Ember
17		W 17	S 17	S 16 Trinity 18	T 17	S 17 Ember
18	S 17 Trinity 5	T 18		M 17	F 18	
	M 18	F 19	S 18 Trinity 14	T 18	S 19	S 18 Advent 4
19 Trinity 1	T 19	S 20	M 19	W 19		M 19
20	W 20		T 20	T 20	S 20 Trinity 23	T 20
21	T 21	S 21 Trinity 10	W 21 Ember	F 21	M 21	W 21
22	F 22	M 22	T 22	S 22	T 22	T 22
23	S 23	T 23	F 23 Ember		W 23	F 23
24 Nat. J. Bap		W 24	S 24 Ember	S 23 Trinity 19	T 24	S 24
25	S 24 Trinity 6	T 25		M 24	F 25	
	M 25	F 26	S 25 Trinity 15	T 25	S 26	S 25 Christmas
26 Trinity 2	T 26	S 27	M 26	W 26		M 26
27	W 27		T 27	T 27	S 27 Advent 1	T 27
28	T 28	S 28 Trinity 11	W 28	F 28	M 28	W 28
29	F 29	M 29	T 29 Michael A.	S 29	T 29	T 29
30	S 30	T 30	F 30		W 30	F 30
		W 31		S 30 Trinity 20		S 31
	S 31 Trinity 7			M 31		

Table 28

Old Style years **504**, 583, **588**, 667, 678, 751, 762, 773, 835, 846, 857, **868**, 930, 941, **952**, 1025, **1036**, 1115, **1120**, 1199, 121C
1283, 1294, 1305, 1367, 1378, 1389, **1400**, 1462, 1473, **1484**, 1557, **1568**, 1647, **1652**, 1731, 1742

Leap Years		January	February	March	April	May
January	February					
T 1	S 1 Epiph. 4	F 1	M 1	M 1	T 1	S 1
F 2	M 2 Purific. M.	S 2	T 2 Purific. M.	T 2 Shrove Tu.	F 2	
S 3	T 3		W 3	W 3 Ash Wed.	S 3	
	W 4		T 4	T 4		S 2 Easter 2
	T 5	S 3	F 5	F 5		M 3
S 4	F 6	M 4	s 6	s 6	S 4 Passion	T 4
M 5	s 7	T 5			M 5	W 5
T 6 Epiphany		W 6 Epiphany			T 6	T 6
W 7		T 7	S 7 Epiph. 5	S 7 Quadrag.	W 7	F 7
T 8	S 8 Epiph. 5	F 8	M 8	M 8	T 8	S 8
F 9	M 9	S 9	T 9	T 9	F 9	
S 10	T 10		W 10	w 10 Ember	S 10	
	W 11		T 11	T 11		S 9 Easter 3
S 11 Epiph. 1	T 12	S 10 Epiph. 1	F 12	F 12 Ember	S 11 Palm	M 10
M 12	F 13	M 11	S 13	s 13 Ember	M 12	T 11
T 13 Hilary	s 14	T 12			T 13	W 12
W 14		w 13 Hilary	S 14 Septuag.	S 14 Lent 2	W 14	T 13
T 15	S 15 Septuag.	T 14	M 15	M 15	T 15	F 14
F 16	M 16	F 15	T 16	T 16	F 16 Good Fri.	S 15
S 17	T 17	s 16	W 17	W 17	S 17	
	W 18		T 18	T 18		S 16 Easter 4
S 18 Epiph. 2	T 19	S 17 Epiph. 2	F 19	F 19		M 17
M 19	F 20	M 18	S 20	S 20	S 18 **Easter Day**	T 18
T 20	S 21	T 19			M 19	W 19
W 21		W 20			T 20	T 20
T 22		T 21	S 21 Sexages.	S 21 Lent 3	W 21	F 21
F 23	S 22 Sexages.	F 22	M 22	M 22	T 22	S 22
S 24	M 23	S 23	T 23	T 23	F 23	
	T 24		w 24 Matthias	W 24	S 24	
	w 25 Matthias	S 24 Epiph. 3	T 25	T 25 Annunc.		S 23 Rogation
S 25 Epiph. 3	T 26	M 25	F 26	F 26	S 25 Quasimodo	M 24
M 26	F 27	T 26	S 27	S 27	M 26	T 25
T 27	s 28	T 26			T 27	w 26
w 28		W 27			w 28	T 27 Ascension
T 29	S 29 Quinquag.	T 28	S 28 Quinquag.	S 28 Lent 4	T 29	F 28
F 30		F 29		M 29	F 30	s 29
S 31		S 30		T 30		
				W 31		S 30 Ascens. 1
		S 31 Epiph. 4				M 31

138

FOR COMMON YEARS
FOR LEAP YEARS (*in bold figures*)
New Style years 1593, **1604**, 1677, 1683, **1688**, 1745, **1756**, 1802, 1813, **1824**, 1897, 1954, 1965, **1976**

June	July	August	September	October	November	December
T 1	T 1	S 1 Trinity 7	W 1	F 1	M 1	W 1
W 2	F 2	M 2	T 2	S 2	T 2	T 2
T 3	S 3	T 3	F 3		W 3	F 3
F 4		W 4	S 4	S 3 Trinity 16	T 4	S 4
S 5	S 4 Trinity 3	T 5		M 4	F 5	
	M 5	F 6	S 5 Trinity 12	T 5	S 6	S 5 Advent 2
S 6 Whit Sun.	T 6	S 7	M 6	W 6		M 6
M 7	W 7		T 7	T 7	S 7 Trinity 21	T 7
T 8	T 8	S 8 Trinity 8	W 8	F 8	M 8	W 8
W 9 Ember	F 9	M 9	T 9	S 9	T 9	T 9
T 10	S 10	T 10	F 10		W 10	F 10
F 11 Ember		W 11	S 11	S 10 Trinity 17	T 11 Martin	S 11
S 12 Ember	S 11 Trinity 4	T 12		M 11	F 12	
	M 12	F 13	S 12 Trinity 13	T 12	S 13	S 12 Advent 3
S 13 Trinity	T 13	S 14	M 13	W 13		M 13
M 14	W 14		T 14 Exalt. C.	T 14	S 14 Trinity 22	T 14
T 15	T 15	S 15 Trinity 9	W 15 Ember	F 15	M 15	W 15 Ember
W 16	F 16	M 16	T 16	S 16	T 16	T 16
T 17 Corpus C.	S 17	T 17	F 17 Ember		W 17	F 17 Ember
F 18		W 18	S 18 Ember	S 17 Trinity 18	T 18	S 18 Ember
S 19	S 18 Trinity 5	T 19		M 18	F 19	
	M 19	F 20	S 19 Trinity 14	T 19	S 20	S 19 Advent 4
S 20 Trinity 1	T 20	S 21	M 20	W 20		M 20
M 21	W 21		T 21	T 21	S 21 Trinity 23	T 21
T 22	T 22	S 22 Trinity 10	W 22	F 22	M 22	W 22
W 23	F 23	M 23	T 23	S 23	T 23	T 23
T 24 Nat. J. Bap	S 24	T 24	F 24		W 24	F 24
F 25		W 25	S 25	S 24 Trinity 19	T 25	S 25 Christmas
S 26	S 25 Trinity 6	T 26		M 25	F 26	
	M 26	F 27	S 26 Trinity 15	T 26	S 27	S 26
S 27 Trinity 2	T 27	S 28	M 27	W 27		M 27
M 28	W 28		T 28	T 28	S 28 Advent 1	T 28
T 29	T 29	S 29 Trinity 11	W 29 Michael A.	F 29	M 29	W 29
W 30	F 30	M 30	T 30	S 30	T 30	T 30
	S 31	T 31				F 31
				S 31 Trinity 20		

Table 29

DOMINICAL LETTER I
,, ,, EI

Old Style years 515, **520**, 526, 599, 610, 621, 683, 694, 705, **716**, 767, 778, 789, **800**, 862, 873, **884**, 957, 963, **968**, 1047, 105
1058, 1131, 1142, 1153, 1215, 1226, 1237, **1248**, 1299, 1310, 1321, **1332**, 1394, 1405, **1416**, 1489, 1495, **1500**, 1579, 158
1590, 1663, 1674, 1685, 1747

Leap Years						
January	February	January	February	March	April	May
W 1	S 1	T 1	S 1 Epiph. 4	S 1 Quinquag.	W 1	F 1
T 2	F 2	F 2	M 2 Purific. M.	M 2	T 2	S 2
F 3	S 2 Epiph. 4	S 3	T 3	T 3 Shrove Tu.	F 3	
S 4	M 3		W 4	W 4 Ash Wed.	S 4	S 3 Easter 2
	T 4	S 4	T 5	T 5		M 4
S 5	W 5	M 5	F 6	F 6	S 5 Passion	T 5
M 6 Epiphany	T 6	T 6 Epiphany	S 7	S 7	M 6	W 6
T 7	F 7	W 7			T 7	T 7
W 8	S 8	T 8	S 8 Epiph. 5	S 8 Quadrag.	W 8	F 8
T 9		F 9	M 9	M 9	T 9	S 9
F 10	S 9 Epiph. 5	S 10	T 10	T 10	F 10	
S 11	M 10		W 11	W 11 Ember	S 11	S 10 Easter 3
	T 11	S 11 Epiph. 1	T 12	T 12		M 11
S 12 Epiph. 1	W 12	M 12	F 13	F 13 Ember	S 12 Palm	T 12
M 13 Hilary	T 13	T 13 Hilary	S 14	S 14 Ember	M 13	W 13
T 14	F 14	W 14			T 14	T 14
W 15	S 15	T 15	S 15 Septuag.	S 15 Lent 2	W 15	F 15
T 16		F 16	M 16	M 16	T 16	S 16
F 17	S 16 Septuag.	S 17	T 17	T 17	F 17 Good Fri.	
S 18	M 17		W 18	W 18	S 18	S 17 Easter 4
	T 18	S 18 Epiph. 2	T 19	T 19		M 18
S 19 Epiph. 2	W 19	M 19	F 20	F 20	S 19 **Easter Day**	T 19
M 20	T 20	T 20	S 21	S 21	M 20	W 20
T 21	F 21	W 21			T 21	T 21
W 22	S 22	T 22	S 22 Sexages.	S 22 Lent 3	W 22	F 22
T 23		F 23	M 23	M 23	T 23	S 23
F 24	S 23 Sexages.	S 24	T 24 Matthias	T 24	F 24	
S 25	M 24		W 25	W 25 Annunc.	S 25	S 24 Rogation
	T 25 Matthias	S 25 Epiph. 3	T 26	T 26		M 25
S 26 Epiph. 3	W 26	M 26	F 27	F 27	S 26 Quasimodo	T 26
M 27	T 27	T 27	S 28	S 28	M 27	W 27
T 28	F 28	W 28			T 28	T 28 Ascension
W 29	S 29	T 29		S 29 Lent 4	W 29	F 29
T 30		F 30		M 30	T 30	S 30
F 31		S 31		T 31		
						S 31 Ascens. 1

COMMON YEARS
LEAP YEARS (*in bold figures*)
Style years 1609, 1615, **1620**, 1699, 1767, **1772**, 1778, 1829, 1835, **1840**, **1908**, 1981, 1987, **1992**

June	July	August	September	October	November	December
1	W 1	S 1 Lammas	T 1	T 1	**S** 1 Trinity 20	T 1
2	T 2		W 2	F 2	M 2	W 2
3	F 3	**S** 2 Trinity 7	T 3	S 3	T 3	T 3
4	S 4	M 3	F 4		W 4	F 4
5		T 4	S 5		T 5	S 5
6	**S** 5 Trinity 3	W 5		**S** 4 Trinity 16	F 6	
	M 6	T 6	**S** 6 Trinity 12	M 5	S 7	**S** 6 Advent 2
7 Whit Sun.	T 7	F 7	M 7	T 6		M 7
8	W 8	S 8	T 8	W 7	**S** 8 Trinity 21	T 8
9	T 9		W 9	T 8	M 9	W 9
10 Ember	F 10	**S** 9 Trinity 8	T 10	F 9	T 10	T 10
11	S 11	M 10	F 11	S 10	W 11 Martin	F 11
12 Ember		T 11	S 12		T 12	S 12
13 Ember	**S** 12 Trinity 4	W 12		**S** 11 Trinity 17	F 13	
	M 13	T 13	**S** 13 Trinity 13	M 12	S 14	**S** 13 Advent 3
14 Trinity	T 14	F 14	M 14 Exalt. C.	T 13		M 14
15	W 15	S 15	T 15	W 14	**S** 15 Trinity 22	T 15
16	T 16		W 16 Ember	T 15	M 16	W 16 Ember
17	F 17	**S** 16 Trinity 9	T 17	F 16	T 17	T 17
18 Corpus C.	S 18	M 17	F 18 Ember	S 17	W 18	F 18 Ember
19		T 18	S 19 Ember		T 19	S 19 Ember
20	**S** 19 Trinity 5	W 19		**S** 18 Trinity 18	F 20	
	M 20	T 20	**S** 20 Trinity 14	M 19	S 21	**S** 20 Advent 4
21 Trinity 1	T 21	F 21	M 21	T 20		M 21
22	W 22	S 22	T 22	W 21	**S** 22 Trinity 23	T 22
23	T 23		W 23	T 22	M 23	W 23
24 Nat. J. Bap	F 24	**S** 23 Trinity 10	T 24	F 23	T 24	T 24
25	S 25	M 24	F 25	S 24	W 25	F 25 Christmas
26		T 25	S 26		T 26	S 26
27	**S** 26 Trinity 6	W 26		**S** 25 Trinity 19	F 27	
	M 27	T 27	**S** 27 Trinity 15	M 26	S 28	**S** 27
28 Trinity 2	T 28	F 28	M 28	T 27		M 28
29	W 29	S 29	T 29 Michael A.	W 28	**S** 29 Advent 1	T 29
30	T 30		W 30	T 29	M 30	W 30
	F 31	**S** 30 Trinity 11		F 30		T 31
		M 31		S 31		

Table 30   EASTER DAY
DOMINICAL LETTER
,,   ,,

Old Style years 531, 542, 553, 615, 626, 637, **648**, 710, 721, **732**, 805, **816**, 895, **900**, 979, 990, 1063, 1074, 1085, 1147, 1
1169, **1180**, 1242, 1253, **1264**, 1337, **1348**, 1427, **1432**, 1511, 1522, 1595, 1606, 1617, 1679, 1690, 1701, **1712**

| Leap Years | | January | February | March | April | May |
January	February					
T 1	F 1	W 1	S 1	S 1	T 1	T 1
W 2	s 2 Purific. M.	T 2			W 2	F 2
T 3		F 3	S 2 Epiph. 4	S 2 Quinquag.	T 3	s 3
F 4	S 3 Epiph. 4	s 4	M 3	M 3	F 4	
s 5	M 4		T 4	T 4 Shrove Tu.	s 5	S 4 Easter 2
	T 5	S 5	W 5	w 5 Ash Wed.		M 5
S 6 Epiphany	w 6	M 6 Epiphany	T 6	T 6	S 6 Passion	T 6
M 7	T 7	T 7	F 7	F 7	M 7	W 7
T 8	F 8	W 8	s 8	s 8	T 8	T 8
W 9	S 9	T 9			W 9	F 9
T 10		F 10	S 9 Epiph. 5	S 9 Quadrag.	T 10	S 10
F 11	S 10 Epiph. 5	S 11	M 10	M 10	F 11	
S 12	M 11		T 11	T 11	S 12	S 11 Easter 3
	T 12	S 12 Epiph. 1	W 12	w 12 Ember		M 12
S 13 Epiph. 1	W 13	M 13 Hilary	T 13	T 13	S 13 Palm	T 13
M 14	T 14	T 14	F 14	F 14 Ember	M 14	W 14
T 15	F 15	W 15	s 15	s 15 Ember	T 15	T 15
W 16	s 16	T 16			W 16	F 16
T 17		F 17	S 16 Septuag.	S 16 Lent 2	T 17	s 17
F 18	S 17 Septuag.	s 18	M 17	M 17	F 18 Good Fri.	
s 19	M 18		T 18	T 18	s 19	S 18 Easter 4
	T 19	S 19 Epiph. 2	W 19	W 19		M 19
S 20 Epiph. 2	W 20	M 20	T 20	T 20	S 20 **Easter Day**	T 20
M 21	T 21	T 21	F 21	F 21	M 21	W 21
T 22	F 22	W 22	s 22	s 22	T 22	F 22
W 23	s 23	T 23			W 23	s 24
T 24		F 24	S 23 Sexages.	S 23 Lent 3	T 24	
F 25	S 24 Sexages.	s 25	M 24 Matthias	M 24	F 25	S 25 Rogation
s 26	M 25 Matthias		T 25	T 25 Annunc.	s 26	M 26
	T 26	S 26 Epiph. 3	W 26	W 26		T 27
S 27 Epiph. 3	W 27	M 27	T 27	T 27	S 27 Quasimodo	W 28
M 28	T 28	T 28	F 28	F 28	M 28	T 29 Ascension
T 29	F 29	W 29		s 29	T 29	F 30
W 30		T 30			W 30	s 31
T 31		F 31		S 30 Lent 4		
				M 31		

r COMMON YEARS
r LEAP YEARS (*in bold figures*)
w Style years 1631, 1642, 1710, 1783, 1794, 1851, 1862, 1919, **1924**, 1930

June	July	August	September	October	November	December
1 Ascens.	T 1	F 1 Lammas	M 1	W 1	S 1	M 1
2	W 2	S 2	T 2	T 2	S 2 Trinity 20	T 2
3	T 3	S 3 Trinity 7	W 3	F 3	M 3	W 3
4	F 4	M 4	T 4	S 4	T 4	T 4
5	S 5	T 5	F 5	S 5 Trinity 16	W 5	F 5
6	S 6 Trinity 3	W 6	S 6	M 6	T 6	S 6
7	M 7	T 7	S 7 Trinity 12	T 7	F 7	S 7 Advent 2
8 Whit Sun.	T 8	F 8	M 8	W 8	S 8	M 8
9	W 9	S 9	T 9	T 9	S 9 Trinity 21	T 9
10	T 10	S 10 Trinity 8	W 10	F 10	M 10	W 10
11 Ember	F 11	M 11	T 11	S 11	T 11 Martin	T 11
12	S 12	T 12	F 12	S 12 Trinity 17	W 12	F 12
13 Ember	S 13 Trinity 4	W 13	S 13	M 13	T 13	S 13
14 Ember	M 14	T 14	S 14 Trinity 13	T 14	F 14	S 14 Advent 3
15 Trinity	T 15	F 15	M 15	W 15	S 15	M 15
16	W 16	S 16	T 16	T 16	S 16 Trinity 22	T 16
17	T 17	S 17 Trinity 9	W 17 Ember	F 17	M 17	W 17 Ember
18	F 18	M 18	T 18	S 18	T 18	T 18
19 Corpus C.	S 19	T 19	F 19 Ember	S 19 Trinity 18	W 19	F 19 Ember
20	S 20 Trinity 5	W 20	S 20 Ember	M 20	T 20	S 20 Ember
21	M 21	T 21	S 21 Trinity 14	T 21	F 21	S 21 Advent 4
22 Trinity 1	T 22	F 22	M 22	W 22	S 22	M 22
23	W 23	S 23	T 23	T 23	S 23 Trinity 23	T 23
24 Nat. J. Bap	T 24	S 24 Trinity 10	W 24	F 24	M 24	W 24
25	F 25	M 25	T 25	S 25	T 25	T 25 Christmas
26	S 26	T 26	F 26	S 26 Trinity 19	W 26	F 26
27	S 27 Trinity 6	W 27	S 27	M 27	T 27	S 27
28	M 28	T 28	S 28 Trinity 15	T 28	F 28	S 28
29 Trinity 2	T 29	F 29	M 29 Michael A.	W 29	S 29	M 29
30	W 30	S 30	T 30	T 30	S 30 Advent 1	T 30
	T 31	S 31 Trinity 11		F 31		W 31

Table 31   EASTER DAY

Old Style years 558, 569, **580,** 653, **664, 748,** 827, 911, 922, 995, 1006, 1017, 1090, 1101, **1112,** 1185, **1196, 1280,** 1359, 14
1454, 1527, 1538, 1549, 1622, 1633, **1644,** 1717, **1728**

Leap Years

January

M 1
T 2
W 3
T 4
F 5
s 6 Epiphany
S 7 Epiph. 1
M 8
T 9
W 10
T 11
F 12
s 13 Hilary
S 14 Epiph. 2
M 15
T 16
W 17
T 18
F 19
S 20
S 21 Epiph. 3
M 22
T 23
W 24
T 25
F 26
S 27
S 28 Epiph. 4
M 29
T 30
W 31

February

T 1
F 2 Purific. M.
S 3
S 4 Epiph. 5
M 5
T 6
W 7
T 8
F 9
S 10
S 11 Epiph. 6
M 12
T 13
W 14
T 15
F 16
S 17
S 18 Septuag.
M 19
T 20
W 21
T 22
F 23
S 24
S 25 Sexages.
M 26
T 27
W 28
T 29

January

T 1
W 2
T 3
F 4
S 5
S 6 Epiphany
M 7
T 8
W 9
T 10
F 11
S 12
S 13 Epiph. 1
M 14
T 15
W 16
T 17
F 18
s 19
S 20 Epiph. 2
M 21
T 22
W 23
T 24
F 25
s 26
S 27 Epiph. 3
M 28
T 29
W 30
T 31

February

F 1
s 2 Purific. M.
S 3 Epiph. 4
M 4
T 5
w 6
T 7
F 8
s 9
S 10 Epiph. 5
M 11
T 12
w 13
T 14
F 15
s 16
S 17 Septuag.
M 18
T 19
W 20
T 21
F 22
s 23
S 24 Sexages.
M 25
T 26
W 27
T 28

March

F 1
s 2
S 3 Quinquag.
M 4
T 5 Shrove Tu.
w 6 Ash Wed.
T 7
F 8
s 9
S 10 Quadrag.
M 11
T 12
w 13 Ember
T 14
F 15 Ember
s 16 Ember
S 17 Lent 2
M 18
T 19
W 20
T 21
F 22
s 23
S 24 Lent 3
M 25 Annunc.
T 26
W 27
T 28
F 29
s 30
S 31 Lent 4

April

M 1
T 2
W 3
T 4
F 5
s 6
S 7 Passion
M 8
T 9
W 10
T 11
F 12
s 13
S 14 Palm
M 15
T 16
W 17
T 18
F 19 Good Fri.
S 20
S 21 **Easter Day**
M 22
T 23
W 24
T 25
F 26
S 27
S 28 Quasimodo
M 29
T 30

May

W 1
T 2
F 3
s 4
S 5 Easter 2
M 6
T 7
W 8
T 9
F 10
S 11
S 12 Easter 3
M 13
T 14
W 15
T 16
F 17
s 18
S 19 Easter 4
M 20
T 21
W 22
T 23
F 24
s 25
S 26 Rogation
M 27
T 28
W 29
T 30 Ascension
F 31

FOR COMMON YEARS
FOR LEAP YEARS (*in bold figures*)
New Style years 1585, 1647, 1658, 1669, **1680**, 1715, 1726, 1737, 1867, 1878, 1889, 1935, 1946, 1957

June	July	August	September	October	November	December
S 1	M 1	T 1 Lammas	S 1 Trinity 11	T 1	F 1	S 1 Advent 1
	T 2	F 2	M 2	W 2	S 2	M 2
S 2 Ascens. 1	W 3	S 3	T 3	T 3		T 3
M 3	T 4		W 4	F 4	S 3 Trinity 20	W 4
T 4	F 5	S 4 Trinity 7	T 5	S 5	M 4	T 5
W 5	S 6	M 5	F 6		T 5	F 6
T 6		T 6	S 7	S 6 Trinity 16	W 6	S 7
F 7	S 7 Trinity 3	W 7		M 7	T 7	
S 8	M 8	T 8	S 8 Trinity 12	T 8	F 8	S 8 Advent 2
	T 9	F 9	M 9	W 9	S 9	M 9
S 9 Whit Sun.	W 10	S 10	T 10	T 10		T 10
M 10	T 11		W 11	F 11	S 10 Trinity 21	W 11
T 11	F 12	S 11 Trinity 8	T 12	S 12	M 11 Martin	T 12
W 12 Ember	S 13	M 12	F 13		T 12	F 13
T 13		T 13	S 14 Exalt. C.	S 13 Trinity 17	W 13	S 14
F 14 Ember	S 14 Trinity 4	W 14		M 14	T 14	
S 15 Ember	M 15	T 15	S 15 Trinity 13	T 15	F 15	S 15 Advent 3
	T 16	F 16	M 16	W 16	S 16	M 16
S 16 Trinity	W 17	S 17	T 17	T 17		T 17
M 17	T 18		W 18 Ember	F 18	S 17 Trinity 22	W 18 Ember
T 18	F 19	S 18 Trinity 9	T 19	S 19	M 18	T 19
W 19	S 20	M 19	F 20 Ember		T 19	F 20 Ember
T 20 Corpus C.		T 20	S 21 Ember	S 20 Trinity 18	W 20	S 21 Ember
F 21	S 21 Trinity 5	W 21		M 21	T 21	
S 22	M 22	T 22	S 22 Trinity 14	T 22	F 22	S 22 Advent 4
	T 23	F 23	M 23	W 23	S 23	M 23
S 23 Trinity 1	W 24	S 24	T 24	T 24		T 24
M 24 Nat. J. Bap	T 25		W 25	F 25	S 24 Trinity 23	W 25 Christmas
T 25	F 26	S 25 Trinity 10	T 26	S 26	M 25	T 26
W 26	S 27	M 26	F 27		T 26	F 27
T 27		T 27	S 28	S 27 Trinity 19	W 27	S 28
F 28	S 28 Trinity 6	W 28		M 28	T 28	
S 29	M 29	T 29	S 29 Trinity 15	T 29	F 29	S 29
	T 30	F 30	M 30	W 30	S 30	M 30
S 30 Trinity 2	W 31	S 31		T 31		T 31

Table 32

DOMINICAL LETTER (
,,   ,,   A(

Old Style years 501, **512, 596,** 675, 759, 770, 843, 854, 865, 938, 949, **960,** 1033, **1044, 1128,** 1207, 1291, 1302, 1375, 138(
1397, 1470, 1481, **1492,** 1565, **1576, 1660,** 1739

Leap Years January	Leap Years February	January	February	March	April	May
S 1	W 1	M 1	T 1	T 1	S 1 Lent 4	T 1
M 2	T 2 Purific. M.	T 2	F 2 Purific. M.	F 2	M 2	W 2
T 3	F 3	W 3	S 3	S 3	T 3	T 3
W 4	S 4	T 4			W 4	F 4
T 5		F 5	S 4 Epiph. 5	S 4 Quinquag.	T 5	S 5
F 6 Epiphany	S 5 Epiph. 5	s 6 Epiphany	M 5	M 5	F 6	
S 7	M 6		T 6	T 6 Shrove Tu.	s 7	S 6 Easter 2
	T 7	S 7 Epiph. 1	W 7	w 7 Ash Wed.		M 7
S 8 Epiph. 1	W 8	M 8	T 8	T 8	S 8 Passion	T 8
M 9	T 9	T 9	F 9	F 9	M 9	W 9
T 10	F 10	W 10	S 10	S 10	T 10	T 10
W 11	S 11	T 11			W 11	F 11
T 12		F 12	S 11 Epiph. 6	S 11 Quadrag.	T 12	S 12
F 13 Hilary	S 12 Epiph. 6	s 13 Hilary	M 12	M 12	F 13	
S 14	M 13		T 13	T 13	S 14	S 13 Easter 3
	T 14	S 14 Epiph. 2	W 14	w 14 Ember		M 14
S 15 Epiph. 2	W 15	M 15	T 15	T 15	S 15 Palm	T 15
M 16	T 16	T 16	F 16	F 16 Ember	M 16	W 16
T 17	F 17	W 17	s 17	s 17 Ember	T 17	T 17
w 18	s 18	T 18			W 18	F 18
T 19		F 19	S 18 Septuag.	S 18 Lent 2	T 19	s 19
F 20	S 19 Septuag.	S 20	M 19	M 19	F 20 Good Fri.	
S 21	M 20		T 20	T 20	S 21	S 20 Easter 4
	T 21	S 21 Epiph. 3	W 21	W 21		M 21
S 22 Epiph. 3	W 22	M 22	T 22	T 22	S 22 **Easter Day**	T 22
M 23	T 23	T 23	F 23	F 23	M 23	W 23
T 24	F 24	W 24	s 24 Matthias	s 24	T 24	T 24
W 25	s 25 Matthias	T 25			W 25	F 25
T 26		F 26	S 25 Sexages.	S 25 Lent 3	T 26	s 26
F 27	S 26 Sexages.	S 27	M 26	M 26	F 27	
s 28	M 27		T 27	T 27	s 28	S 27 Rogation
	T 28	S 28 Epiph. 4	w 28	w 28		M 28
S 29 Epiph. 4	W 29	M 29		T 29	S 29 Quasimodo	T 29
M 30		T 30		F 30	M 30	W 30
T 31		W 31		S 31		T 31 Ascension

OR COMMON YEARS
OR LEAP YEARS (*in bold figures*)
ew Style years 1590, 1601, **1612**, 1685, **1696**, 1753, **1764**, 1810, 1821, **1832**, 1962, 1973, **1984**

June	July	August	September	October	November	December
1	S 1 Trinity 2	W 1 Lammas	S 1	M 1	T 1	S 1
2	M 2	T 2		T 2	F 2	
	T 3	F 3	S 2 Trinity 11	W 3	S 3	S 2 Advent 1
3 Ascens. 1	W 4	S 4	M 3	T 4		M 3
4	T 5		T 4	F 5	S 4 Trinity 20	T 4
5	F 6	S 5 Trinity 7	W 5	S 6	M 5	W 5
6	S 7	M 6	T 6		T 6	T 6
7		T 7	F 7	S 7 Trinity 16	W 7	F 7
8	S 8 Trinity 3	W 8	S 8	M 8	T 8	S 8
9	M 9	T 9		T 9	F 9	
	T 10	F 10	S 9 Trinity 12	W 10	S 10	S 9 Advent 2
10 Whit Sun.	W 11	S 11	M 10	T 11		M 10
11	T 12		T 11	F 12	S 11 Trinity 21	T 11
12	F 13	S 12 Trinity 8	W 12	S 13	M 12	W 12
13 Ember	S 14	M 13	T 13		T 13	T 13
14		T 14	F 14 Exalt. C.	S 14 Trinity 17	W 14	F 14
15 Ember	S 15 Trinity 4	W 15	S 15	M 15	T 15	S 15
16 Ember	M 16	T 16		T 16	F 16	
	T 17	F 17	S 16 Trinity 13	W 17	S 17	S 16 Advent 3
17 Trinity	W 18	S 18	M 17	T 18		M 17
18	T 19		T 18	F 19	S 18 Trinity 22	T 18
19	F 20	S 19 Trinity 9	W 19 Ember	S 20	M 19	W 19 Ember
20	S 21	M 20	T 20		T 20	T 20
21 Corpus C.		T 21	F 21 Ember	S 21 Trinity 18	W 21	F 21 Ember
22	S 22 Trinity 5	W 22	S 22 Ember	M 22	T 22	S 22 Ember
23	M 23	T 23		T 23	F 23	
	T 24	F 24	S 23 Trinity 14	W 24	S 24	S 23 Advent 4
24 Trinity 1	W 25	S 25	M 24	T 25		M 24
25	T 26		T 25	F 26	S 25 Trinity 23	T 25 Christmas
26	F 27	S 26 Trinity 10	W 26	S 27	M 26	W 26
27	S 28	M 27	T 27		T 27	T 27
28		T 28	F 28	S 28 Trinity 19	W 28	F 28
29	S 29 Trinity 6	W 29	S 29 Michael A.	M 29	T 29	S 29
30	M 30	T 30		T 30	F 30	
	T 31	F 31	S 30 Trinity 15	W 31		S 30
						M 31

Table 33

DOMINICAL LETTER

,, ,, B

Old Style years 607, 691, 702, 786, 797, 881, **892, 976,** 1139, 1223, 1234, 1318, 1329, 1413, **1424, 1508,** 16

Leap Years		January	February	March	April	May
January	February					
S 1	T 1	S 1	W 1	W 1	S 1	M 1
	w 2 Purific. M.	M 2	T 2 Purific. M.	T 2		T 2
S 2	T 3	T 3	F 3	F 3	S 2 Lent 4	W 3
M 3	F 4	W 4	S 4	S 4	M 3	T 4
T 4	S 5	T 5			T 4	F 5
W 5		F 6 Epiphany			W 5	S 6
T 6 Epiphany	S 6 Epiph. 5	S 7	S 5 Epiph. 5	S 5 Quinquag.	T 6	
F 7	M 7		M 6	M 6	F 7	S 7 Easter 2
S 8	T 8	S 8 Epiph. 1	T 7	T 7 Shrove Tu.	S 8	M 8
	W 9	M 9	W 8	w 8 Ash Wed.		T 9
S 9 Epiph. 1	T 10	T 10	T 9	T 9	S 9 Passion	W 10
M 10	F 11	W 11	F 10	F 10	M 10	T 11
T 11	S 12	T 12	S 11	S 11	T 11	F 12
W 12		F 13 Hilary			W 12	S 13
T 13 Hilary	S 13 Epiph. 6	S 14	S 12 Epiph. 6	S 12 Quadrag.	T 13	
F 14	M 14		M 13	M 13	F 14	S 14 Easter 3
S 15	T 15	S 15 Epiph. 2	T 14	T 14	S 15	M 15
	w 16	M 16	W 15	w 15 Ember		T 16
S 16 Epiph. 2	T 17	T 17	T 16	T 16	S 16 Palm	W 17
M 17	F 18	W 18	F 17	F 17 Ember	M 17	T 18
T 18	S 19	T 19	S 18	s 18 Ember	T 18	F 19
W 19		F 20			W 19	S 20
T 20	S 20 Septuag.	S 21	S 19 Septuag.	S 19 Lent 2	T 20	
F 21	M 21		M 20	M 20	F 21 Good Fri.	S 21 Easter 4
S 22	T 22	S 22 Epiph. 3	T 21	T 21	S 22	M 22
	w 23	M 23	W 22	W 22		T 23
S 23 Epiph. 3	T 24	T 24	T 23	T 23	S 23 **Easter Day**	W 24
M 24	F 25 Matthias	W 25	F 24 Matthias	F 24	M 24	T 25
T 25	S 26	T 26	S 25	s 25 Annunc.	T 25	F 26
W 26		F 27			W 26	S 27
T 27	S 27 Sexages.	S 28	S 26 Sexages.	S 26 Lent 3	T 27	
F 28	M 28		M 27	M 27	F 28	S 28 Rogation
S 29	T 29	S 29 Epiph. 4	T 28	T 28	S 29	M 29
		M 30		W 29		T 30
S 30 Epiph. 4		T 31		T 30	S 30 Quasimodo	W 31
M 31				F 31		

148

OR COMMON YEARS
OR LEAP YEARS (*in bold figures*)

ew Style years **1628, 1848,** 1905, **1916, 2000**

June	July	August	September	October	November	December
1 Ascension	S 1	T 1 Lammas	F 1	**S** 1 Trinity 15	W 1	F 1
2	W 2	W 2	S 2	M 2	T 2	S 2
3	**S** 2 Trinity 2	T 3	.	T 3	F 3	
	M 3	F 4	**S** 3 Trinity 11	W 4	S 4	**S** 3 Advent 1
4 Ascens. 1	T 4	S 5	M 4	T 5		M 4
5	W 5		T 5	F 6	**S** 5 Trinity 20	T 5
6	T 6	**S** 6 Trinity 7	W 6	S 7	M 6	W 6
7	F 7	M 7	T 7		T 7	T 7
8	S 8	T 8	F 8	**S** 8 Trinity 16	W 8	F 8
9		W 9	S 9	M 9	T 9	S 9
10	**S** 9 Trinity 3	T 10		T 10	F 10	
	M 10	F 11	**S** 10 Trinity 12	W 11	S 11 Martin	**S** 10 Advent 2
11 Whit Sun.	T 11	S 12	M 11	T 12		M 11
12	W 12		T 12	F 13	**S** 12 Trinity 21	T 12
13	T 13	**S** 13 Trinity 8	W 13	S 14	M 13	W 13
14 Ember	F 14	M 14	T 14 Exalt. C.		T 14	T 14
15	S 15	T 15	F 15	**S** 15 Trinity 17	W 15	F 15
16 Ember		W 16	S 16	M 16	T 16	S 16
17 Ember	**S** 16 Trinity 4	T 17		T 17	F 17	
	M 17	F 18	**S** 17 Trinity 13	W 18	S 18	**S** 17 Advent 3
18 Trinity	T 18	S 19	M 18	T 19		M 18
19	W 19		T 19	F 20	**S** 19 Trinity 22	T 19
20	T 20	**S** 20 Trinity 9	W 20 Ember	S 21	M 20	W 20 Ember
21	F 21	M 21	T 21		T 21	T 21
22 Corpus C.	S 22	T 22	F 22 Ember	**S** 22 Trinity 18	W 22	F 22 Ember
23		W 23	S 23 Ember	M 23	T 23	S 23 Ember
24 Nat. J. Bap	**S** 23 Trinity 5	T 24		T 24	F 24	
	M 24	F 25	**S** 24 Trinity 14	W 25	S 25	**S** 24 Advent 4
S 25 Trinity 1	T 25	S 26	M 25	T 26		M 25 Christmas
26	W 26		T 26	F 27	**S** 26 Trinity 23	T 26
27	T 27	**S** 27 Trinity 10	W 27	S 28	M 27	W 27
28	F 28	M 28	T 28		T 28	T 28
29	S 29	T 29	F 29 Michael A.	**S** 29 Trinity 19	W 29	F 29
30		W 30	S 30	M 30	T 30	S 30
	S 30 Trinity 6	T 31		T 31		
	M 31					**S** 31

Table 34

Old Style years 539, 550, 634, 645, 729, **740**, **824**, 987, 1071, 1082, 1166, 1177, 1261, **1272**, **1356**, 1519, 1603, 1614, 1698, 1709.

Leap Years		January	February	March	April	May
January	February					

Leap Years – January
F 1
S 2
S 3
M 4
T 5
W 6 Epiphany
T 7
F 8
S 9
S 10 Epiph. 1
M 11
T 12
W 13 Hilary
T 14
F 15
S 16
S 17 Epiph. 2
M 18
T 19
W 20
T 21
F 22
S 23
S 24 Epiph. 3
M 25
T 26
W 27
T 28
F 29
S 30
S 31 Epiph. 4

Leap Years – February
M 1
T 2 Purific. M.
W 3
T 4
F 5
S 6
S 7 Epiph. 5
M 8
T 9
W 10
T 11
F 12
S 13
S 14 Epiph. 6
M 15
T 16
W 17
T 18
F 19
S 20
S 21 Septuag.
M 22
T 23
W 24
T 25 Matthias
F 26
S 27
S 28 Sexages.
M 29

January
S 1
S 2
M 3
T 4
W 5
T 6 Epiphany
F 7
S 8
S 9 Epiph. 1
M 10
T 11
W 12
T 13 Hilary
F 14
S 15
S 16 Epiph. 2
M 17
T 18
W 19
T 20
F 21
S 22
S 23 Epiph. 3
M 24
T 25
W 26
T 27
F 28
S 29
S 30 Epiph. 4
M 31

February
T 1
W 2 Purific. M.
T 3
F 4
S 5
S 6 Epiph. 5
M 7
T 8
W 9
T 10
F 11
S 12
S 13 Epiph. 6
M 14
T 15
W 16
T 17
F 18
S 19
S 20 Septuag.
M 21
T 22
W 23
T 24 Matthias
F 25
S 26
S 27 Sexages.
M 28

March
T 1
W 2
T 3
F 4
S 5
S 6 Quinquag.
M 7
T 8 Shrove Tu.
W 9 Ash Wed.
T 10
F 11
S 12
S 13 Quadrag.
M 14
T 15
W 16 Ember
T 17
F 18 Ember
S 19 Ember
S 20 Lent 2
M 21
T 22
W 23
T 24
F 25 Annunc.
S 26
S 27 Lent 3
M 28
T 29
W 30
T 31

April
F 1
S 2
S 3 Lent 4
M 4
T 5
W 6
T 7
F 8
S 9
S 10 Passion
M 11
T 12
W 13
T 14
F 15
S 16
S 17 Palm
M 18
T 19
W 20
T 21
F 22 Good Fri.
S 23
S 24 **Easter Day**
M 25
T 26
W 27
T 28
F 29
S 30

May
S 1 Quasimodo
M 2
T 3
W 4
T 5
F 6
S 7
S 8 Easter 2
M 9
T 10
W 11
T 12
F 13
S 14
S 15 Easter 3
M 16
T 17
W 18
T 19
F 20
S 21
S 22 Easter 4
M 23
T 24
W 25
T 26
F 27
S 28
S 29 Rogation
M 30
T 31

r Common Years
r Leap Years (*in bold figures*)
w Style years 1639, 1707, 1791, 1859

June	July	August	September	October	November	December
1	F 1	M 1 Lammas	T 1	S 1	T 1	T 1
2 Ascension	S 2	T 2	F 2	F 2	W 2	F 2
3		W 3	S 3	S 3	T 3	S 3
4	S 3 Trinity 2	T 4		S 2 Trinity 15	F 4	
	M 4	F 5	S 4 Trinity 11	M 3	S 5	S 4 Advent 2
5 Ascens. 1	T 5	S 6	M 5	T 4		M 5
6	W 6		T 6	W 5		T 6
7	T 7	S 7 Trinity 7	W 7	T 6	S 6 Trinity 20	W 7
8	F 8	M 8	T 8	F 7	M 7	T 8
9	S 9	T 9	F 9	S 8	T 8	F 9
10		W 10	S 10		W 9	S 10
11	S 10 Trinity 3	T 11		S 9 Trinity 16	T 10	
	M 11	F 12	S 11 Trinity 12	M 10	F 11 Martin	S 11 Advent 3
12 Whit Sun.	T 12	S 13	M 12	T 11	S 12	M 12
13	W 13		T 13	W 12		T 13
14	T 14	S 14 Trinity 8	W 14 Exalt. C.	T 13	S 13 Trinity 21	W 14 Ember
15 Ember	F 15	M 15	T 15	F 14	M 14	T 15
16	S 16	T 16	F 16	S 15	T 15	F 16 Ember
17 Ember		W 17	S 17		W 16	S 17 Ember
18 Ember	S 17 Trinity 4	T 18		S 16 Trinity 17	T 17	
	M 18	F 19	S 18 Trinity 13	M 17	F 18	S 18 Advent 4
19 Trinity	T 19	S 20	M 19	T 18	S 19	M 19
20	W 20		T 20	W 19		T 20
21	T 21	S 21 Trinity 9	W 21 Ember	T 20	S 20 Trinity 22	W 21
22	F 22	M 22	T 22	F 21	M 21	T 22
23 Corpus C.	S 23	T 23	F 23 Ember	S 22	T 22	F 23
24 Nat. J. Bap		W 24	S 24 Ember		W 23	S 24
25	S 24 Trinity 5	T 25		S 23 Trinity 18	T 24	
	M 25	F 26	S 25 Trinity 14	M 24	F 25	S 25 Christmas
26 Trinity 1	T 26	S 27	M 26	T 25	S 26	M 26
27	W 27		T 27	W 26		T 27
28	T 28	S 28 Trinity 10	W 28	T 27	S 27 Advent 1	W 28
29	F 29	M 29	T 29 Michael A.	F 28	M 28	T 29
30	S 30	T 30	F 30	S 29	T 29	F 30
		W 31			W 30	S 31
	S 31 Trinity 6			S 30 Trinity 19		
				M 31		

Table 35   EASTER DAY

Leap Years		January	February	March	April	May
January	February					
T 1	S 1 Epiph. 4	F 1	M 1	M 1	T 1	S 1
F 2	M 2 Purific. M.	S 2	T 2 Purific. M.	T 2	F 2	
S 3	T 3		W 3	W 3	S 3	S 2 Quasimod
	W 4	S 3	T 4	T 4		M 3
S 4	T 5	M 4	F 5	F 5	S 4 Lent 4	T 4
M 5	F 6	T 5	S 6	S 6	M 5	W 5
T 6 Epiphany	S 7	W 6 Epiphany			T 6	T 6
W 7		T 7	S 7 Epiph. 5	S 7 Quinquag.	W 7	F 7
T 8	S 8 Epiph. 5	F 8	M 8	M 8	T 8	S 8
F 9	M 9	S 9	T 9	T 9 Shrove Tu.	F 9	
S 10	T 10		W 10	W 10 Ash Wed.	S 10	S 9 Easter 2
	W 11	S 10 Epiph. 1	T 11	T 11		M 10
S 11 Epiph. 1	T 12	M 11	F 12	F 12	S 11 Passion	T 11
M 12	F 13	T 12	S 13	S 13	M 12	W 12
T 13 Hilary	S 14	W 13 Hilary			T 13	T 13
W 14		T 14	S 14 Epiph. 6	S 14 Quadrag.	W 14	F 14
T 15	S 15 Epiph. 6	F 15	M 15	M 15	T 15	S 15
F 16	M 16	S 16	T 16	T 16	F 16	
S 17	T 17		W 17	W 17 Ember	S 17	S 16 Easter 3
	W 18	S 17 Epiph. 2	T 18	T 18		M 17
S 18 Epiph. 2	T 19	M 18	F 19	F 19 Ember	S 18 Palm	T 18
M 19	F 20	T 19	S 20	S 20 Ember	M 19	W 19
T 20	S 21	W 20			T 20	T 20
W 21		T 21	S 21 Septuag.	S 21 Lent 2	W 21	F 21
T 22	S 22 Septuag.	F 22	M 22	M 22	T 22	S 22
F 23	M 23	S 23	T 23	T 23	F 23 Good Fri.	
S 24	T 24		W 24 Matthias	W 24	S 24	S 23 Easter 4
	W 25 Matthias	S 24 Epiph. 3	T 25	T 25 Annunc.		M 24
S 25 Epiph. 3	T 26	M 25	F 26	F 26	S 25 **Easter Day**	T 25
M 26	F 27	T 26	S 27	S 27	M 26	W 26
T 27	S 28	W 27			T 27	T 27
W 28		T 28	S 28 Sexages.	S 28 Lent 3	W 28	F 28
T 29	S 29 Sexages.	F 29		M 29	T 29	S 29
F 30		S 30		T 30	F 30	
S 31				W 31		S 30 Rogation
		S 31 Epiph. 4				M 31

r Common Years
r Leap Years (*in bold figures*)

w Style years 1582 (after 15 Oct.), 1666, 1734, 1886, 1943

June	July	August	September	October	November	December
1	T 1	S 1 Trinity 6	W 1	F 1	M 1	W 1
2	F 2	M 2	T 2	S 2	T 2	T 2
3 Ascension	S 3	T 3	F 3	W 3	W 3	F 3
4		W 4	S 4	T 4	T 4	S 4
5	S 4 Trinity 2	T 5		S 3 Trinity 15	F 5	
	M 5	F 6	S 5 Trinity 11	M 4	S 6	S 5 Advent 2
6 Ascens. 1	T 6	S 7	M 6	T 5		M 6
7	W 7		T 7	W 6		T 7
8	T 8	S 8 Trinity 7	W 8	T 7	S 7 Trinity 20	W 8
9	F 9	M 9	T 9	F 8	M 8	T 9
10	S 10	T 10	F 10	S 9	T 9	F 10
11		W 11	S 11		W 10	S 11
12	S 11 Trinity 3	T 12		S 10 Trinity 16	T 11 Martin	
	M 12	F 13	S 12 Trinity 12	M 11	F 12	S 12 Advent 3
13 Whit Sun.	T 13	S 14	M 13	T 12	S 13	M 13
14	M 14		T 14 Exalt. C.	W 13		T 14
15	T 15	S 15 Trinity 8	W 15 Ember	T 14	S 14 Trinity 21	W 15 Ember
16 Ember	F 16	M 16	T 16	F 15	M 15	T 16
17	S 17	T 17	F 17 Ember	S 16	T 16	F 17 Ember
18 Ember		W 18	S 18 Ember		W 17	S 18 Ember
19 Ember	S 18 Trinity 4	T 19		S 17 Trinity 17	T 18	
	M 19	F 20	S 19 Trinity 13	M 18	F 19	S 19 Advent 4
20 Trinity	T 20	S 21	M 20	T 19	S 20	M 20
21	W 21		T 21	W 20		T 21
22	T 22	S 22 Trinity 9	W 22	T 21	S 21 Trinity 22	W 22
23	F 23	M 23	T 23	F 22	M 22	T 23
24 Corpus C.	S 24	T 24	F 24	S 23	T 23	F 24
25		W 25	S 25		W 24	S 25 Christmas
26	S 25 Trinity 5	T 26		S 24 Trinity 18	T 25	
	M 26	F 27	S 26 Trinity 14	M 25	F 26	S 26
27 Trinity 1	T 27	S 28	M 27	T 26	S 27	M 27
28	W 28		T 28	W 27		T 28
29	T 29	S 29 Trinity 10	W 29 Michael A.	T 28	S 28 Advent 1	W 29
30	F 30	M 30	T 30	F 29	M 29	T 30
	S 31	T 31		S 30	T 30	F 31
				S 31 Trinity 19		

Table 36   ENGLISH CALENDAR for 1752.

In this year New Style was adopted in England.   Eleven days were dropped out of the calendar in
began with 1 January following 31 December 1751.   The Dominical Letters for this year are three:
was D, and that from 14 September to 31 December was A.   Easter Day in 1752 was calculated

January	February	March	April	May	June
W 1	S 1	S 1 Lent 3	W 1	F 1	M 1
T 2		M 2	T 2	S 2	T 2
F 3	S 2 Sexages.	T 3	F 3		W 3
S 4	M 3	W 4	S 4	S 3 Rogation	T 4
	T 4	T 5		M 4	F 5
S 5	W 5	F 6	S 5 Easter 1	T 5	S 6
M 6 Epiphany	T 6	S 7	M 6	W 6	
T 7	F 7		T 7	T 7 Ascension	S 7 Trinity 2
W 8	S 8	S 8 Lent 4	W 8	F 8	M 8
T 9		M 9	T 9	S 9	T 9
F 10	S 9 Quinquag.	T 10	F 10		W 10
S 11	M 10	W 11	S 11	S 10 Ascens. 1	T 11
	T 11 Shrove Tu.	T 12		M 11	F 12
S 12 Epiph. 1	W 12 Ash Wed.	F 13	S 12 Easter 2	T 12	S 13
M 13 Hilary	T 13	S 14	M 13	W 13	
T 14	F 14		T 14	T 14	S 14 Trinity 3
W 15	S 15	S 15 Passion	W 15	F 15	M 15
T 16		M 16	T 16	S 16	T 16
F 17	S 16 Quadrag.	T 17	F 17		W 17
S 18	M 17	M 18	S 18	S 17 Whit Sun.	T 18
	T 18	T 19		M 18	F 19
S 19 Epiph. 2	W 19	F 20	S 19 Easter 3	T 19	S 20
M 20	T 20	S 21	M 20	W 20	
T 21	F 21		T 21	T 21	S 21 Trinity 4
W 22	S 22	S 22 Palm	W 22	F 22	M 22
T 23		M 23	T 23	S 23	T 23
F 24	S 23 Lent 2	T 24	F 24		W 24 Nat. J. Bap
S 25	M 24	W 25 Annunc.	S 25	S 24 Trinity	T 25
	T 25 Matthias	T 26		M 25	F 26
S 26 Septuag.	W 26	F 27 Good Fri.	S 26 Easter 4	T 26	S 27
M 27	T 27	S 28	M 27	W 27	
T 28	F 28		T 28	T 28 Corpus C.	S 28 Trinity 5
W 29	S 29	S 29 Easter Day	W 29	F 29	M 29
T 30		M 30	T 30	S 30	T 30
F 31		T 31		S 31 Trinity 1	

September, the day after Wednesday, 2 September, being called Thursday, 14 September. The year since it was a Leap Year, the Letter for January and February was E, that from 1 March to 2 September according to Old Style ; Easter Day for 1753 (Table 32) was calculated according to New Style.

July	August	September	October	November	December
W 1	S 1	T 1	S 1 Trinity 17	W 1	F 1
T 2		W 2	M 2	T 2	S 2
F 3	S 2 Trinity 10	Eleven days omitted	T 3	F 3	
S 4	M 3	T 14	W 4	S 4	S 3 Advent 1
	T 4	F 15	T 5		M 4
S 5 Trinity 6	W 5	S 16	F 6	S 5 Trinity 22	T 5
M 6	T 6		S 7	M 6	W 6
T 7	F 7	S 17 Trinity 15		T 7	T 7
W 8	S 8	M 18	S 8 Trinity 18	W 8	F 8
T 9		T 19	M 9	T 9	S 9
F 10	S 9 Trinity 11	W 20	T 10	F 10	
S 11	M 10	T 21	W 11	S 11	S 10 Advent 2
	T 11	F 22	T 12		M 11
S 12 Trinity 7	W 12	S 23	F 13	S 12 Trinity 23	T 12
M 13	T 13		S 14	M 13	W 13
T 14	F 14	S 24 Trinity 16		T 14	T 14
W 15	S 15	M 25	S 15 Trinity 19	W 15	F 15
T 16		T 26	M 16	T 16	S 16
F 17	S 16 Trinity 12	W 27	T 17	F 17	
S 18	M 17	T 28	W 18	S 18	S 17 Advent 3
	T 18	F 29 Michael A.	T 19		M 18
S 19 Trinity 8	W 19	S 30	F 20	S 19 Trinity 24	T 19
M 20	T 20		S 21	M 20	W 20
T 21	F 21			T 21	T 21
W 22	S 22		S 22 Trinity 20	W 22	F 22
T 23			M 23	T 23	S 23
F 24	S 23 Trinity 13		T 24	F 24	
S 25	M 24		W 25	S 25	S 24 Advent 4
	T 25		T 26		M 25 Christmas
S 26 Trinity 9	W 26		F 27	S 26 Trinity 25	T 26
M 27	T 27		S 28	M 27	W 27
T 28	F 28			T 28	T 28
W 29	S 29		S 29 Trinity 21	W 29	F 29
T 30			M 30	T 30	S 30
F 31	S 30 Trinity 14		T 31		
	M 31				S 31

A.D.	Easter	A.D.	Easter	A.D.	Easter	A.D.	Easter	A.D.	Easter	A.D.	Easter
500	April 2	550	April 24	600	April 10	650	March 28	700	April 11	750	March 29
501	April 22	551	April 9	601	March 26	651	April 17	701	April 3	751	April 18
502	April 14	552	March 31	602	April 15	652	April 1	702	April 23	752	April 9
503	March 30	553	April 20	603	April 7	653	April 21	703	April 8	753	March 25
504	April 18	554	April 5	604	March 22	654	April 13	704	March 30	754	April 14
505	April 10	555	March 28	605	April 11	655	March 29	705	April 19	755	April 6
506	March 26	556	April 16	606	April 3	656	April 17	706	April 4	756	March 28
507	April 15	557	April 1	607	April 23	657	April 9	707	March 27	757	April 10
508	April 6	558	April 21	608	April 7	658	March 25	708	April 15	758	April 2
509	March 22	559	April 13	609	March 30	659	April 14	709	March 31	759	April 22
510	April 11	560	March 28	610	April 19	660	April 5	710	April 20	760	April 6
511	April 3	561	April 17	611	April 4	661	March 28	711	April 12	761	March 29
512	April 22	562	April 9	612	March 26	662	April 10	712	April 3	762	April 18
513	April 7	563	March 25	613	April 15	663	April 2	713	April 16	763	April 3
514	March 30	564	April 13	614	March 31	664	April 21	714	April 8	764	March 25
515	April 19	565	April 5	615	April 20	665	April 6	715	March 31	765	April 14
516	April 3	566	March 28	616	April 11	666	March 29	716	April 19	766	April 6
517	March 26	567	April 10	617	April 3	667	April 18	717	April 4	767	April 19
518	April 15	568	April 1	618	April 16	668	April 9	718	March 27	768	April 10
519	March 31	569	April 21	619	April 8	669	March 25	719	April 16	769	April 2
520	April 19	570	April 6	620	March 30	670	April 14	720	March 31	770	April 22
521	April 11	571	March 29	621	April 19	671	April 6	721	April 20	771	April 7
522	April 3	572	April 17	622	April 4	672	April 25	722	April 12	772	March 29
523	April 16	573	April 9	623	March 27	673	April 10	723	March 28	773	April 18
524	April 7	574	March 25	624	April 15	674	April 2	724	April 16	774	April 3
525	March 30	575	April 14	625	March 31	675	April 22	725	April 8	775	March 26
526	April 19	576	April 5	626	April 20	676	April 6	726	March 24	776	April 14
527	April 4	577	April 25	627	April 12	677	March 29	727	April 13	777	March 30
528	March 26	578	April 10	628	March 27	678	April 18	728	April 4	778	April 19
529	April 15	579	April 2	629	April 16	679	April 3	729	April 24	779	April 11
530	March 31	580	April 21	630	April 8	680	March 25	730	April 9	780	March 26
531	April 20	581	April 6	631	March 24	681	April 14	731	April 1	781	April 15
532	April 11	582	March 29	632	April 12	682	March 30	732	April 20	782	April 7
533	March 27	583	April 18	633	April 4	683	April 19	733	April 5	783	March 23
534	April 16	584	April 2	634	April 24	684	April 10	734	March 28	784	April 11
535	April 8	585	March 25	635	April 9	685	March 26	735	April 17	785	April 3
536	March 23	586	April 14	636	March 31	686	April 15	736	April 8	786	April 23
537	April 12	587	March 30	637	April 20	687	April 7	737	March 24	787	April 8
538	April 4	588	April 18	638	April 5	688	March 29	738	April 13	788	March 30
539	April 24	589	April 10	639	March 28	689	April 11	739	April 5	789	April 19
540	April 8	590	March 26	640	April 16	690	April 3	740	April 24	790	April 11
541	March 31	591	April 15	641	April 8	691	April 23	741	April 9	791	March 27
542	April 20	592	April 6	642	March 24	692	April 14	742	April 1	792	April 15
543	April 5	593	March 29	643	April 13	693	March 30	743	April 14	793	April 7
544	March 27	594	April 11	644	April 4	694	April 19	744	April 5	794	March 23
545	April 16	595	April 3	645	April 24	695	April 11	745	March 28	795	April 12
546	April 8	596	April 22	646	April 9	696	March 26	746	April 17	796	April 3
547	March 24	597	April 14	647	April 1	697	April 15	747	April 2	797	April 23
548	April 12	598	March 30	648	April 20	698	April 7	748	April 21	798	April 8
549	April 4	599	April 19	649	April 5	699	March 23	749	April 13	799	March 31

OF EASTER DAYS

A.D.	Easter	A.D.	Easter	A.D.	Easter	A.D.	Easter	A.D.	Easter	A.D.	Easter
800	April 19	850	April 6	900	April 20	950	April 7	1000	March 31	1050	April 15
801	April 4	851	March 22	901	April 12	951	March 30	1001	April 13	1051	March 31
802	March 27	852	April 10	902	March 28	952	April 18	1002	April 5	1052	April 19
803	April 16	853	April 2	903	April 17	953	April 3	1003	March 28	1053	April 11
804	March 31	854	April 22	904	April 8	954	March 26	1004	April 16	1054	April 3
805	April 20	855	April 7	905	March 31	955	April 15	1005	April 1	1055	April 16
806	April 12	856	March 29	906	April 13	956	April 6	1006	April 21	1056	April 7
807	March 28	857	April 18	907	April 5	957	April 19	1007	April 6	1057	March 30
808	April 16	858	April 3	908	March 27	958	April 11	1008	March 28	1058	April 19
809	April 8	859	March 26	909	April 16	959	April 3	1009	April 17	1059	April 4
810	March 31	860	April 14	910	April 1	960	April 22	1010	April 9	1060	March 26
811	April 13	861	April 6	911	April 21	961	April 7	1011	March 25	1061	April 15
812	April 4	862	April 19	912	April 12	962	March 30	1012	April 13	1062	March 31
813	March 27	863	April 11	913	March 28	963	April 19	1013	April 5	1063	April 20
814	April 16	864	April 2	914	April 17	964	April 3	1014	April 25	1064	April 11
815	April 1	865	April 22	915	April 9	965	March 26	1015	April 10	1065	March 27
816	April 20	866	April 7	916	March 24	966	April 15	1016	April 1	1066	April 16
817	April 12	867	March 30	917	April 13	967	March 31	1017	April 21	1067	April 8
818	March 28	868	April 18	918	April 5	968	April 19	1018	April 6	1068	March 23
819	April 17	869	April 3	919	April 25	969	April 11	1019	March 29	1069	April 12
820	April 8	870	March 26	920	April 9	970	March 27	1020	April 17	1070	April 4
821	March 24	871	April 15	921	April 1	971	April 16	1021	April 2	1071	April 24
822	April 13	872	March 30	922	April 21	972	April 7	1022	March 25	1072	April 8
823	April 5	873	April 19	923	April 6	973	March 23	1023	April 14	1073	March 31
824	April 24	874	April 11	924	March 28	974	April 12	1024	April 5	1074	April 20
825	April 9	875	March 27	925	April 17	975	April 4	1025	April 18	1075	April 5
826	April 1	876	April 15	926	April 2	976	April 23	1026	April 10	1076	March 27
827	April 21	877	April 7	927	March 25	977	April 8	1027	March 26	1077	April 16
828	April 5	878	March 23	928	April 13	978	March 31	1028	April 14	1078	April 8
829	March 28	879	April 12	929	April 5	979	April 20	1029	April 6	1079	March 24
830	April 17	880	April 3	930	April 18	980	April 11	1030	March 29	1080	April 12
831	April 2	881	April 23	931	April 10	981	March 27	1031	April 11	1081	April 4
832	March 24	882	April 8	932	April 1	982	April 16	1032	April 2	1082	April 24
833	April 13	883	March 31	933	April 14	983	April 8	1033	April 22	1083	April 9
834	April 5	884	April 19	934	April 6	984	March 23	1034	April 14	1084	March 31
835	April 18	885	April 11	935	March 29	985	April 12	1035	March 30	1085	April 20
836	April 9	886	March 27	936	April 17	986	April 4	1036	April 18	1086	April 5
837	April 1	887	April 16	937	April 2	987	April 24	1037	April 10	1087	March 28
838	April 14	888	April 7	938	April 22	988	April 8	1038	March 26	1088	April 16
839	April 6	889	March 23	939	April 14	989	March 31	1039	April 15	1089	April 1
840	March 28	890	April 12	940	March 29	990	April 20	1040	April 6	1090	April 21
841	April 17	891	April 4	941	April 18	991	April 5	1041	March 22	1091	April 13
842	April 2	892	April 23	942	April 10	992	March 27	1042	April 11	1092	March 28
843	April 22	893	April 8	943	March 26	993	April 16	1043	April 3	1093	April 17
844	April 13	894	March 31	944	April 14	994	April 1	1044	April 22	1094	April 9
845	March 29	895	April 20	945	April 6	995	April 21	1045	April 7	1095	March 25
846	April 18	896	April 4	946	March 22	996	April 12	1046	March 30	1096	April 13
847	April 10	897	March 27	947	April 11	997	March 28	1047	April 19	1097	April 5
848	March 25	898	April 16	948	April 2	998	April 17	1048	April 3	1098	March 28
849	April 14	899	April 1	949	April 22	999	April 9	1049	March 26	1099	April 10

A.D.	Easter	A.D.	Easter	A.D.	Easter	A.D.	Easter	A.D	Easter	A.D.	Easter
1100	April 1	1150	April 16	1200	April 9	1250	March 27	1300	April 10	1350	March 28
1101	April 21	1151	April 8	1201	March 25	1251	April 16	1301	April 2	1351	April 17
1102	April 6	1152	March 30	1202	April 14	1252	March 31	1302	April 22	1352	April 8
1103	March 29	1153	April 19	1203	April 6	1253	April 20	1303	April 7	1353	March 24
1104	April 17	1154	April 4	1204	April 25	1254	April 12	1304	March 29	1354	April 13
1105	April 9	1155	March 27	1205	April 10	1255	March 28	1305	April 18	1355	April 5
1106	March 25	1156	April 15	1206	April 2	1256	April 16	1306	April 3	1356	April 24
1107	April 14	1157	March 31	1207	April 22	1257	April 8	1307	March 26	1357	April 9
1108	April 5	1158	April 20	1208	April 6	1258	March 24	1308	April 14	1358	April 1
1109	April 25	1159	April 12	1209	March 29	1259	April 13	1309	March 30	1359	April 21
1110	April 10	1160	March 27	1210	April 18	1260	April 4	1310	April 19	1360	April 5
1111	April 2	1161	April 16	1211	April 3	1261	April 24	1311	April 11	1361	March 28
1112	April 21	1162	April 8	1212	March 25	1262	April 9	1312	March 26	1362	April 17
1113	April 6	1163	March 24	1213	April 14	1263	April 1	1313	April 15	1363	April 2
1114	March 29	1164	April 12	1214	March 30	1264	April 20	1314	April 7	1364	March 24
1115	April 18	1165	April 4	1215	April 19	1265	April 5	1315	March 23	1365	April 13
1116	April 2	1166	April 24	1216	April 10	1266	March 28	1316	April 11	1366	April 5
1117	March 25	1167	April 9	1217	March 26	1267	April 17	1317	April 3	1367	April 18
1118	April 14	1168	March 31	1218	April 15	1268	April 8	1318	April 23	1368	April 9
1119	March 30	1169	April 20	1219	April 7	1269	March 24	1319	April 8	1369	April 1
1120	April 18	1170	April 5	1220	March 29	1270	April 13	1320	March 30	1370	April 14
1121	April 10	1171	March 28	1221	April 11	1271	April 5	1321	April 19	1371	April 6
1122	March 26	1172	April 16	1222	April 3	1272	April 24	1322	April 11	1372	March 28
1123	April 15	1173	April 8	1223	April 23	1273	April 9	1323	March 27	1373	April 17
1124	April 6	1174	March 24	1224	April 14	1274	April 1	1324	April 15	1374	April 2
1125	March 29	1175	April 13	1225	March 30	1275	April 14	1325	April 7	1375	April 22
1126	April 11	1176	April 4	1226	April 19	1276	April 5	1326	March 23	1376	April 13
1127	April 3	1177	April 24	1227	April 11	1277	March 28	1327	April 12	1377	March 29
1128	April 22	1178	April 9	1228	March 26	1278	April 17	1328	April 3	1378	April 18
1129	April 14	1179	April 1	1229	April 15	1279	April 2	1329	April 23	1379	April 10
1130	March 30	1180	April 20	1230	April 7	1280	April 21	1330	April 8	1380	March 25
1131	April 19	1181	April 5	1231	March 23	1281	April 13	1331	March 31	1381	April 14
1132	April 10	1182	March 28	1232	April 11	1282	March 29	1332	April 19	1382	April 6
1133	March 26	1183	April 17	1233	April 3	1283	April 18	1333	April 4	1383	March 22
1134	April 15	1184	April 1	1234	April 23	1284	April 9	1334	March 27	1384	April 10
1135	April 7	1185	April 21	1235	April 8	1285	March 25	1335	April 16	1385	April 2
1136	March 22	1186	April 13	1236	March 30	1286	April 14	1336	March 31	1386	April 22
1137	April 11	1187	March 29	1237	April 19	1287	April 6	1337	April 20	1387	April 7
1138	April 3	1188	April 17	1238	April 4	1288	March 28	1338	April 12	1388	March 29
1139	April 23	1189	April 9	1239	March 27	1289	April 10	1339	March 28	1389	April 18
1140	April 7	1190	March 25	1240	April 15	1290	April 2	1340	April 16	1390	April 3
1141	March 30	1191	April 14	1241	March 31	1291	April 22	1341	April 8	1391	March 26
1142	April 19	1192	April 5	1242	April 20	1292	April 6	1342	March 31	1392	April 14
1143	April 4	1193	March 28	1243	April 12	1293	March 29	1343	April 13	1393	April 6
1144	March 26	1194	April 10	1244	April 3	1294	April 18	1344	April 4	1394	April 19
1145	April 15	1195	April 2	1245	April 16	1295	April 3	1345	March 27	1395	April 11
1146	March 31	1196	April 21	1246	April 8	1296	March 25	1346	April 16	1396	April 2
1147	April 20	1197	April 6	1247	March 31	1297	April 14	1347	April 1	1397	April 22
1148	April 11	1198	March 29	1248	April 19	1298	April 6	1348	April 20	1398	April 7
1149	April 3	1199	April 18	1249	April 4	1299	April 19	1349	April 12	1399	March 30

A.D.	Easter	A.D.	Easter	A.D.	Easter	A.D.	Easter	A.D.	Easter	A.D.	Easter
1400	April 18	1450	April 5	**1500**	April 19	1550	April 6	**1600**	March 23	1650	April 14
1401	April 3	1451	April 25	1501	April 11	1551	March 29	1601	April 12	1651	March 30
1402	March 26	**1452**	April 9	1502	March 27	**1552**	April 17	1602	April 4	**1652**	April 18
1403	April 15	1453	April 1	1503	April 16	1553	April 2	1603	April 24	1653	April 10
1404	March 30	1454	April 21	**1504**	April 7	1554	March 25	**1604**	April 8	1654	March 26
1405	April 19	1455	April 6	1505	March 23	1555	April 14	1605	March 31	1655	April 15
1406	April 11	**1456**	March 28	1506	April 12	**1556**	April 5	1606	April 20	**1656**	April 6
1407	March 27	1457	April 17	1507	April 4	1557	April 18	1607	April 5	1657	March 29
1408	April 15	1458	April 2	**1508**	April 23	1558	April 10	**1608**	March 27	1658	April 11
1409	April 7	1459	March 25	1509	April 8	1559	March 26	1609	April 16	1659	April 3
1410	March 23	**1460**	April 13	1510	March 31	**1560**	April 14	1610	April 8	**1660**	April 22
1411	April 12	1461	April 5	1511	April 20	1561	April 6	1611	March 24	1661	April 14
1412	April 3	1462	April 18	**1512**	April 11	1562	March 29	**1612**	April 12	1662	March 30
1413	April 23	1463	April 10	1513	March 27	1563	April 11	1613	April 4	1663	April 19
1414	April 8	**1464**	April 1	1514	April 16	**1564**	April 2	1614	April 24	**1664**	April 10
1415	March 31	1465	April 14	1515	April 8	1565	April 22	1615	April 9	1665	March 26
1416	April 19	1466	April 6	**1516**	March 23	1566	April 14	**1616**	March 31	1666	April 15
1417	April 11	1467	March 29	1517	April 12	1567	March 30	1617	April 20	1667	April 7
1418	March 27	**1468**	April 17	1518	April 4	**1568**	April 18	1618	April 5	**1668**	March 22
1419	April 16	1469	April 2	1519	April 24	1569	April 10	1619	March 28	1669	April 11
1420	April 7	1470	April 22	**1520**	April 8	1570	March 26	**1620**	April 16	1670	April 3
1421	March 23	1471	April 14	1521	March 31	1571	April 15	1621	April 1	1671	April 23
1422	April 12	**1472**	March 29	1522	April 20	**1572**	April 6	1622	April 21	**1672**	April 7
1423	April 4	1473	April 18	1523	April 5	1573	March 22	1623	April 13	1673	March 30
1424	April 23	1474	April 10	**1524**	March 27	1574	April 11	**1624**	March 28	1674	April 19
1425	April 8	1475	March 26	1525	April 16	1575	April 3	1625	April 17	1675	April 4
1426	March 31	**1476**	April 14	1526	April 1	**1576**	April 22	1626	April 9	**1676**	March 26
1427	April 20	1477	April 6	1527	April 21	1577	April 7	1627	March 25	1677	April 15
1428	April 4	1478	March 22	**1528**	April 12	1578	March 30	**1628**	April 13	1678	March 31
1429	March 27	1479	April 11	1529	March 28	1579	April 19	1629	April 5	1679	April 20
1430	April 16	**1480**	April 2	1530	April 17	**1580**	April 3	1630	March 28	**1680**	April 11
1431	April 1	1481	April 22	1531	April 9	1581	March 26	1631	April 10	1681	April 3
1432	April 20	1482	April 7	**1532**	March 31	1582 [1]	April 15	**1632**	April 1	1682	April 16
1433	April 12	1483	March 30	1533	April 13	1583	March 31	1633	April 21	1683	April 8
1434	March 28	**1484**	April 18	1534	April 5	**1584**	April 19	1634	April 6	**1684**	March 30
1435	April 17	1485	April 3	1535	March 28	1585	April 11	1635	March 29	1685	April 19
1436	April 8	1486	March 26	**1536**	April 16	1586	April 3	**1636**	April 17	1686	April 4
1437	March 31	1487	April 15	1537	April 1	1587	April 16	1637	April 9	1687	March 27
1438	April 13	**1488**	April 6	1538	April 21	**1588**	April 7	1638	March 25	**1688**	April 15
1439	April 5	1489	April 19	1539	April 6	1589	March 30	1639	April 14	1689	March 31
1440	March 27	1490	April 11	**1540**	March 28	1590	April 19	**1640**	April 5	1690	April 20
1441	April 16	1491	April 3	1541	April 17	1591	April 4	1641	April 25	1691	April 12
1442	April 1	**1492**	April 22	1542	April 9	**1592**	March 26	1642	April 10	**1692**	March 27
1443	April 21	1493	April 7	1543	March 25	1593	April 15	1643	April 2	1693	April 16
1444	April 12	1494	March 30	**1544**	April 13	1594	March 31	**1644**	April 21	1694	April 8
1445	March 28	1495	April 19	1545	April 5	1595	April 20	1645	April 6	1695	March 24
1446	April 17	1496	April 3	1546	April 25	1596	March 29	1646	March 29	1696	April 12
1447	April 9	1497	March 26	1547	April 10	1597	March 27	1647	April 18	1697	April 4
1448	March 24	1498	April 15	**1548**	April 1	1598	April 16	**1648**	April 2	1698	April 24
1449	April 13	1499	March 31	1549	April 21	1599	April 8	1649	March 25	1699	April 9

[1] See page 161 for Easter Days according to New Style after 1582.

A.D.	Easter	A.D.	Easter	A.D.	Easter	A.D.	Easter	A.D.	Easter	A.D.	Easter
1700	March 31	1750	April 15	1800 [2]	April 13	1850	March 31	**1900** [2]	April 15	1950	April 9
1701	April 20	1751	April 7	1801	April 5	1851	April 20	1901	April 7	1951	March 25
1702	April 5	**1752** [1]	March 29	1802	April 18	**1852**	April 11	1902	March 30	**1952**	April 13
1703	March 28	1753	April 22	1803	April 10	1853	March 27	1903	April 12	1953	April 5
1704	April 16	1754	April 14	**1804**	April 1	1854	April 16	**1904**	April 3	1954	April 18
1705	April 8	1755	March 30	1805	April 14	1855	April 8	1905	April 23	1955	April 10
1706	March 24	**1756**	April 18	1806	April 6	**1856**	March 23	1906	April 15	**1956**	April 1
1707	April 13	1757	April 10	1807	March 29	1857	April 12	1907	March 31	1957	April 21
1708	April 4	1758	March 26	**1808**	April 17	1858	April 4	**1908**	April 19	1958	April 6
1709	April 24	1759	April 15	1809	April 2	1859	April 24	1909	April 11	1959	March 29
1710	April 9	**1760**	April 6	1810	April 22	**1860**	April 8	1910	March 27	**1960**	April 17
1711	April 1	1761	March 22	1811	April 14	1861	March 31	1911	April 16	1961	April 2
1712	April 20	1762	April 11	**1812**	March 29	1862	April 20	**1912**	April 7	1962	April 22
1713	April 5	1763	April 3	1813	April 18	1863	April 5	1913	March 23	1963	April 14
1714	March 28	**1764**	April 22	1814	April 10	**1864**	March 27	1914	April 12	**1964**	March 29
1715	April 17	1765	April 7	1815	March 26	1865	April 16	1915	April 4	1965	April 18
1716	April 1	1766	March 30	**1816**	April 14	1866	April 1	**1916**	April 23	1966	April 10
1717	April 21	1767	April 19	1817	April 6	1867	April 21	1917	April 8	1967	March 26
1718	April 13	**1768**	April 3	1818	March 22	**1868**	April 12	1918	March 31	**1968**	April 14
1719	March 29	1769	March 26	1819	April 11	1869	March 28	1919	April 20	1969	April 6
1720	April 17	1770	April 15	**1820**	April 2	1870	April 17	**1920**	April 4	1970	March 29
1721	April 9	1771	March 31	1821	April 22	1871	April 9	1921	March 27	1971	April 11
1722	March 25	**1772**	April 19	1822	April 7	**1872**	March 31	1922	April 16	**1972**	April 2
1723	April 14	1773	April 11	1823	March 30	1873	April 13	1923	April 1	1973	April 22
1724	April 5	1774	April 3	**1824**	April 18	1874	April 5	**1924**	April 20	1974	April 14
1725	March 28	1775	April 16	1825	April 3	1875	March 28	1925	April 12	1975	March 30
1726	April 10	**1776**	April 7	1826	March 26	**1876**	April 16	1926	April 4	**1976**	April 18
1727	April 2	1777	March 30	1827	April 15	1877	April 1	1927	April 17	1977	April 10
1728	April 21	1778	April 19	**1828**	April 6	1878	April 21	**1928**	April 8	1978	March 26
1729	April 6	1779	April 4	1829	April 19	1879	April 13	1929	March 31	1979	April 15
1730	March 29	**1780**	March 26	1830	April 11	**1880**	March 28	1930	April 20	**1980**	April 6
1731	April 18	1781	April 15	1831	April 3	1881	April 17	1931	April 5	1981	April 19
1732	April 9	1782	March 31	**1832**	April 22	1882	April 9	**1932**	March 27	1982	April 11
1733	March 25	1783	April 20	1833	April 7	1883	March 25	1933	April 16	1983	April 3
1734	April 14	**1784**	April 11	1834	March 30	**1884**	April 13	1934	April 1	**1984**	April 22
1735	April 6	1785	March 27	1835	April 19	1885	April 5	1935	April 21	1985	April 7
1736	April 25	1786	April 16	**1836**	April 3	1886	April 25	**1936**	April 12	1986	March 30
1737	April 10	1787	April 8	1837	March 26	1887	April 10	1937	March 28	1987	April 19
1738	April 2	**1788**	March 23	1838	April 15	**1888**	April 1	1938	April 17	**1988**	April 3
1739	April 22	1789	April 12	1839	March 31	1889	April 21	1939	April 9	1989	March 26
1740	April 6	1790	April 4	**1840**	April 19	1890	April 6	**1940**	March 24	1990	April 15
1741	March 29	1791	April 24	1841	April 11	1891	March 29	1941	April 13	1991	March 31
1742	April 18	**1792**	April 8	1842	March 27	**1892**	April 17	1942	April 5	**1992**	April 19
1743	April 3	1793	March 31	1843	April 16	1893	April 2	1943	April 25	1993	April 11
1744	March 25	1794	April 20	**1844**	April 7	1894	March 25	**1944**	April 9	1994	April 3
1745	April 14	1795	April 5	1845	March 23	1895	April 14	1945	April 1	1995	April 16
1746	March 30	**1796**	March 27	1846	April 12	**1896**	April 5	1946	April 21	**1996**	April 7
1747	April 19	1797	April 16	1847	April 4	1897	April 18	1947	April 6	1997	March 30
1748	April 10	1798	April 8	**1848**	April 23	1898	April 10	**1948**	March 28	1998	April 12
1749	March 26	1799	March 24	1849	April 8	1899	April 2	1949	April 17	1999	April 4
										2000 [3]	April 23

[1] Table 36 provides an English Calendar for 1752. From this point the list gives the date of Easter according to the New Style. For the Julian Easters, A.D. 1753–2000, see Giry, *Manuel*, pp. 206–10.

[2] 1800 and 1900 were not Leap Years.   [3] 2000 will be a Leap Year.

A.D.	Easter	A.D.	Easter	A.D.	Easter	A.D.	Easter	A.D.	Easter
1583 [1]	April 10	**1600**	April 2	1650	April 17	**1700** [2]	April 11	1750	March 29
1584	April 1	1601	April 22	1651	April 9	1701	March 27	1751	April 11
1585	April 21	1602	April 7	**1652**	March 31	1702	April 16	**1752**	April 2
1586	April 6	1603	March 30	1653	April 13	1703	April 8		
1587	March 29	**1604**	April 18	1654	April 5	**1704**	March 23		
1588	April 17	1605	April 10	1655	March 28	1705	April 12		
1589	April 2	1606	March 26	**1656**	April 16	1706	April 4		
1590	April 22	1607	April 15	1657	April 1	1707	April 24		
1591	April 14	**1608**	April 6	1658	April 21	**1708**	April 8		
1592	March 29	1609	April 19	1659	April 13	1709	March 31		
1593	April 18	1610	April 11	**1660**	March 28	1710	April 20		
1594	April 10	1611	April 3	1661	April 17	1711	April 5		
1595	March 26	**1612**	April 22	1662	April 9	**1712**	March 27		
1596	April 14	1613	April 7	1663	March 25	1713	April 16		
1597	April 6	1614	March 30	**1664**	April 13	1714	April 1		
1598	March 22	1615	April 19	1665	April 5	1715	April 21		
1599	April 11	**1616**	April 3	1666	April 25	**1716**	April 12		
		1617	March 26	1667	April 10	1717	March 28		
		1618	April 15	**1668**	April 1	1718	April 17		
		1619	March 31	1669	April 21	1719	April 9		
		1620	April 19	1670	April 6	**1720**	March 31		
		1621	April 11	1671	March 29	1721	April 13		
		1622	March 27	**1672**	April 17	1722	April 5		
		1623	April 16	1673	April 2	1723	March 28		
		1624	April 7	1674	March 25	**1724**	April 16		
		1625	March 30	1675	April 14	1725	April 1		
		1626	April 12	**1676**	April 5	1726	April 21		
		1627	April 4	1677	April 18	1727	April 13		
		1628	April 23	1678	April 10	**1728**	March 28		
		1629	April 15	1679	April 2	1729	April 17		
		1630	March 31	**1680**	April 21	1730	April 9		
		1631	April 20	1681	April 6	1731	March 25		
		1632	April 11	1682	March 29	**1732**	April 13		
		1633	March 27	1683	April 18	1733	April 5		
		1634	April 16	**1684**	April 2	1734	April 25		
		1635	April 8	1685	April 22	1735	April 10		
		1636	March 23	1686	April 14	**1736**	April 1		
		1637	April 12	1687	March 30	1737	April 21		
		1638	April 4	**1688**	April 18	1738	April 6		
		1639	April 24	1689	April 10	1739	March 29		
		1640	April 8	1690	March 26	**1740**	April 17		
		1641	March 31	1691	April 15	1741	April 2		
		1642	April 20	**1692**	April 6	1742	March 25		
		1643	April 5	1693	March 22	1743	April 14		
		1644	March 27	1694	April 11	**1744**	April 5		
		1645	April 16	1695	April 3	1745	April 18		
		1646	April 1	**1696**	April 22	1746	April 10		
		1647	April 21	1697	April 7	1747	April 2		
		1648	April 12	1698	March 30	**1748**	April 14		
		1649	April 4	1699	April 19	1749	April 6		

[1] Gregory XIII's bull directed that ten days should be omitted after 4 Oct. 1582 and that Sunday, 17 Oct. should be treated as the eighteenth Sunday after Pentecost, which agrees with an Easter Day on 25 April. Table No. 35 should therefore be used for the period 15 Oct.–31 Dec. 1582 New Style.   [2] 1700 N.S. was not a Leap Year.

INDEX